IMPERIAL DELUSIONS

Polemics

Stephen Eric Bronner, Series Editor

The books in the Polemics series confront readers with provocative ideas by major figures in the social sciences and humanities on a host of controversial issues and developments. The authors combine a sophisticated argument with a lively and engaging style, making the books interesting to even the most accomplished scholar and appealing to the general reader and student.

Media Wars: News at a Time of Terror
By Danny Schechter

The Collapse of Liberalism:
Why America Needs a New Left
By Charles Noble

Imperial Delusions:
American Militarism and Endless War
By Carl Boggs

Forthcoming Titles

American National Identity in a Post-National Age
By James Sleeper

Animal Rights and Human Evolution
By Steven Best

Corruption
By Robert Fitch

Freud's Foes:
Psychoanalysis, Science, and Resistance
By Kurt Jacobsen

Murdering Myths:
The Real Story Behind the Death Penalty
By Judith Kay

No Free Lunch:
How to Destroy Television as We Know It
By Philip Green

Power and Disruption
By Frances Fox-Piven

Repressive Tolerance:
Second Edition
By Herbert Marcuse

Same Sex Marriage and Democracy
By R. Claire Snyder

Technopolitics and Globalization
By Douglas Kellner

IMPERIAL DELUSIONS

American Militarism and Endless War

CARL BOGGS

ROWMAN & LITTLEFIELD PUBLISHERS, INC.
Lanham • Boulder • New York • Toronto • Oxford

ROWMAN & LITTLEFIELD PUBLISHERS, INC.

Published in the United States of America
by Rowman & Littlefield Publishers, Inc.
A wholly owned subsidiary of The Rowman & Littlefield Publishing Group, Inc.
4501 Forbes Boulevard, Suite 200, Lanham, MD 20706
www.rowmanlittlefield.com

P.O. Box 317, Oxford OX2 9RU, UK

Distributed by NATIONAL BOOK NETWORK

British Library Cataloguing in Publication Information Available

Library of Congress Cataloging-in-Publication Data

Boggs, Carl.
  Imperial delusions : American militarism and endless war / Carl Boggs.
    p. cm. — (Polemics)
  Includes bibliographical references and index.
  ISBN 0-7425-2772-7 (cloth : alk. paper)
  1. Militarism—United States. 2. United States—Military policy. 3. Civil-military
relations—United States. I. Title. II. Series. Polemics (Rowman & Littlefield, Inc.)

E840.4.B64 2005
322'.5'0973090511—dc22

                                                                    2005011764

Printed in the United States of America

To Laurie Nalepa

CONTENTS

PREFACE

This book explores the resurgence of United States militarism in its multiple dimensions—historical, economic, political, cultural, global—as the imperial ethos becomes ever more deeply embedded in the very fabric of American life. At the start of the twenty-first century it seems appropriate to refer to the militarization of both U.S. foreign policy and American society as a whole. Whether or not the nation has become "addicted" to war (and preparation for war), there can be little doubt that warfare motifs, discourses, and priorities increasingly shape all phases of social life, impacting everything from language, media representations, and popular culture to the workplace, forms of consumption, and politics. War is the most profitable area of corporate investment, marketed by public-relations firms, lobbies, political action committees (PACs), think tanks, and foundations, and glorified on TV, in video games, and in film. The impulse toward militarism is embellished by the gun culture, local militias, gangs, and parts of the sports establishment. As an ideology, the contemporary merging of flag-waving patriotism, militarism, and imperial hubris furnishes American citizens with a powerful (if no doubt fleeting) sense of national unity and global purpose. Above all, militarism stands as an enabling mechanism of U.S. Empire, of an expanded Pax Americana—an awesome instrument at the disposal of American elites in their drive toward unchallenged world domination.

There is nothing fundamentally novel about any of this, even as altered historical circumstances create new openings for U.S. global power; the impetus toward colonial exploits through military force goes back to the earliest days of the republic. Since the turn of the last century the U.S. worldwide armed presence—on the seas and land, in the air, and now in outer space—can be said to have no historical parallels, a reality quite at odds with the torrents of propaganda affirming a benevolent, peaceful, democratic U.S. foreign policy. A guiding theme of this book is that U.S. history up to the present contains a *peculiarly* militaristic strand, a phenomenon increasingly visible since the end of World War II. To speak of a "new militarism" thus hardly suggests a radical departure from long-standing patterns but rather an *extension* and *deepening* of those patterns, so that we arrive today at a more aggressive, globalizing definition of "Empire." As explored in the following pages, a revitalized U.S. imperialism and militarism flows from several inter-related factors: a growing mood of American exceptionalism in international affairs, the primacy of military force in U.S. policy, arrogation of the right to intervene around the world, the spread of xenophobic patriotism, further consolidation of the permanent war system. With the end of the cold war, and more dramatically since the terrorist attacks of 9/11, the result is an increasingly militant and arrogant U.S. foreign behavior marked by outright rejection of important global treaties, repeated violations of international law, disregard for the United Nations, elevated assaults on the natural environment, militarization of space, and flagrant acts of military intervention—all giving Pax Americana a refurbished mission. Beneath everything has congealed an ideological fundamentalism grounded in superpatriotism and a rigid neoliberalism in the service of corporate power.

As the United States moves to reshape the geopolitical terrain of the world, with hundreds of military bases in 130 countries added to hundreds of installations stretched across its own territorial confines, the vast majority of Americans refuse to admit their nation possesses anything resembling an Empire. Yet U.S. global expansion is far more ambitious than anything pursued or even imagined by previous imperial powers. It might be argued that the "new militarism" is rooted in a "new imperialism" that aspires to nothing short of world domination, a project earlier outlined by its exuberant proponents and given new life by the Bush II presidency, which has set out to remove all vestiges of ideological and material impediments to worldwide corporate power—by every means at its disposal.

It is hard to resist the conclusion that the United States, its strong fusion of national exceptionalism, patriotic chauvinism, and neoliberal fundamentalism fully in place, has evolved into something of an outlaw, rogue state—the kind of fearsome entity conjured up by its own incessant propaganda. Celebrations of power, violence, and conquest long associated with warfare inevitably take its architects and practitioners into the dark side of human experience, into a zone marked by unbridled fanaticism and destructive ventures requiring a culture of lies, duplicity, and double standards. Militarism as a tool of global power ultimately leads to a jettisoning of fixed and universal values, the corruption of human purpose, the degradation of those who embrace it, and finally social disintegration. As Chris Hedges writes in *War Is a Force That Gives Us Meaning*: "War never creates the society or harmony we desire, especially the harmony we briefly attain during wartime."[1] Here the critical observer is entitled to ask whether the staggering costs and consequences of U.S. imperial domination can possibly be worth any of the goals or ideals invoked as their political justification.

We seem to have reached a point where U.S. leaders see themselves as uniquely entitled to carry out warfare and imperial agendas simply owing to the country's status as the world's lone superpower and its preponderance of military force. In the wake of 9/11 and the onset of Bush's war against terrorism, the trajectory of U.S. militarism encounters fewer limits in time and space as it becomes amorphous and endless, galvanized by the threat of far-flung enemies. As at the height of the cold war, the power structure embellishes an image of the globe where two apocalyptic forces—good versus evil, civilized versus primitive—are locked in a battle to the death. U.S. expansionism is thereby justified through its quest, its apparent *need,* for an increase in both domestic and global power—a quest destined to bring the superpower to work against even its own interests. Empires across history have disintegrated on the shoals of their boundless elite hubris, accelerated by global overreach, internal decay, and collapse of legitimacy, and there is little reason to think that Pax Americana will be able to avoid the same fate. While a feverish nationalism might sustain elite domestic legitimacy temporarily, it cannot secure the same kind of popular support *internationally,* any more than could a United States–managed world economy that sows its own dysfunctions in the form of mounting chaos, poverty, and inequality. To the extent the United States is determined to set itself above the rest of the world, brandishing technologically awesome military power and threatening planetary survival in the process, it winds up subverting its own requirements for international stability and hegemony.

In a perpetual struggle to legitimate their actions, American leaders invoke the familiar and trusted, but increasingly hollow, pretext of exporting democracy and human rights. With the eclipse of the Communist threat, U.S. foreign policy followed the path of "humanitarian intervention," cynically employing seductive motifs like multiculturalism, human rights, and democratic pluralism—all naturally designed for public consumption. Few knowledgeable observers outside the United States take such rhetoric seriously, so its propagandistic merit is confined mainly to the *domestic* sphere, although even here its credibility is waning. "Democracy" becomes another self-serving facade for naked U.S. geopolitical interests, even as its popular credibility has become nearly exhausted, all the more with the fraudulent claims invoked to justify the war on Iraq. Strikingly, the concept of democracy (global or domestic) receives little critical scrutiny within American political discourse, the mass media, or even academia; the democratic humanitarian motives of U.S. foreign policy have become an article of faith, and not just among neoconservatives. Yet even the most cursory inventory of the postwar historical record demonstrates a pervasive legacy of U.S. support for authoritarian regimes across the globe and a rather flagrant contempt for democracy where it hinders (imputed) national interests. Throughout the Middle East and Central Asia the United States has established close ties with a variety of dictators and monarchs willing to collaborate with American geopolitical and neoliberal agendas. The recent armed interventions in the Balkans, Afghanistan, and Iraq have left behind poor, chaotic, violence-ridden societies far removed from even the most generous definition of pluralist democracy.

The case of Iraq is particularly instructive. Framing "preemptive" war as a strike against Saddam Hussein's tyranny and for "liberation," the Bush administration—its assertions regarding terrorist links, weapons of mass destruction, and imminent Iraqi military threats shown to be lies—scandalously trumpets the old myths while corporate boondoggles become more transparent by the day. The recent experience of U.S. involvement in Iraq reveals everything but democratic intent: support for Hussein throughout the 1980s, including his catastrophic war against Iran; two devastating military invasions; more than a decade of United States–led economic sanctions costing hundreds of thousands of lives; surveillance and bombings spanning more than a decade; repeated coup and assassination plots; cynical use of the UN inspections process for intelligence and covert operations; aid to terrorist insurgents; an illegal, costly, and dictatorial military occupation. As elsewhere, U.S. ambitions in Iraq were never about democracy but were and are a function of resource wars, geopolitical strategy, and domestic pressures exerted by a powerful war machine.

The Iraqi disaster, occurring fully within the general trajectory of American global power, illuminates perhaps even more the *fragility* and vulnerability of U.S. hegemony than its potency or invincibility, more the weaknesses than the strengths. A resurgent militarism is both cause and effect of the deepening crisis of legitimacy that befalls domestic and international realms of U.S. imperial power. As I argue in the final chapter, the resort to overpowering military force in the service of expansionary U.S. economic and geopolitical goals is likely to be counterproductive, a sign of eventual if not immediate *decline*. Armed interventions, no matter how so-

phisticated their technology and logistics, cannot permit elites to shape
world politics as they desire where mass support for that military action is
weak or lacking. Great-power operations are bound to provoke challenges
from subordinate or competing nations, not to mention blowback leading
to local resistance and terrorism, thus restricting superpower maneuverabil-
ity. And lopsided domestic spending priorities favoring a bloated Pentagon
budget lead to accelerated decline of the public infrastructure: health services, education, housing, the environment, and broad social programs vital
to the real strength of any society. Increasing assaults from Republicans *and*
Democrats on "government bureaucracy" at the very moment allocations
for military, law enforcement, surveillance, and intelligence functions so dramatically *increase* will only hasten this downward trend, eventually calling
the imperial mission itself into question. Historical experience suggests that
an elite resort to coercive power works against the prospects for strong
hegemony, notably where a legitimation crisis is already present, since hegemony depends more on economic well-being, political stability, cultural dynamism, and widespread civic engagement than on brute force. An elite
preference for military action and authoritarian rule weakens the political,
economic, and cultural imperatives of effective governance. Those imperatives were adequately satisfied in the wake of 9/11, but the situation
changed radically once Bush embraced the war on terrorism as a launching
pad for the Iraq venture, at which point the ideological gulf between the
lone superpower and the rest of the world deepened. We now face a
predicament where the new militarism, taken up with zeal by virtually
every leading American politician, has through its awesome war-making
power already contributed to destabilization of the same global system it aspires to dominate.

A NOTE ON LANGUAGE

Any critical, historically grounded analysis of U.S. foreign and military behavior sooner or later encounters the many built-in distortions, biases, and
transgressions of language peculiar to the topic. George Orwell's famous reference to newspeak as administered discourse suggests that nowhere is this
caveat better advised than in the vocabulary of great-power military interventions, where warfare is typically framed to signify precisely its opposite,
"peace." We have seen how U.S. military planners routinely associated the
most horrific scenarios of death and destruction in Vietnam with images of
peace and stability, all intended for domestic public consumption. Imperial

aggression has forever been characterized by its protagonists as the "liberation" or "civilizing" of supposedly backward, undemocratic populations. Within American political culture today such debauchery of language has reached new levels in both its sophistication and absurdity, the result of a public sphere colonized by spectacles of righteous warfare with its own militarized technocratic language. This vocabulary has been so fully assimilated into public discourse as to become almost invisible, uncritically absorbed into the vocabulary of politicians, the media, government officials, and varied "experts" from across the political spectrum.

One instance of such degraded language is the crystallization of bureaucratic Pentagon discourse—detached, clinical, far removed from the deadly human impact of technologically honed military action. Well known are references to "collateral damage," "high-value targets," and "decapitating strikes," linguistically finessing the horrors of aerial bombardment—a practice common to all wars since Vietnam, when technowar was first refined by the Pentagon. The refrain is aggressive and technocratic, saturated with masculine, often sexual allusions and sports metaphors reflective of the imperial, patriarchal mindset. We encounter the familiar video-game imaging of combat with its spectacular "hits" and "precision attacks," endowed with the wondrous beauty and order of a technocratic, violent society. At yet another level is the intensely partisan language of imperial ideology, identified with U.S. global power and the outgrowth of the country's capacity to enforce linguistic codes. Even reputedly objective scholars and journalists invoke the standpoint "we" and "us" when describing American global behavior, while definitions of "the enemy" and references to "evil" foreign others are often taken at face value from official government propaganda and elite discourse.

In this book I have sought to avoid such linguistic misrepresentations, which deny the very idea of critical scholarship, as much as possible. This matter goes well beyond the question of semantics or style and reflects crucial *political* and ideological biases that, as Orwell knew only too well, are most egregious when it comes to the discourse of war and peace. The great hegemonizing power of contemporary media culture has given this phenomenon new meaning, rendering efforts to demystify imperial, militarized language all the more difficult, yet more imperative. A few illustrations are in order:

- The application of the term "defense" to the massive, and clearly *strategic,* U.S. global military presence obliterates its meaning beyond recognition. Throughout this volume I use more accurate renderings such as "military," "armed forces," and "armed intervention," insofar as "defense" signifies nothing more than efforts to repel attacks or threats against the territorial integrity of the nation—the universally accepted meaning, and the one contained in the UN Charter. From this standpoint, the term "Pentagon spending," for example, seems more appropriate than tepid references to "defense allocations" or the "defense budget," above all when the focus is a nation bent on global domination through military force.

• The constantly invoked terms "we" and "us" in purported objective (or "expert") commentary on U.S. foreign policy are similarly misleading. First, the unabashedly partisan style is more endemic to the sports vernacular, where loyal hometown fans and supporters are expected to cheer for their favorite teams—although even here the more respectable journalistic ethos has been to avoid cheerleading styles on the perfectly logical grounds that they distort more than clarify the reportage. Second, the fanciful notion of an ecumenical "we" in military decision making obscures the crucial distinction between the real authors of a policy (some combination of Washington and corporate elites) and the vast majority of people, who tend to be indifferent or opposed to the policy, or are simply propagandized into following along. In this vein to say that "we" attacked Iraq or decided to militarize space or snubbed an international treaty makes no sense; in fact "they" (ruling elites) are the agents in question.

• There are frequent allusions in the public discourse to the U.S. war "with" Iraq or conflict "with" nations deemed to be "trouble spots" or "crisis zones," a seemingly innocuous linguistic turn of phrase that misrepresents blatantly one-sided superpower attacks on smaller, weaker nations as a tragic struggle of roughly equal forces caught up in an unavoidable contest of political and military wills. The notion conveyed is that of a benevolent, patient, peace-loving superpower reluctantly dragged into wars it would much rather avoid. For clearer meaning, the more active formulation "against" should replace "with," as in "the United States decided to wage war *against* Iraq" (or Panama or Yugoslavia). This linguistic shift makes even more sense when the superpower military action in question amounts to a clear violation of the UN Charter and international law. It is easy enough to see how absurd it would be if a historian wrote that Nazi Germany found itself at war or in a state of conflict "with" Poland, Czechoslovakia, or the Soviet Union.

- The phrase "preemptive attack," supposedly introduced by the Bush administration to justify its military action against Iraq, has no conceptual or linguistic meaning where the targeted nation—small, weak, distant, largely defenseless—poses no conceivable military threat and logically could not do so owing to extraordinary U.S. armed superiority. Since to militarily "preempt" means to take action in order to prevent an imminent enemy attack, the word's usage (adopted uncritically in American public discourse) has propaganda value only and should be bracketed in quotes.

- As indicated throughout this book, what is usually described as "terrorism" has many faces corresponding to various contexts and interpretations, even while the dominant political culture endows it with a *single* meaning derived largely from official government phraseology. There is no agreed-upon definition of "terrorism," much less any general theory of how and why people resort to violence for political ends, nor is the dictionary rendering of much help. The prevailing terminology stresses local and small-group (or individual) violence directed against the status quo or state power, ignoring forms of *state* terrorism or "friendly" acts of violence, or those used to defend existing power relations. The only explanation for such a one-sided definition is ideological bias, since linguistic consistency is nowhere to be found. Because the United States has long been involved in warfare against foreign countries, often targeting urban and civilian infrastructures, imposing deadly economic sanctions, supporting brutal dictatorships, funding and training death squads, and setting up military camps for violent insurgency in Latin America and elsewhere, it would be impossible to arrive at a definition of terrorism that excludes U.S. global behavior.

- One hears daily mention in American politics and media culture of "evil" forces, as in "evil tyrants," "evil terrorists," "evil belief systems," "evil enemies out to destroy Western civilization," "evil empires," and of course "evil nations"—as in Bush's familiar "axis of evil" encompassing the terrible threesome of Iran, Iraq, and North Korea. The world is said to be overrun by "evildoers" ready to carry out barbaric acts against innocent people, and there is an undeniable kernel of truth to this. Yet where politicians and media in the United States are concerned, "evil" is defined as something uniformly alien, foreign, external, the manifestation of horrible deeds carried out by and through other cultures, religions, or nations. In its mundane historical reality, however, the line between good and evil is far more blurred than this simplistic dichotomy would have us believe. Thus if "evil" is meant to cover acts of violence leading to horrible loss of human life, then the architects of U.S. military interventions are surely no less culpable than the plotters of 9/11; based on the carnage it brought to Vietnam alone the United States would have to be ranked at the top of the world's evildoers. Still another problem with the fixation on evil is that the human action in question is abruptly and capriciously removed from its larger social and historical *context*, framing violent acts in support of repressive power as morally equivalent to those same methods used to resist or fight it, or to achieve such goals as national independence and democratic rights. The easy demonizing of *others'* motives and actions as undistilled evil, a familiar ploy of U.S. leaders and opinion makers, turns out to be linguistically meaningless and politically self-serving.

• The media and politicians are fond of distinguishing between "unilateral" (bad) and "multilateral" (good) military options, a binary opposition especially invoked by liberals and progressives critical of Bush for his supposedly go-it-alone unilateralism in Iraq. Within this framework it is simply assumed that U.S. global interests and strategic agendas (themselves scarcely questioned) are best served if other crucial actors such as UN Security Council members can somehow be brought around to support them. At present, however, this linguistic nicety is quite hollow given how the United States routinely employs its vast economic, political, and military power to influence, manipulate, and dominate all actors on the global scene, countries and international agencies alike. It has mobilized with greater or lesser degrees of difficulty a "multilateral" support for its agendas, however immoral or disastrous those agendas might be. Viewed thusly, "multilateralism" refers not so much to a "coalition of the willing" as to a superpower-dominated alliance (rendering also the very term "coalition" useless). Owing to one-sided power relations, to the great reach of U.S. Empire, a true multilateralism involving equal, voluntary participation behind a global common good is presently unthinkable. And the familiar differentiation never makes clear why "multilateralism" *by definition* should be endowed with positive connotations.

Other such linguistic abuses permeate the public sphere, a function not simply of government (or media) propaganda but of long-standing, deeply ingrained forms of ideological hegemony that cut across the political spectrum and shape the broader cultural arena. Imperial agendas have come to be routinely taken for granted—among liberals and conservatives, Democrats and Republicans alike, and even among many progressives. In this book I have sought to correct provincial bias of this sort, in the interest of both lucid exposition and critical scrutiny, without advancing any sanctified claim of neutrality or impartiality. This is by no means an easy task, given how thoroughly public discourse is colonized by corporate and imperial agendas.

ACKNOWLEDGMENTS

This project is the outgrowth of an anthology on U.S. militarism I assembled for the journal *New Political Science* (*NPS*), which appeared in March 2002. I wish to thank members of the Caucus for a New Political Science, and especially the journal editor George Katsiaficas, for valuable support and assistance in this work. In 2003 the *NPS* collection was extensively broadened and revised, reappearing as a volume titled *Masters of War: Militarism and Blowback in an Era of American Empire*, published by Routledge. The contributions not only of Katsiaficas but of Routledge editors Eric Nelson and Angela Chnapko—along with the thirteen other writers for that volume—were critically valuable in helping frame my research and writing for *Imperial Delusions*. Two of my own essays contained in *Masters of War*—an introductory piece on globalization and Empire and a lengthier article on the legacy of U.S. war crimes—are incorporated here in substantially revised form.

A special thanks is owed to Stephen Bronner, who encouraged and helped guide this project from the outset. Peter McLaren and Manfred Steger read earlier drafts of the manuscript and offered extensive, insightful suggestions for improvement. Mary Carpenter and then Laura Roberts Gottlieb at Rowman & Littlefield provided ongoing encouragement and assistance. Darrin Ford and Ani Alfredson Newman furnished abundant and much-needed research assistance. Numerous colleagues and friends extended their much-valued support: Mona Afridi, Eduardo Arismendi-Pardi, Dennis Boggs, Monica Carbajal, Doug Hadsell, Chalmers Johnson, Shahriar Kalhor, Jeff Lustig, Karen Offitzer, Michael Parenti, Tom Pollard, Hamoud Sahli, John Sanbonmatsu, Igor Subbotin, Brady Sullivan, and Milt Wolpin. The hospitable owner and employees of Panini/Prebica Café in Marina del Rey, California, where large portions of this book were written, went out of their way to provide a congenial working environment along with great coffee. Finally, I wish to express my deepest thanks to Laurie Nalepa, whose strong intellectual and emotional support has lent this project a special meaning from beginning to end.

INTRODUCTION

The ceaseless global expansion of U.S. military power since the early 1940s is matched by an astonishing public refusal to incorporate an understanding of that power into the various discourses—political, educational, media, cultural. The more omnipresent that power has become, the more it permeates virtually every corner of international and domestic life, the more it seems to be ignored or deflected, suppressed or forgotten, kept safely outside the established public sphere. The notion of a U.S. militarism appears to conflict with two prevailing American myths: the idea that all societal institutions are open and democratic, and the belief that U.S. foreign policy is shaped by benign, even noble motives and interests. The undeniable legacy of militarism that has pervaded, in some ways transformed, the main arenas of American life—political, economic, cultural, intellectual—has been overwhelmed by the force of patriotic ideology, imperial arrogance, media spectacles, academic apologies, and (more recently) post-9/11 fears and insecurities over terrorism. As the world's lone superpower moves to consolidate its global domination, a stratagem laid out in many documents and statements and given life by elite interventions around the globe, critical analysis largely vanishes from sight, subordinated by an ensemble of celebratory and self-serving platitudes.

If a recycled but upgraded Pax Americana departs somewhat from classical imperialism in a period of accelerated capitalist globalization, the pursuit of its agendas requires the broadened use of military force—or at least the *threat* of such force—which means that Empire will be sustained through what the well-worn maxim terms "by any means necessary"—with possibly horrific consequences for the world. Integral to the logic of a New World Order created and managed by the United States (and a few of its allies) is perpetual growth of the Pentagon system and the war economy, the greatest threat today to world peace and perhaps even planetary survival. Yet virtually the entire political culture remains in a state of denial regarding Empire, detached from all the risks, costs, and consequences of a militarism veering out of control. Sadly enough, this syndrome engulfs not only mainstream discourses but *oppositional* discourses as well.

The contradictions between the actuality of U.S. military power and the insular public political environment it inhabits could not be more glaring. Never has such an awesome military machine so dominated the world or its own social order, its dimensions so vast that they have become easy to ignore, as if part of the natural landscape, a taken-for-granted reality. Strangely, even by the end of the twentieth century, the long and bloody legacy of U.S. imperialism and militarism—beginning with the first westward push—was obscure to most Americans, whose view was distorted by school textbooks, official political discourse, the mass media, even scholarly writings, except for a few well-known critics like Noam Chomsky, Howard Zinn, Michael Parenti, Edward Herman, Chalmers Johnson, and Michael Klare. The recent "discovery" of U.S. military power here and there across the ideological spectrum has been met by a chorus of grateful voices, hopeful that the Pentagon is up to slaying new dragons in the form of rogue states and terrorists.

The most systematic and critical earlier recognition of the Pentagon system came from a scholar writing in the mid-1950s: C. Wright Mills, in his classic *Power Elite* (1956), anticipated the dangers of U.S. militarism to a degree scarcely matched even in intellectual works written much later—at a time when the military-industrial complex was far more ensconced and menacing than when Mills was writing. Mills' work, along with the somewhat later contributions of Fred Cook, Seymour Melman, and Harry Magdoff, stood virtually alone in its uncompromising critique of the U.S. war economy, providing future ammunition to the new Left and succeeding antiwar movements. These conceptual breakthroughs, however, would be largely abandoned throughout the 1980s and 1990s owing in part to the famous "Vietnam syndrome," in part to the growing backlash against movements of the 1960s, in part to an increasing focus on domestic issues. Aside from a small nucleus of radical intellectuals, it seemed no longer fashionable to indulge in discourses related to U.S. imperial power, now considered beyond the pale of rational debate.

Much of what Mills wrote before his untimely death in 1963 was less a reflection on the existing state of affairs than a prophetic look to the future. Writing in the early days of the cold war, he was not entirely able to foresee the length and intensity of the U.S.–Soviet rivalry, the horrors of counterinsurgency war in Indochina, or later military interventions that would help legitimate American imperial expansion. Mills did, nonetheless, grasp a fundamental logic of U.S. capitalism grounded in relentless pursuit of wealth and power across the globe—a pursuit necessitating a huge military machine. For Mills, the power elite was comprised of people "in command of the major hierarchies and organizations of modern society. They rule the big corporations. They run the machinery of state and claim its prerogatives. They direct the military establishment."[1] As he put it:

> During modern times, and especially in the U.S., men had come to look upon history as a peaceful continuum interrupted by war. But now, the American elite does not have any real image of peace. . . . The only seriously accepted plan for "peace" is the fully loaded pistol. In short war or a high state of war preparedness is felt to be the normal and seemingly permanent condition of the U.S.[2]

Mills saw that the Pentagon had already become a behemoth political and economic structure in its own right, its elites increasingly prepared to view world politics in distinctly military terms. And like Melman later, he understood the crucial role of science and technology in buttressing the war economy. Mills viewed the Pentagon system as far more than an instrument of foreign policy; it would be integral to the development of a militarized society and culture. Thus: "American militarism, in fully developed form, would mean the triumph in all areas of life of the military metaphysics, and hence the subordination to it of all other ways of life."[3] That such tendencies were little more than embryonic at the time Mills was writing lends his insights even greater power.

What Mills saw in the 1950s was, oddly enough, a military-industrial complex that few others were able to see—then or later. The structural and ideological features of the Pentagon system have been in place since roughly the time of Pearl Harbor. U.S. military spending remained more or less constant throughout the cold war years, at $300 billion in constant fiscal year 2000 dollars, fell modestly and briefly during the 1990s, and then rose dramatically after 9/11, with projected levels of $500 billion by 2008. U.S. military forces remain scattered across the globe, in more than one hundred countries at nearly one thousand installations, with several hundred ships deployed in the major oceans and seas and a massive air fleet ready to attack at a moment's notice—all armed with enough nuclear weaponry to destroy the earth many times over. With Star Wars, moreover, the United States is the only nation dedicated to a full-fledged militarization of space, enhancing its surveillance, intelligence, and strike capabilities. As of 2003 the Pentagon accounted for nearly 45 percent of total world military spending, triple what Russia and China together allocate, more than the next *nine* nations combined, and roughly twenty-five times the military outlays of all designated rogue states taken together. The United States is likely to spend hundreds of billions of dollars maintaining its armed presence in the Middle East, much of it going to the occupation of Iraq as part of the U.S. effort to "remap" the region. Since 1990 the United States has sold nearly $200 billion in arms to 140 countries, and it plans vast new sales in connection with the eastward expansion of NATO. When framed by an increasingly aggressive geopolitical strategy, defined as full-spectrum dominance, it is easy to see how these elements of militarism have provided U.S. elites with enough power to block rival centers of power—yet another meaning of the New World Order.

As Mills was the first to foresee, the war economy, the Pentagon bureaucracy, and an aggressive foreign policy converge within the same matrix of development; they share an identical logic. Since World War II the U.S. military has provided an international shield for Western corporate and financial interests, more globalized today than ever. At the same time, military Keynesianism as a form of state capitalism has furnished a major stimulus for domestic economic growth on a foundation of scientific and technological innovation wedded to enormous corporate profits. As Noam Chomsky observes, "It is difficult to imagine a system better designed for the benefit of the privileged few than the military system."[4] Legitimated by the need to wage global combat against a series of "enemies," the Pentagon system establishes a nearly ideal unity of state, economy, and armed forces—a unity not matched by any other nation.

The deflected and sublimated discourse of U.S. militarism has become one of the tragedies of American public life, obscuring from view the terrible costs and consequences of Empire: millions of human casualties resulting from a legacy of foreign interventions, trillions of dollars in resources drained from the national treasury, ecological devastation, ongoing threat of nuclear catastrophe, militarization of society, evisceration of democratic practices, corruption of international agencies and institutions. While such realities might seem obvious enough to any rational observer, they have received little attention within the established public sphere, reflecting a poverty of discourse that is simultaneously political, intellectual, and cultural. The post-9/11 milieu has simply deepened this retreat, even as the role of the U.S. military in world politics becomes the object of heightened (but uncritical) attention. What Mills viewed as rather axiomatic in the 1950s is met today either with silence or celebratory acceptance.

This gulf between discourse and reality is nowhere more obvious than in an educational system that seems explicitly designed to mystify social awareness; the topic of U.S. imperial and military power, except where occasionally celebrated, is largely taboo. This is just as true for university-level reading as in high school or the lower grades. A survey of thirty-six widely used college texts in the fields of history, political science, and sociology—those disciplines expected to address the U.S. role in world affairs—reveals some fascinating but disturbing information. No fewer than twenty-seven of these required course readings, ranging in length from three hundred to six hundred pages, contain absolutely *nothing* about the American military in *any* of its dimensions. The nine remaining texts present only minimal references, usually no more than one paragraph and never more than three pages, all totally lacking in critical perspective. Such remarkable invisibility of U.S. military power extends beyond classroom texts to well-known history and social science volumes that set out to explore major issues in contemporary American historical development.

Strangely enough, it is the discipline of political science—dedicated to the study of *politics*—that has the most egregious record in its avoidance of military-related discourses. For reasons hard to fathom, the only subfields that take up the concerns of military power and armed interventions are comparative politics and international relations, that is, areas that focus on nations and cultures *other* than the United States. The main professional journal, the *American Political Science Review (APSR)*, is noteworthy for completely ignoring questions of military power: for example, in the four decades since the United States first launched its military assault on Indochina, arguably a watershed event in postwar American life, the *APSR* published exactly *one* article on the Vietnam War and its consequences. A frequently used text over many years in political science and sociology is Thomas Dye's *Power and Society*, which contains just one chapter on power among nations but nothing on the Pentagon system, aside from a fleeting reference to the Vietnam syndrome in which only American casualties are mentioned. In the more than three hundred pages of Leon Baradat's *Political Ideologies* (2000), there is nothing on the military; in Sidney Tarrow's otherwise excellent volume *Power in Movement* (2000) the topic is never taken up in 240 pages; in a text by Michael Roskin et. al., *Political Science: An Introduction* (2000), there is no more than a brief paragraph (out of five hundred pages) on the role of the president as commander in chief of the armed forces; and James Q. Wilson's highly respected *American Government* (2000) has no reference to the military in its thirteen chapters.

Within the subfield of international relations the situation is better, but only slightly: the question of U.S. military power here cannot be sidestepped altogether. Yet in the nine chapters of Robert Keohane's and Elinor Ostrom's widely respected volume *Local Commons and Global Interdependence* (1995) one finds scarcely a word about the U.S. military and its legacy of armed interventions around the world. Similarly, in the anthology *Global Politics in a Changing World* (2000), edited by Richard Mansbach and Edward Rhodes, with its eighty-one contributions, there is not a single entry dealing with this topic. In Joshua Goldstein's *International Relations* (1999) we finally come across a book that includes as much as a full chapter on the military, but even here one finds nary a reference to American global or military power. James Danzigger's well-known *Understanding the Political World* (1998) contains absolutely nothing regarding the military, war, or armed interventions in its seventeen chapters.

The state of affairs in sociology and history might be expected to be an improvement over political science, since these disciplines are known to have more intellectual breadth and critical perspective, attracting faculty and students outside mainstream discourses. On close investigation, however, the differences turn out to be marginal. In Kai Erikson's *Sociological Visions* (1997), there is no mention of U.S. military power, while in James Farganis's *Readings in Social Theory* (2000)—with no fewer than forty contributors—the topic is not deemed worthy of coverage. In Jon Shepard's classic text *Sociology* (1990) one searches in vain through nineteen long chapters for any military references. David Newman's generally fine volume *Sociology* (2002) covers more than 450 pages, but none of them are devoted to the study of U.S. military power. More critical works are just as silent: thus Roberta Garner's *Contemporary Movements and Ideologies* (1999) presents absolutely nothing on the American military, its foreign ventures and global presence, or on peace and anti-intervention movements central to any study of social change. In Steven Vago's *Social Change* (1996), the issue of military power is completely absent from its 380 pages, while the same is true of Malcolm Waters' *Modern Sociological Theory* (1994). One of the more familiar texts for undergraduate students in social and political theory is George Ritzer's excellent *Modern Sociological Theory* (1996), which covers vast expanses of important theoretical work spanning an entire century. Ritzer explores an immense variety of theories, from Marxism through critical theory, postmodernism, feminism, cultural studies, and neo-Marxism, addressing topics such as corporate power, class relations, bureaucracy, race and gender relations, the family, and social change—but *nothing* on the military in its 520 pages. This discursive vacuum is all the more remarkable given the otherwise sophisticated, far-reaching, and *critical* quality of the text. The lacunae in Ritzer's book reveal a deeper problem within the field of sociology itself: there are subfields covering virtually every realm of human life but there is no "sociology of the military," just as there is nothing of the sort within any other scholarly discipline. It turns out that Mills, one of great sociological thinkers of the twentieth century, has been largely forgotten within his own discipline, as if questions of power were somehow too embarrassing or too controversial to pose.

Books written for more general readerships, including best sellers, usually offer no better treatment of the subject matter. Thus Benjamin Barber's critically acclaimed *Jihad vs. McWorld* (1997) contains nothing on the U.S. military despite its avowed emphasis on unraveling the core issues of global conflict. Much the same could be said of other respected texts: Michael Sandel's *Democracy's Discontent* (1996), Ronald Inglehart's *Modernization and Postmodernization* (1997), Robert Putnam's *Bowling Alone* (2000), Francis Fukuyama's *The Great Disruption* (1999), and William Domhoff's revised version of *Who Rules America?* (2002). Three other well-received volumes—Fukuyama's *The Last Man and the End of History* (1992), Samuel Huntington's *The Clash of Civilizations* (1997), and Michael Hardt and Antonio Negri's *Empire* (2001)—do in fact incorporate abundant references to U.S. global and military power, but in each case that power is viewed more or less uncritically, as a positive force behind world order, justice, democracy, even peace. The absence of any critical perspective on the U.S. military role in global politics here is particularly noteworthy given that the books explicitly confront issues of power, conflict, and violence in the contemporary world.

One of the most popular textbooks in political sociology and related fields for more than thirty years has been G. William Domhoff's *Who Rules America?* which has gone through several editions and revisions since it first appeared and has exposed hundreds of thousands, perhaps millions, of students to the complex workings of the American power structure. Inspired by Marxist categories of class and power, the book has deeply influenced an entire generation of progressive intellectuals owing to its lucid conceptual framework and its strong empirical foundations. Domhoff's single-minded focus is on power in all its ramifications. His work is an investigation of who occupies vital institutional positions and who exerts influence on decision making in various arenas of public life. His main thesis is that "the corporations, banks, and agribusiness form a corporate community that shapes the federal government on the policy issues of interest to it, issues that have a major impact on the income, job security, and well-being of most other Americans."[5] Rejecting more conventional approaches to power, such as pluralism, Domhoff argues for a "class domination theory of power" in the United States, meaning that the commands of the upper class are "carried out with relatively little resistance, which is possible because that group or class has been able to establish the rules and customs through which everyday life is conducted." He shows that corporations wield extraordinary power over virtually every aspect of American society.[6]

One problem with Domhoff's book is that, astonishingly, there is no reference to military power throughout its 250 pages—that is, absolutely *no* reference. The Pentagon system; permanent war economy; interlocking relationship among government, corporations, and the military; the ongoing militarization of society; U.S. global power—all of this remains absent from Domhoff's many detailed investigations of power and its impact on investment, jobs, income, and the overall well-being of the general population. He includes a lengthy discussion of the "special-interest process" but includes nothing about the largest and most consequential "special interest" of all, the Pentagon. Influences on the "policy-making process" are examined in great detail, but the military is nowhere to be seen. Toward the end of *Who Rules America?* (in chapter 8) Domhoff looks at "the big picture" of power relations in the United States but somehow allows the realities of military power to escape from view; the Pentagon simply vanishes, even as its hundreds of business contractors in actuality occupy center stage. The author's keen sensitivity to matters of *power* appears to fail at a certain moment. Somehow the largest military apparatus in history, with its enormous impact on politics, education, the media, work, and culture, goes unnoticed. Could this be a mere oversight? Domhoff is one of the sociologists who was supposed to inherit the mantle of C. Wright Mills, but he seems to have forgotten some of his mentor's most insightful contributions.

As in most scholarly fields, academic specialists in American foreign policy and international relations profess scientific objectivity but generally identify with U.S. ambitions in the global arena—often performing as cheerleaders—as can be readily detected in such journals as *Foreign Affairs* and *World Politics*. Within this paradigm U.S. military power is always deployed for right and noble purposes, despite limits and miscalculations here and there. Many such academics construct a world in which U.S. armed force is marginal, often vanishing into the global backstage, where it is scarcely deserving of systematic analysis; it lurks in the background as a benevolent force. One example is a recent work by Robert Jervis, whose presidential address to the American Political Science Association in 2001 was published, in extended form, in the March 2002 issue of *APSR*. Jervis is one of the most widely published and respected scholars in the area of international relations and teaches at Columbia University. His article "Theories of War in an Era of Leading-Power Peace" draws on hundreds of sources, proffers a number of insightful theoretical generalizations about war and peace, and surveys the global landscape with historical grace. Yet the article is remarkable for its utterly total failure to confront the reality of U.S. superpower domination and the country's readiness to use military power to secure its economic and geopolitical interests. Even before the end of the cold war this fact of international life should have been axiomatic for any serious interpretation of developments in world politics.

Jervis argues that in a historical context where states possess modern armies and nuclear weapons it is hard for anyone to believe that war could make sense. "If war were not so dreadful," he writes, "it could be considered as an instrument for national enrichment; if peace did not seem to bring national well-being, violence would at least be contemplated; that military victory is no longer seen as a positive value both contributes to and is in part explained by the high perceived costs of war."[7] Given such conditions, today there is a precipitous decline of militarism, an epochal move away from global "realism," away from the tendency of nation-states to solve problems by means of armed intervention: world politics is shaped increasingly by norms of compromise, consideration for the interests of others, respect for law, and a shunning of violence coinciding with the rise of pacifistic democratic values.[8] As Jervis puts it, the main threat to peaceful relations at present is that populations might "become bored by the rich, peaceful world and come to desire glory, honor, and extreme nationalism once again," although this is unlikely owing to the fact that peaceful outlooks are "highly stable, being sustained by constant socialization and supporting the peace that serves the [developed] Community so well."[9] Moreover, the very motives that historically undergirded war have been eroded: "Relative economic advantage was sought in the past in part because it contributed to military security. This no longer being the case, the possibilities for cooperation are increased."[10]

Fundamental to Jervis's understanding of modern warfare is a range of highly questionable assumptions concerning the trajectory of U.S. foreign and military policy. Thus he assumes that American leaders pursue constructive agendas consistent with values of peace, democracy, and cooperation while renouncing warfare as being too costly, and that the general population has been socialized into attitudes conducive to peaceful international relations. For example: "The United States is defending not traditional interests, let alone vital ones, but [is] . . . upholding values such as democracy, self-determination, and rejection of coercion as a means of changing the status quo."[11] Jervis argues that, in contrast with the imperialism of previous eras, present-day U.S. global hegemony is not only peaceful but "seems uncoerced and accepted by most states" largely because "the common realization that all-out war would be irrational provides a license for threats and lower levels of violence."[12] Further, while the "American ability to lead military operations" might cause resentments and frictions, it does furnish a potent resource for the international community.[13] The very existence of such a community today casts serious doubt on theories indicating that "leading powers" are always willing to use military force as they struggle for geopolitical leverage in an era of uncoerced peace without centralized authority.

If Jervis simply wanted to insist that warfare among the most developed nations is far less likely than in the past, his conclusions—though rather commonplace by now—would be valid enough. Also valid would be the notion that such countries lack the economic incentives to wage military action against each other, even assuming conflict would ever reach such intensity. His stronger generalizations, however, not only lack empirical substantiation but can be easily shown to run directly against the grain of stubborn historical realities. A precipitous decline in global violence, or militarism? Emergence of a noncoercive U.S. global hegemony? A benevolent American role in world affairs, its leaders dedicated to peaceful, democratic, cooperative values? The increased willingness of U.S. leaders to adopt a compromising stance in the international arena? While Jervis's theoretical work may represent the leading edge of mainstream academic writing, its connection with real-world developments and events—before and after 9/11—is nothing short of mystical. How does he explain the unprecedented levels of U.S. economic, political, and military power that enable what has become the single hegemon to dominate international financial and trade activities through the strength of its transnational corporations and banks, to exert unchallenged leverage within the International Monetary Fund (IMF), World Bank, and World Trade Organization (WTO), to dominate and corrupt the United Nations, and to intervene with superior armed strength virtually without impunity anywhere it chooses? How does he account for the horrendous costs and consequences of American Empire? Of course an entirely different kind of framework from that offered by Jervis is needed, one more consonant with the actuality of U.S. global domination and the plainly stated intentions of U.S. leaders to pursue that domination by all means at their disposal. Such a framework would permit a fuller grasp of actual U.S. behavior in the world: repeated military interventions in violation of the UN Charter and international law; use of cruel economic sanctions against "rogue states," with murderous outcomes for civilian populations; abrogation of one international treaty after another deemed to be in conflict with the national interest; stockpiling of weapons of mass destruction while threatening other countries for possession of the same; refusal to participate in the International Criminal Tribunal; the illegal militarization of space; continuous support for proxy wars, death squads, terrorist groups, and brutal dictatorships around the globe. Democracy? Peace? Compromise? Human rights? For the American superpower, these notions exist only as mythical abstractions obliterated by the realities of imperial and military domination—realities that political elites themselves now overtly champion.

U.S. national interests, like those of any regime that possesses economic, political, and military supremacy, do not lie in the direction of all-out warfare, which is bloody and costly. The United States would clearly prefer a New World Order in which its enormous privilege can be sustained in a peaceful, stable fashion, without need for coercive intervention. But in a global arena characterized by vast material inequality, widespread repression, chaos, the diffusion of horrific weapons, and growing resistance to superpower domination, such dreams are illusory. As for the fanciful notion that modern warfare (enforced by the nuclear umbrella) renders military action less likely—the result has been, and will continue to be, exactly the opposite. This was plain enough for any observer to notice even before the events of 9/11. During the postwar years, in fact, the refinements of technowar, such as more awesome and efficient aerial bombardment, along with remote missile targeting and space-based intelligence, have made entering into combat a much *easier* decision for militarily advanced nations like the United States, which prefers to attack weak, poor, relatively defenseless countries like Afghanistan, Panama, Iraq, Serbia. Among other things, technowar minimizes casualties suffered by the aggressor. In such circumstances the norms of cooperation, nonviolence, and lawful behavior are jettisoned in favor of ruthless military violence that may accept few limits or restraints. The universe depicted by Jervis—an essentially harmonious, peaceful, and cooperative order governed by well-intentioned American leaders, punctured now and then by minor local wars—is pure mythology, a construction of simple apologetics for unbridled U.S. global power, rather than a sober analysis that addresses the harsh realities of Empire. There is nothing in Jervis's framework that could have anticipated the terrorist attacks of 9/11 or the continuing deadly cycle of militarism and terrorism that haunts the world, much less the U.S. imperial invasion of Iraq—quite in contrast to, for example, the work of Chalmers Johnson, Noam Chomsky, and Tariq Ali. Here we find yet another sad reminder of the impoverished discourse of militarism and war pervading American political culture at the start of the twenty-first century.

The abundant commentary on globalization, integral to an understanding of recent antiglobalization movements beginning with the late 1999 Seattle protests, has followed a similar discursive pattern: the U.S. military winds up invisible within an otherwise massive, worldwide power structure. The deepening of planetary corporate expansion, globalization simply refers to the incessant spread of capital across national boundaries into every corner of the globe, characterized by enhanced flows of money, resources, information, and trade. Of course the capitalist economy has been for centuries a world market and financial system; its novelty today involves dramatic increases of volume and speed, along with the system's greater penetration into regions of the periphery. Central to globalization is the progressive commodification of the world that, in the end, is shaped and controlled by transnational corporate power working through huge firms, banks, leading states, and such international agencies as the WTO, World Bank, and the IMF.

The failure to grasp the importance of U.S. military power, visible across the ideological spectrum, assumes many forms. A common thread is that the process is unifying the world into a single mode of production, integrating diverse regions, nations, and cultures into a more or less commodified whole. Taken to their logical extremes, globalization theories embrace the notion of a relatively abstract, autonomous development toward full-scale marketization of economies, political systems, and cultures. Within this framework the subversion or perhaps end of the nation-state is often prophesied and is considered a function of increasing transnational capitalist *economic* power. Thus William Robinson refers to the emergence of an "interstate system" generating new forms of "collective authority for a global ruling class" embodied in a transnational state. He writes that "globalization has increasingly eroded national boundaries, and made it structurally impossible for individual nations to sustain independent, or even autonomous, economies, polities, and social structures."[14] Deriving inspiration from Marx, Robinson argues that, in global as in domestic terms, the modern state is rooted in a system of production and class relations; the state exists as a "constellation of class forces." From this standpoint, globalization supersedes the nation-state as a "thing," paving the way toward an emergent (transnational) ruling class.[15] One result of this process is the decline of U.S. supremacy, insofar as this new global class now performs functions of a world hegemon.[16] Leslie Sklair envisions a roughly similar line of development, stripping away the vestiges of the old state system and generating conditions of a transnational capitalist class that mobilizes people and resources across the globe in its insatiable drive for markets and profits. The new class is made up of corporate executives, globalizing bureaucrats, politicians, globalizing professionals, and consumerist elites operating through economic, political, and cultural spheres; the class reproduces itself by means of a "culture-ideology of consumerism."[17]

Arguments of this sort, embracing a unifying, homogenizing process of capitalist globalization, permeate the bulk of both mainstream and critical thinking on the global economy, increasingly so since the 1990s. They provide much of the inspiration for antiglobalization activism throughout the world. Despite their focus on the inequities and dysfunctions of corporate power, however, the theories and the movements alike tend to downplay, if not ignore altogether, the predominant role of U.S. *nation-state* power in defining, shaping, and managing the contours of economic globalization. Not only the vast leverage of U.S.–based corporations and banks, but also the capacity of American elites to dominate world institutions, speaks volumes: while states in general might be subordinated to the workings of the global economy, this is emphatically not true for the United States. This tendency to devalue U.S. national power applies in more extreme form to the military, which receives surprisingly little attention even among leading critics of corporate globalization—a theme to be taken up more fully in chapter 1.

From Thomas I. Friedman's *The Lexus and the Olive Tree* to Michael Hardt and Antonio Negri's *Empire*,[18] from conservative to radical, schemas of globalization appear to resonate with prevailing assumptions regarding the U.S. role in world politics—namely, that the United States is essentially a benevolent superpower whose elites are committed to liberal democracy and humanitarian values, resorting to military power only when absolutely necessary, to make life on the planet more just and peaceful. There are flaws and mistakes to be found in American policy, but the policy itself—indeed the entire developmental path—embraces noble ends. The motif of globalization, stressing as it does general historical processes and universal norms along with the devaluing of nation-state power, is perfectly congruent with these premises and, moreover, easily coheres with widely diverse theoretical outlooks. In the case of Hardt and Negri, their arguments underpinning the idea of a benign Empire (further explored in chapter 1) are derived from a variety of sources: neo-Marxism, anarchism, liberalism, postmodernism. A preoccupation with the ostensibly free flow of markets, shared in some way by all these theories, coincides with a strong bias against taking up the issue of military power, even in some cases corporate and governmental power; the coercive side of Empire somehow vanishes. Such modes of thinking have gotten much stronger since 9/11.

Postmodern discourses, figuring heavily in *Empire* owing to its reliance on Michel Foucault's model of dispersed power, stress decentered forms of authority and social relations, diversity, and fluidity tied to abstract historical processes that, in this context, merge nicely with globalization motifs. Its nearly mystical approach to international politics in effect conceals the self-interested, blatant, violent exercise of American national power. The concept of Empire, vague enough in itself, is meant to reinforce the idea of U.S. military power acting on behalf of the general interest, for universal values. Powerful class, institutional, and national interests more or less vanish from sight. (Hardt and Negri's book will be discussed more fully in the next chapter.) As for Marxism, its emphasis on the causal role of underlying economic factors, production, and class relations—surely vital enough in analyzing corporate domination—often relegates the question of military power (seemingly no matter how large the military) to epiphenomenal or secondary status, sometimes ignoring it altogether. History and politics are a product of the clash of social forces, with the military figuring as no more than an instrument of class rule. While sensitive to themes of revolution and armed intervention in general, the Marxist tradition has usually stopped short of *systematic* exploration of military power as such. There is indeed no Marxist sociology of the military, as there is of religion, the family, race relations, politics, culture, and so forth. The most powerful critiques of U.S. militarism, following Mills, have in fact recently come from sources largely *outside* of Marxism—Seymour Melman, Noam Chomsky, Chalmers Johnson—a circumstance that seems hardly accidental. While Chomsky identifies firmly with the anarchist tradition, his work actually stands out as exceptional, insofar as anarchism has historically confronted virtually every form of domination *but* the military, as any familiarity with the literature quickly reveals. In the case of Murray Bookchin, the most revered anarchist theorist in the United States and perhaps the world, one looks in vain for even peripheral references to military power or U.S. global domination in his abundant work.[19] The conventional anarchist focus on distinctly *local* power relations, on the spontaneous energy of grassroots struggles—along with its well-known hostility to the political-governmental realm—clashes with efforts to analyze complex global forces including militarism.

What is true of decidedly *critical* viewpoints like Marxism, anarchism, and postmodernism can readily be extended to mainstream liberal discourses. There is indeed something of a consensus shared by such writers as Alvin and Heidi Toffler, Thomas Friedman, Samuel Huntington, and Francis Fukuyama that both liberal capitalism and economic globalization inevitably give rise to an era of human rights, peace, and democracy on a foundation of open markets and trade, technological development, and consumerism.[20] Liberals do concede that globalization reinforces U.S. global hegemony, but this is axiomatically viewed as a good thing, since the American model, with its embodiment of all these good values, is to be emulated worldwide. Military force is simply another instrument needed to ensure the integrity of this model against all challengers. It is precisely on this basis that Washington elites claim the right to intervene anywhere and any time that evil threatens the harmonious order of global market relations or U.S. geopolitical interests. Liberals (a term that applies to Democrats and Republicans alike) dismiss all competing ideologies as irrational, extremist, a mad refusal to go along with the dictates of history governed by Pax Americana. In the case of Fukuyama, Huntington, and kindred writers who take for granted the "peaceful behavior of democracies," liberal democracy is seen as such retrograde tendencies as imperialism, war, and militarism. In Fukuyama's words: "Liberal democracy replaces the irrational desire to be recognized as greater than others with a rational desire to be recognized as equal. A world made up of liberal-democracies, then, should have much less incentive for war, since all nations would reciprocally recognize one another's legitimacy."[21] War is viewed as the archaic product of "aristocratic masters" who possess a yen for exploitation and domination, whereas "civil peace is brought about by liberals."[22] Why the most established, most powerful liberal democracy in the world also has the longest and most brutal record of militarism among all nations is not explained by such theories; they simply mystify the historical reality. In any event, one finds among liberals of this stripe a more overt, even brazen defense of U.S. military power and imperial designs than among the more critical proponents of globalization, who often sidestep the question altogether.

Matters have changed somewhat, however, since the NATO attack on Yugoslavia, and more emphatically since 9/11 and the onset of the war on terrorism: American liberals and progressives in large numbers have come to more fervently embrace the blessings of the New World Order and with it the role of U.S. military power. Oddly, even with the ascension of Bush's more blatant willingness to intervene in the service of global domination, liberals and progressives have adopted increasingly *uncritical* views of U.S. militarism in the service of Empire. Many have been outright celebratory. For most, U.S.–initiated wars (as in Yugoslavia, Afghanistan, and Iraq) have suddenly been transformed into "good wars" in the tradition of World War II; the horrible lessons of Indochina (or the Vietnam syndrome) have seemingly been purged from historical memory in a world filled with terrible demons to be slayed. The closure of public debate means that ruling elites will have greater autonomy to carry out aggressive foreign and military strategies. A case in point: with the United States perched to attack Iraq in fall 2002, the midterm election campaign was totally devoid of any debates related to the inevitable costs and consequences of war, not to mention the morality of invading a sovereign nation. The war on terrorism shaped all public discourse.

How could such a highly developed, prosperous, literate nation with vast resources in education and communication have arrived at such a disastrous state of affairs—for the United States and the world? How could the political process be so lacking in democratic sensibilities, in moral concerns, in global accountability? The answer must begin with the overarching theme presented in this book: the lack stems from public and intellectual failure to confront the actualities of U.S. military power and the Empire it supports, owing to a deep historical legacy of imperialism, racism, military conquest, and patriotism. Whatever its great advantages as a superpower, the United States has an embarrassingly impoverished and provincial political culture, most visible in global affairs. If this historical legacy seemed to wane after the Vietnam defeat, it has come back with a resurgence over the past decade, and especially since 9/11. In many ways American nationalism, denied by the pundits and intellectuals, constitutes the most powerful source of domestic legitimation. Surely chauvinism, xenophobia, and arrogance enable the vast majority of Americans to take on a cavalier attitude toward war, enabling them to largely ignore the vast costs and consequences involved. As with Iraq, the visitation on other countries of callous feelings toward death and destruction becomes the norm. Elements of the right wing find intrinsic value, even catharsis, in warfare presumably waged for noble ends, while liberals join in the hunt for foreign devils, whether Communists or terrorists. For both, a blind, uncritical support of Israel combined with addiction to the war economy fits into the equation. Cold warriors, along with many on the progressive Left, have for years been obsessed with fighting the ghosts of Stalin and locating the most recent evil dictator to be destroyed by U.S. military force. They too are overcome by a violent, arrogant, patriotic mind-set. The bearers of liberalism, globalization theory, and postmodernism often distance themselves from the imperial outlook, but, as we have seen, their framework sidesteps the overwhelming reality of U.S. military power where it does not glorify such power. Meanwhile, the architects of imperial power and military aggression have more room to maneuver in pursuit of U.S. global domination.

1

THE RISE OF THE
MILITARY BEHEMOTH

The United States has become the domain of a virulent militarism in
defense of an expanding Empire, the dynamic agency of a system of
economic, political, and military domination without parallel in human
history. If America is now the land of the world's last imperial power, that
status increasingly depends on the capacity to rule every corner of the
earth by armed force. Of course the U.S. legacy of colonial power reaches
back to the earliest days of the new republic. Yet the current historical situation is best understood as both rooted in the past and a significant am-
plification of that past, marking an epochal shift in global politics. The
new militarism constitutes a daunting, seemingly unyielding reality of
our time, a phenomenon destined to influence every aspect of historical
development and social life well into the future, through the twenty-first
century and perhaps beyond. References to such terms as "globalization,"
"war," "terrorism," and "world domination" make sense only in the context of the massive resources, technology, and armed might of the American superpower, in possession of the most gargantuan military apparatus
ever, one that extends throughout the world and into space, with a Pentagon budget greater than the military budgets of the next nine countries
combined. For the U.S. Empire to effectively reproduce itself over time,
however, it will require considerable domestic sources of ideological and
material supports—a deepening mass patriotic mobilization behind military power and imperial expansion. As an inevitable by-product of this
development we can expect a progressively militarized society and culture along with a further narrowing of the public sphere, with potentially
devastating consequences for the nations of the world, the global environment, political democracy, the American people, indeed the very fate
of the earth.

THE HISTORICAL TRAJECTORY

To speak of a distinctive *American* militarism at the start of the twenty-first century may seem odd to those attached to the abundant myths of U.S. political education, something in sharp contrast to the peace-loving, altruistic, democratic sensibilities generally understood to define the nation's historical experience. After all, there have been no dramatic military coups or juntas since the founding of the republic, nor has the power of generals and admirals ever overwhelmed the integrity of civilian political rule. Indeed the military has always performed essentially instrumental functions, in the service of institutions, laws, and ideals that lie presumably beyond the scope of Pentagon decision making. The U.S. military, in other words, has been subordinated to the liberal-democratic principles of freedom, citizen participation, national self-determination, and constitutional governance, both domestically and abroad. The time-honored preoccupation with national security, heightened in the aftermath of the September 11, 2001, terrorist attacks, has taken on meaning within this framework. President Woodrow Wilson's view of a strong America "making the world safe for democracy" seemed to capture the spirit and essence of U.S. foreign and military policy during the twentieth century, as did later apparently selfless and democratic motives during the World War II struggle against fascism. At the same time, the U.S. was never particularly known for its string of foreign conquests or network of colonies around the globe, as were earlier Spanish, French, and British empires. Few Americans today would entertain the notion of a U.S. empire or the idea that their country stands for anything but peaceful, democratic, humanitarian ends. As for the concept of militarism, that could describe only such demons as Napoleon or Hitler or Saddam Hussein. Moreover, whatever role the military has played throughout American history would ostensibly be diminishing at a time when globalization, rooted in specifically economic interests and discourses (growth, trade, investment, markets, etc.) would appear to supersede the old-fashioned, clumsy, costly, destructive tools of military violence—a major reason, perhaps, why the specter of U.S. global military power has (at least before 9/11) commanded surprisingly limited attention from scholars, journalists, and politicians.

The uncomfortable and depressing historical reality, unfortunately, scarcely fits this kind of fanciful mythology: U.S. militarism remains more alive than ever, more potent, far-reaching, and menacing than even at the height of the cold war—a generalization likely to take on greater validity in the wake of 9/11 and its upshot, the war on terrorism that Bush promised to extend indefinitely across the globe. Consider that in just fourteen years the United States has carried out significant direct military interventions no less than six times: Panama, Iraq (twice), Somalia, the Balkans, Afghanistan. Other potential targets are on the Pentagon drawing board, including Iran,

Syria, and North Korea. A tradition of military power and conquest runs long and deep, providing added thrust to the contemporary expansion of U.S. imperial rule through a combination of economic, political, cultural, and military vehicles, often concealed behind a facade of democratic structures and above all discourses. As Howard Zinn writes, "aggressive expansion was a constant of national ideology and policy," which, of course, uniformly depended on lofty moral claims and justifications.[1] The actual history is one of conquest and dominion, of territorial aggrandizement and imposition of social order through outright coercion—genocidal wars against Indian tribes, the theft of land from Mexico and Spain, and the invasion of Russia after World War I, followed by a succession of bloody military interventions in Korea, Indochina, Central America, the Caribbean, the Persian Gulf, and the Balkans—not to mention countless proxy wars, covert actions, and other interventions waged in scores of nations.

U.S. colonial expansion, mixed with elements of corporate power, militarism, and racism, has historically unfolded beneath the veneer of Enlightenment rationality, with its ideals of social progress, modernity, democracy, and economic growth tied to advances in science and technology. While outwardly espousing peace and cooperation, American ruling elites have championed an ideology of militarism and lauded the (always necessary) pursuit of war, recognizing the value of armed might in the assertion of U.S. economic and geopolitical interests. Though scarcely written about in high-school or even college textbooks, American nationalism has always been ethnocentric, messianic, and arrogant, tied as it has been to an ethos of expansion and conquest. Upholding a worldview that stresses legal and moral precepts, elites themselves have never bothered with such matters, preferring instead the agenda of gunboats, marine invasions, aerial bombardments, and other expressions of brute armed power to go along with the routines of economic calculation and plunder. Beneath high-sounding ideals has been the mundane actuality of a ruthless, manipulative realpolitik that, when practiced by other nations, has been scornfully attacked for its naked, Machiavellian self-interest. This dark side of U.S. foreign and military policy is hardly aberrant, a function of mistakes or miscalculations, but has been integral to the developmental process itself, justified by some privileged mandate: national interest, God, Manifest Destiny, the Monroe Doctrine, the American Century, the struggle against an evil Communism, or simply the virtues of freedom and democracy that must be spread around the world. Such mandates have been, for the most part, taken as holy imperatives by all sectors of the power structure, just as today Republicans and Democrats alike affirm the priorities of Empire, the right of military intervention, the permanent war economy.

Today the ethos of militarism—of conquest, domination, and violence—permeates the American economy, political institutions, culture, and of course foreign policy. This is no longer simply a matter of Pentagon power. It could hardly be otherwise given the country's position as sole remaining super-power, combined with its long historical trajectory. The United States has un-rivaled military control over the world's landmasses, sea lanes, and air spaces, with great aspirations toward the colonization of outer space, revealing in great relief what Chalmers Johnson refers to as "an imperial project that the Cold War obscured."[2] Consuming (in 2004) roughly $400 billion yearly, the sprawling Pentagon system deploys troops in more than five hundred major bases around the globe, crucial to monitoring and protecting the New World Order. As in the past, American global power today requires ongoing infra-structural development, resource mobilization, massive research and develop-ment, general preparedness, a huge communications network, and recurrent armed interventions, suggesting that it was Theodore Roosevelt and not Woodrow Wilson who may have best capsulized the thrust of U.S. global pol-itics. Speaking in 1897, just seven years after the Wounded Knee massacre of Sioux men, women, and children and only a year before the United States would go to war against Spain as the first step toward Empire, Roosevelt com-mented: "In strict confidence . . . I should welcome almost any war, for I think this country needs one."[3] For Roosevelt, as for most subsequent American leaders, war never amounted to the opposite of peace but rather was viewed as a redemptive, purifying, ennobling form of human activity, just another ex-tension of modernity and progress. The only difference separating Roosevelt from most subsequent presidents is the former's greater candor.

As the United States continues to celebrate the virtues of international order, human rights, and democracy—never missing an opportunity to lec-ture nations like China and Cuba for their human-rights abuses—its ruling elites have become increasingly reckless and violent, brazenly violating every global norm they pretend to uphold. In world politics the United States has become an outlaw country, the rogue state of all rogue states, in-tent on transforming the process of globalization into the building blocks of empire and military domination, so far with considerable success. In spring 1999 the United States, working beneath the NATO umbrella, bombed Yu-goslavia for seventy-nine consecutive days, destroying factories, apartment buildings, schools, hospitals, water-treatment plants, electrical and commu-nications systems, and transportation networks, nearly wiping out the civil-ian infrastructure—a blatant act of military aggression violating every canon of international law, including the UN Charter and even the NATO Char-ter itself. Bombs were dropped on densely populated urban areas. Antiper-sonnel bombs were used on both civilian and military targets, along with various projectiles tipped with depleted uranium. Justified as a "humanitar-ian" intervention to counter Serb "ethnic cleansing" in Kosovo, the war was designed to strengthen NATO's eastward expansion and secure U.S. and Western geopolitical ambitions in the Balkans—a vital region linking Europe with the Middle East. In certain respects NATO's attack on Serbia can be understood as the first war carried out in defense of the global market system,[4] requiring few if any casualties among the aggressors.

The great "efficiency" with which the United States and its allies rained death and destruction on Yugoslavia was made possible in part by lessons drawn from the Persian Gulf War and, to a lesser extent, the 1989 Panama invasion. The Gulf War of 1991 was conducted as essentially a technowar massacre of Iraqis, viewed in the United States as media spectacle and patriotic celebration. Over the next twelve years the war continued largely through periodic U.S. and British bombing missions and harsh economic sanctions ostensibly intended to make Hussein jettison his weapons of mass destruction and move toward arms reductions. With no Soviet military response to worry about, the United States entered the post–cold war era by bombing this poor, nearly defenseless, but resource-rich nation of twenty-three million into oblivion. The first Gulf War, with its intensified militaristic ideology fueled by worship of high-tech weaponry, came to approximate the "perfect war." A venture to protect mainly Western oil interests, the intervention was cloaked in high-sounding rhetoric about national self-determination, human rights, and the need to restrain another Hitler-like demon. The mass media, ever obedient to Pentagon agendas, perpetuated this mythology by means of a continuous barrage of lies, distortions, caricatures, and sensational images that would have made the old Hearst press rather proud.[5] The first Gulf War and its aftermath cost the lives of hundreds of thousands of Iraqis, the majority of them civilian.

The 1991 Gulf War might be viewed as a dress rehearsal for the full-scale invasion and occupation of Iraq twelve years later, which released pent-up frustrations of neoconservative "defense intellectuals" over the earlier Bush decision to stop short of regime change. Obsessed with overthrow of Hussein even without UN endorsement and the support of nations like France, Germany, and Russia, the United States in 2002 invoked the "Bush Doctrine" of preemptive strike to finish off its crusade for economic and geopolitical control of the Gulf region. Once again, these real strategic objectives were pursued under cover of a series of largely fraudulent claims—that Iraqi weapons of mass destruction (WMD) posed an imminent threat to the United States and the world, that Iraq was on the verge of developing nuclear weapons, that Hussein was connected with al Qaeda, and so forth. In the recycled Gulf War the U.S. military quickly pulverized the disorganized resistance, hit hard at the nation's infrastructure, and declared victory in just three weeks—though occupation of a defeated but generally hostile population would prove to be an entirely different matter. As of early summer 2004, the military action had cost more than fifty thousand military and civilian lives combined, leaving a nation already debilitated by three wars and economic sanctions in shambles. Recalling some of the worst excesses of nineteenth-century Western imperialism, the United States simply took over Iraq by force, set up its own governing body, imposed martial law, and severely limited other international presences in the country. The parallels between the Indian wars of previous centuries and the second Gulf War to extend the New World Order is too obvious to overlook.

The criminal and hypocritical nature of such U.S. military aggression deserves far more attention than it has received in the domestic media, academic world, and political arena, where objections are usually limited to instrumental concerns of timing, costs, and mobilizing support. The popular media in particular, more than ever an extension of corporate and governmental power, seem to have abandoned any critical role in society. In the Gulf circumstances, no doubt the Iraqis did retain some WMD capabilities, but from every credible report—following many years of international inspections—they were tiny by global standards, especially in comparison with such states as Israel. More to the point, the moralizing, hectoring demands of American leaders for Iraqi accountability sound preposterous in view of the fact that the United States has for many decades been in the forefront of producing, selling, deploying, and *using* WMD. Indeed Iraq itself was once a beneficiary of American weapons-making largesse. We know that the United States has conducted far more nuclear tests than any other country, disseminating vast amounts of radiation beneath and above the ground. It carried out devastating chemical warfare in Vietnam with lethal devices manufactured by Monsanto, Dow, and DuPont, dumping millions of pounds of Agent Orange, napalm, white phosphorous, and other toxins into a fragile ecosystem, where they will remain for many decades. It used terrifying fuel-air bombs over Iraq and Afghanistan. It carried out terror bombings of densely populated cities at the end of World War II, using special incendiary devices to produce firestorms, including a massive raid on Tokyo with nearly 1,100 bombers just a day before the armistice was signed.[6] The atomic leveling of Hiroshima and Nagasaki in the final days of the war clearly had no military value. Throughout the postwar era American leaders consistently made the first moves in the arms race with the USSR, managing to keep ahead while stimulating new phases in the balance of terror at every turn. When it comes to weapons of mass destruction, the United States can readily lay claim to the status of world champion.

The military operations against Iraq, Yugoslavia, and Afghanistan, along with the earlier quick invasion of Panama, were part of a U.S. foreign policy shift intended to exorcise the demons of the Indochina defeat—to purge the Vietnam syndrome, representing defeat and impotence—as well as lay the foundations of U.S. global supremacy. A powerfully resurgent military, accompanied by a strong resolve to use it, would presumably restore national pride. The Pentagon would be given considerably greater freedom of maneuver in a post–cold war universe filled with new challenges. In the case of

Vietnam, the United States behaved with little moral constraint, dumping seven million tons of bombs on the country, leaving an unparalleled legacy of destruction in a poor Third World nation. What overcoming the Vietnam syndrome meant in this context was the obsession with getting beyond military failure and learning the crucial lesson of defeat: namely, break the old reliance on ground warfare by adopting high-tech (mostly aerial) weaponry. While politically "rational" in certain respects, this is a recipe for rekindled militarism, which has become an integral feature of the New World Order. Yet it is a militarism that, dedicated as ever to consolidation of Empire, acquires important new dimensions that will be explored throughout this book.

The new militarism is best understood within the historical convergence of the end of the cold war, rise of the United States as single world hegemon, high-tech warfare, corporate-driven globalization, and, more recently, the aftershock of major terrorist attacks. We have an unprecedented concentration of economic and political power in the hands of a small stratum of elites, ruling through transnational corporations and such global agencies as the World Bank, IMF, WTO, and even the UN. Except for the United States and possibly a few other G-8 nations, the vast global economy has moved beyond the effective reach of local and national decision-making bodies; the international arena is authoritarian to the core. At the same time, the world system as a whole—and the many countries within it—is beset with fragmentation, chaos, instability, and violence (civic and state) that often lacks ideological definition.[7] The signs are abundantly clear: they include the growing divide between rich and poor (both within and between countries), massive social dislocations, local warfare, acts of terrorism and the threat of nuclear war, the spread of new diseases, the proliferation of dangerous weapons including, of course, WMD. Such a Hobbesian state of nature provides an ideal setting for military intervention, for assertion of a dictatorial Leviathan in a context where "order" (read: New World Order) threatens to unravel. For the custodians of U.S. national power, "threat" is equated with any stirrings of independence, ideological deviations, or challenges to American domination within the global system.

From an ideological standpoint, the U.S. Empire will have some difficulty sustaining itself within a matrix of market relations, instrumental rationality, consumerism, and the rampant local disorder that infuses the whole panorama of global corporate colonization. The inevitable loss of community, social infrastructure, ecological balance, and democratic practices is bound to nourish conditions of social polarization, violent conflict, upheaval, and blowback—consequences fruitful to the growth of popular movements but also to a virulent superpower response, as we have already seen. Efforts to resolve these contradictions by military force, as the United States is regularly poised to do, only generate further, perhaps more explosive, contradictions on a world scale.

In the midst of dramatic changes in global politics, in the aftermath of the Soviet collapse and the waning of the cold war, and despite several years of Pentagon downsizing and modernization, U.S. militarism at the start of the new century is more robust and expansionary than ever. The renewed threat of global terrorism, precipitating heightened American vigilance and action, has merely *reinforced* this tendency. U.S. foreign policy is tied to the same long-standing agendas—permanent war economy, pursuit of geopolitical supremacy, continuing search for new enemies—that held sway throughout the cold war era. While forms of intervention remain local, they have become systemic, ruthless, and globally defined at a time when high-tech warfare renders military ventures more cruelly one-sided and less costly for the superpower. Here "globalization" takes on yet another meaning—a process integral to the struggle of American elites to remake the world according to neoliberal, corporate priorities. Familiar past enemies (Communists, Fascists) are replaced by a new set of demons: rogue states, terrorists, local tyrants, drug traffickers, and the like. Imperial stratagems take different forms, including manipulation of international bodies (UN, WTO, World Bank, etc.), covert actions, global surveillance, political and diplomatic initiatives, and economic sanctions, with military intervention always lurking in the background, ready to come to the forefront. Political atrophy throughout the international arena helps to further clear away obstacles to U.S. pursuit of global domination.[8]

As Noam Chomsky argues, the 1990s witnessed a new phase of international relations: shrouded in moralizing discourses of peace and human rights, American policy makers, setting themselves up as guardians of the world system, reached a point of flagrant disregard for global laws and conventions seen as standing in the way of their own interests.[9] Every instance of U.S. armed intervention in the 1980s and 1990s constitutes a gross violation of regional treaties and laws, not to mention the UN Charter itself, which prohibits military aggression against sovereign nations (for example, Grenada, Nicaragua, Panama, Serbia, Afghanistan, and Iraq). In any event, the United States has consistently shown contempt for international bodies, agreements, and procedures, all the more so as it has gained unchallenged domination—a point developed further in chapter 5.

The "Clinton Doctrine" of the 1990s fits the pattern of an aggressive foreign policy in the service of neoliberal arrangements tied to free trade, privatization, deregulation, social cutbacks, and open foreign investment. As the first president of the new global era, Clinton visited more than seventy countries, set up the WTO, pushed through NAFTA, boosted the international budget, maintained high levels of Pentagon spending, militarized the drug wars in South America, continued the military/economic assault on Iraq, laid the groundwork for "humanitarian" interventions, bombed the Sudan and Afghanistan, and carried out warfare in the Balkans. His doctrine actually broadened the parameters of U.S. military operations, despite talk of Pentagon reductions, arms limitations, base closings, and armed-services demobilizations—all done under the auspices of military modernization. Meanwhile, the United States failed to confront such growing international problems as poverty, disease, and human-rights abuses within or outside regions under its influence, in fact lending support to nations (Israel, Turkey, Indonesia, Colombia, Pakistan) recognized as the worst abusers. During the Clinton years, moreover, the United States balked at paying its UN dues, rejected a ban on land mines, dragged its feet on nuclear reductions, and kept alive the Reagan-Bush Star Wars program. Enthused by the prospect of total surveillance of the world, Clinton raised intelligence spending to new levels ($70 billion officially), with new emphasis on the supersecret National Security Agency. The planned, systematic, and near-total destruction of the Serb economy must be considered one of the most egregious war crimes of the postwar years.

Clinton's brand of globalism was quickly ratified by the incoming Bush administration, when Secretary of State Colin Powell, speaking in January 2001, announced the possibility of using American forces anywhere in defense of national interests and a neoliberal order regarded as morally and politically superior to any conceivable rival. Powell asserted that the United States occupies a special niche in its historic commitment to worldwide peace, prosperity, and democracy—all guaranteed by the great achievements of corporate capitalism and backed by fearsome military might—echoing almost word for word what Secretary of State Madeleine Albright had repeated throughout the Clinton presidency. Powell blithely commented that "other systems do not work. We are going to show a vision to the world of the value system of America." He added: "The U.S. has a special role in the world and should not adhere to every international agreement and convention that someone thinks to propose."[10] For the U.S. power structure, at least, economic globalization and military power are part of the same logic.

Soon after Bush II assumed office, the United States turned its back on the Kyoto global warming accords, endorsed Clinton's rejection of the land-mine treaty, refused to go along with the universal ban on biological weapons, was in the process of abrogating the 1972 Anti-Ballistic Missile arms-control treaty, and dismissed the International Criminal Court set up in Rome as counter to U.S. national interests. Further, by virtue of its pursuit of Star Wars the United States was violating the landmark 1967 Outer Space Treaty prohibiting the militarization of space. Bush also floated proposals to terminate environmental standards concerning Pentagon operations within the country and around the world. This arrogant, reckless, indeed lawless outlook was designed precisely to give the U.S. military a freer hand in policing the globe. If the first Bush administration gave us the New World Order, the second Bush presidency in its brief tenure has laid out a global strategy rooted in a new militarism geared to the defense of that same order.

The new militarism is located at the intersection of globalization and the entrenchment of U.S. economic, political, and military power—a matrix well beyond the question of who specifically is involved in elite decision making. Democrats and Republicans, with just a few exceptions, are in full agreement on this larger trajectory. The confluence of processes mentioned above has taken the United States to the apex of the world system. The United States stands alone in its vast capacity to wield economic, institutional, and coercive instruments to get what it wants in a world of chaos. The refinement of technowar endows military combat with a certain routinized, impersonal quality, while high-tech communications allow for modes of surveillance and control, making Orwell's predictions of a Big Brother apparatus seem rather tepid. The U.S. military option is emboldened by a mixture of factors: local chaos within the global system, challenges from rogue states, the threat of terrorism, the proliferation of WMD, the imminent rise of potential competing national powers, and the all-important struggle for material resources (oil, water, timber, minerals, etc.) at a time when scarcity, population pressures, and ecological crisis can be expected to generate new stresses and rivalries. As Michael Klare writes: "Whereas international conflict was until recently governed by political and ideological considerations, the wars of the future will largely be fought over the possession and control of vital economic goods—especially resources needed for the functioning of modern industrial societies."[11] As the largest consumer of material resources by far, the United States finds itself in the deepest predicament, one reason its elites are so anxious to sustain maximum military power and flexibility.

The result has been a more aggressive U.S. foreign policy reliant on worldwide mobility, technological warfare, surveillance, and an ongoing search for new villains—who, in the wake of 9/11, will be rather easy to locate. Stepped-up militarization of the drug wars, as in Plan Colombia, which justifies a long-term U.S. presence in resource-laden South America, fits this pattern. Plan Colombia, designed to get rid of both coca production and armed insurgency, brought new levels of U.S. economic and military aid, including a network of "advisers," into the region. In Colombia as in several other countries, drug lords and narco traffickers provide ideal demons, although military operatives cannot easily distinguish between armed units and civilian populations.

Whatever the locale or particular objectives at stake, U.S. imperialism is the product of a long and continuous history: from start to present the trajectory has involved a convergence of propertied interests, colonial vision, territorial expansion, and militarism. World War II gave the United States the international superiority it had sought earlier. During the postwar years a series of wars and interventions has brought the American military apparatus to a position of unchallenged global power, solidified by the collapse of the Soviet bloc—leaving only Russian weaponry as a major concern for U.S. national security. The Pentagon system is held together by a powerful ensemble of corporate, governmental, and military elites, legitimated by bipartisan support, patriotism, and the massive influence of the media. Despite the apparent breadth of this legitimation, in fact U.S. elites comprise a narrow, insular stratum attached to an equally narrow (neoliberal) ideology that enjoys far less support globally than domestically. By the early twenty-first century the United States has reached the point of having greater power across the global landscape than any nation in history. One major outcome of so much power is the increased prospect of strong resistance to Empire, of blowback in one form or another, most dramatically visible in the terrorist attacks of 9/11. Another is the growing difficulty of establishing democratic controls over globalized corporate, political, and military decision-making structures.

With the ascension of Bush II to the presidency, the events of 9/11, the global war on terrorism, and the quick invasion of Iraq, the very *idea* of U.S. Empire is becoming widely accepted more or less across the political spectrum. Indeed elites no longer seem much troubled by the reference. If mainstream liberals and conservatives feel uncomfortable with the label, preferring the more detached rhetoric of the New World Order, neoconservatives increasingly dispense with any qualms about the role of U.S. imperial power—it might be ruthless and violent but it is necessary, ultimately benevolent, something now and then to celebrate.[12] Of course leftists have for decades identified Empire as the logical outgrowth of capitalism, with its incessant search for markets, cheap labor, and raw materials. The difference now is that Empire has come to signify a more established fact of international relations, an objective, seemingly irreversible development. To the degree this is so, the phenomenon cannot be understood in terms of specific administrations, leaders, and policies, for it is rooted deeply in history, beyond the decisions of specific presidents or legislatures.

The problem for Empire, however, is that it sharply conflicts with the stated, legitimating ideals of American politics—democracy, rule of law, consensual government, rights, and so forth—insofar as it embraces just the opposite: unbridled power, authoritarian rule, horrific violence, abandonment of ethical and legal constraints. Intrinsic to Empire is a coercive world system dominated by the United States and held together by concentrated economic, political, and military power, rather than by general market processes, democratic governance, or the glue of ideological hegemony. Empire is reproduced by means of economic leverage, political manipulation, secret deliberations, surveillance and control, covert actions, and of course military intervention. The closest historical model for this is the lengthy

U.S. imperial domination of Latin America, where rule was typically anything but consensual and participatory. True enough, the Roman and
British empires rested on widespread coercion, but the scope was more limited and their capacity to project every mode of power across the entire
globe was far weaker.

While the situation has dramatically changed since 9/11, therefore, it
is possible to establish an imperial continuity leading up to and into the
Bush II administration. If Bush validates and embellishes the shift toward a
new militarism, this may be less a matter of substance than of *style*: he shares
with Clinton and other predecessors exactly the same imperial project in
defense of U.S. geopolitical and corporate interests. To be sure, Bush has
pursued this aim more aggressively, more overtly, perhaps even more recklessly than could be said of Clinton. At the same time, it is hard to forget
that the Clinton presidency was manifestly conservative, notably in foreign
policy. Clinton firmly believed that expansion of U.S. power should rest on
a base of multilateralism, broad international consent, a respect for UN conventions, and economic imperatives. He wanted to avoid behaving in such
a way as to alienate large regions of the world. By early 2003, Bush, incited
by 9/11 and the war on terrorism, and with the idea of indulging the neocons, had already launched perhaps the most aggressive U.S. foreign policy
ever. His chosen instrument—military action—had already undermined the
fragile world system. His initiatives turned out to be bold, uncompromising,
unilateral, and dismissive of the language of democratic legitimation. It is
easy to detect a line of continuity from the Monroe Doctrine to the "Bush
Doctrine."

Under Bush and the neocons, however, American global power remains in many ways fragile and vulnerable, as the increasing reliance on coercive methods inevitably reflects. After 9/11 the United States became
hell-bent on a course of vengeful action, the sign of a retributive and indeed
weakened national ego—the same ideological syndrome underlying historical Fascism in countries like Italy and Germany.[13] Bush's primary mode of
international policy has been to strike back, to punish, to make amends for
the past, downplaying the political, economic, and above all *ideological* requirements for world order. While Bush has adeptly inflamed and exploited
nationalism for political and military purposes, he has essentially shown
contempt for that very world order, flaunting power at the UN, making a
travesty of international law and treaties, and justifying military aggression
on the basis of a phony concept of preemptive war. There is serious doubt
that the present U.S. modus operandi will be compatible with the conditions needed for global domination—a theme that will be explored more
fully in the concluding chapter. In many ways Bush's recklessness could do
more to *subvert* than to reproduce U.S. imperial power. The new militarism
is Janus-faced: achieving short-term armed victories, it affirms the efficacy

of brute force but simultaneously undercuts the requirements for *ideological hegemony* needed for stable Empire over time.

As U.S. military power veers out of control, beyond the reach of democratic mechanisms or countervailing forces, the *consequences* of such power flexed throughout the Empire will likewise be uncontrollable. At the time of this writing (summer 2004) American forces are looking to solidify their harsh occupation of Iraq in the midst of continuing fierce resistance, just as the Pentagon is drawing up "contingency plans" for military action in such nations as Syria, North Korea, and Iran (plans likely to be put on hold as long as the Iraq quagmire deepens). U.S. domination breeds instability, resistance, and blowback even as the country's institutional power expands. The twenty-first century figures to be a time of increasing blowback, as Chalmers Johnson argues. The struggle to achieve and maintain global domination is sure to bring, in response, a perpetual spiral of authoritarianism, decay, violence, insurgency—and indeed terrorism. If the U.S. military can deliver massive blows anywhere with relatively few *immediate* risks and costs, blowback follows a more protracted, torturous, uncertain path: local attacks on U.S. targets, proliferation of "incidents," popular movements, terrorism, sabotage, guerrilla insurgency, and simply mounting general revulsion toward U.S. power wherever it is experienced.

The problem is that military power alone, whatever its geographical scope or technological capacity, cannot supply its own legitimacy or build the firmaments of global stability over the long run—as popular insurgencies against superior armed strength in Vietnam, South Africa, Algeria, and Israel have demonstrated. Effective political governance, in contrast to authoritarian rule in its different guises, requires ideological hegemony. The very logic of military domination ensures ongoing chaos and resistance, as the nightmare of U.S. occupation in Iraq has quickly and (for the elites) shockingly revealed. U.S. militarism has also met with terrorist episodes in Saudi Arabia and Morocco, insurgencies in the Philippines and Colombia, and deep anti-American sentiment in France, Germany, Russia, China, and Indonesia, to name only a few countries. It spurred worldwide antiwar mobilizations in the period leading up to the war on Iraq. Michael Hardt and Antonio Negri refer to the explosive "novelty" of the new imperialist situation: "Empire creates a greater potential for revolution than did the modern regimes of power because it presents us, alongside the machine of command, with an alternative: the set of all the exploited and subjugated, a multitude that is directly opposed to Empire, with no mediation between them."[14]

Viewed in this context, the new militarism—sure to be fueled by an interminable U.S. war on terrorism—can be understood despite its novelty as an extension of the American past, a further expression of the frontier ethos of conquest and domination, in which war against impediments to "progress" and national interests is pursued as a sacred right and duty. There will always be "good" wars to be fought and won by leaders of an Empire. While embedded in a certain institutional rationality, this is nothing less than the culture of an outlaw nation that, in an era when the threat of mass-destruction weapons is greater than ever, represents the greatest danger to world peace, perhaps even planetary survival.

GLOBALIZATION AND EMPIRE

The expansion of a globalized capitalist system and the consolidation of U.S. Empire are processes that have unfolded hand in hand over the past few decades. Economic globalization is best viewed as the systemic development of corporate power across national borders in perpetual search of markets, raw materials, low-cost labor, and technological advantage—all made possible by the growing mobility of capital and facilitated by increasingly fluid conditions of trade, communications, and information sharing. An outgrowth of preceding centuries of economic development spreading from Europe outward, this process has dramatically increased its speed and breadth since the 1970s, further solidifying the world system along with its leading national and international centers of power. At its existing pace this form of corporate expansion is sweeping away everything before it, allowing for the unprecedented flourishing of market relations in even the most isolated regions of the globe, as Marx and Engels long ago anticipated in the *Communist Manifesto*.[15] These epic trends within the economy, however, have no parallel in the sphere of *politics*, where what we observe is something altogether different: the decline of local and national decision making, erosion of long-standing political ideologies, and failure of an international system of governance to take hold. The appearance of worldwide diversity and fragmentation is now overshadowed by a homogenizing logic brought about by transnational corporate rule, with its unifying thrust toward commodification of the planet. We are in the midst of a profoundly depoliticizing shift of forces in which the global domain triumphs over the local, the commodity supersedes autonomous social life, standardization prevails over diversity—and, above all, economics takes precedence over politics. It is precisely within this historical trajectory—the triumph of global corporate power along with the shrinking of politics—that the militarism of Empire asserts itself.

The seemingly unified global economy, presumed essence of the New World Order, barely conceals its own sharpening contradictions, as we have seen. At the start of the new century roughly 80 percent of the world's population lives in poor countries that control less than 20 percent of the total resources and wealth. The assets of the three richest people in the world amount to more than the combined gross domestic products of the fifty least developed nations, while some 350 global billionaires have amassed an income equivalent to that of two and a half billion people. The richest one-fifth consume nearly 90 percent of all global resources at a time when one-quarter of the planet is illiterate, one-third lacks clean water, and two-thirds have no adequate sewage. The neoliberal market hegemony championed by transnational corporations and ruling elites of the G–8 nations is meant to ameliorate these severe imbalances and inequities, all of them worsening by the day, as well as any serious challenges to corporate domination itself. In pursuit of such domination, corporate-driven globalization anticipates nothing short of a neoliberal "end of history" presided over by the WTO, IMF, and World Bank operating in tandem with the transnationals. Global-ization thus represents a mechanism, however imbalanced and uneven, for solving crises generated by systemic dysfunctions and conflicts. Globalism is designed to manage and rationalize class relations, forms of production and work, and the relationship between human beings and the environment—without any effective Keynesian *political* agency. If unbridled corporate power can give rise to chaos and violence, then a smooth functioning of the global order based on universal governing criteria becomes the structural antidote. In the absence of viable governing mechanisms, however—and owing to the anarchic tendencies of world capitalism—military solutions will seem all too tempting, especially with such a huge apparatus already in place.

The global system creates a heightened division of labor, with produc-tion, finance, and commerce in many ways decentralized while their man-agement is further *centralized,* located in the headquarters of transnational corporations and their host nations in North America, Europe, and Japan. This level of concentrated power is unprecedented, as are its consequences. One phenomenon that allows for simultaneous integration and decentral-ization of the world economy is the rapid advance of informational tech-nology. While proponents of this system envision a new era of prosperity and democracy fueled by material growth across the globe, the reality has been something quite different: massive social dislocations, growing ex-tremes of rich and poor, increasing disconnection between centers of eco-nomic decision making and political structures that previously nourished local participation and democratic citizenship. Larger zones of human exis-tence wind up subordinated to the supposed laws and dictates of the inter-national market, with the concerns of labor, health, human rights, and the environment pushed beyond the reach of public intervention—one disas-trous outcome of the evisceration of public life in the age of neoliberal domination. The more accentuated the power, the more difficult will be the task of mounting popular challenges to market preeminence over society and nature. Today the goal of "public" institutions like the WTO, IMF, and

World Bank is essentially to safeguard capitalist development by rationalizing the framework for investment, production, and trade, with other agendas (related to labor, the environment, and human rights, for example) devalued. With diminished political resources available to local structures and groups, the negative effects of unrestrained corporate expansion will be difficult to confront. On one side this blockage has given rise to a series of popular antiglobalization movements that gained momentum in late 1999. On the other side it opens the door to renewed (U.S.) militarism in circumstances where smooth functioning of the New World Order breaks down or comes under challenge.

A New World Order will have serious problems sustaining itself within the matrix of market relations, instrumental rationality, consumerism, and rampant individualism that infuses the whole panorama of corporate colonization. The social and political disorder that accompany bureaucratic order nourish conditions of polarization, upheaval, and violence, with catastrophe perhaps not too far over the horizon. These features are built into a capitalist trajectory geared to an endless search for markets, profits, open investment and trade, maximized growth, and new areas of the planet to explore and colonize. The social Darwinian ethos intrinsic to this developmental model is reflected not only in economics but at all levels of social and political life, including in the world of politics. Material processes take on a life of their own, undermining the ecosystem as they destroy forests and soil; pollute the land, air, and water; produce global warming; deplete natural resources; and leave behind a large belt of blighted communities and cities. Planetary devastation is endemic to capitalist globalism and the political atrophy it brings: in the absence of effective worldwide mechanisms for public intervention, lacking genuine regulatory controls, the system veers toward escalating crisis and possible breakdown. At the same time, the power of local states, labor, community groups, and social movements to reverse this pattern has been compromised by the enlarged scope of corporate and imperial power. New rules of governance for the global economy are lacking, while structures needed to establish such rules are either weakened (the UN) or fully subordinated to the power structure.

One possible avenue out of this morass, for ruling elites if not for the fate of the earth and its inhabitants, would be the emergence of a new transnational class ready to consolidate the world economy on new ideological and institutional footing. The outcome might be similar to the ascendancy of social-democratic parties in Europe and elsewhere during the twentieth century—parties dedicated to refurbishing and managing capitalism along Keynesian welfare-state lines. In some quarters it is predicted, or at least hoped, that a governing apparatus with similar functions will emerge globally. The very trajectory of global capitalism, with its anarchic and self-destructive tendencies, would seem to force such an outcome.

According to Leslie Sklair and kindred globalization theorists, we are today witnessing the appearance, uneven and still fragmented, of precisely this kind of transnational capitalist class (TCC), which presides over an integrative process conceived, organized, promoted, and defended by streamlined economic, political, and cultural instruments. As Sklair puts it, "Globalization is driven by identifiable actors working through institutions they own and control." Using global systems theory, he suggests that "the most important transnational forces are the transnational corporations, the transnational capitalist class, and the culture-ideology of consumerism. The power and authority of the members of the transnational capitalist class derive from the corporations they own and control."[16] This new class is beginning to constitute itself as a "transnational dominant class" in some spheres of globalization, evolving to the level where it has assumed institutional control over market processes often regarded as self-regulating or anarchic. From this premise Sklair argues that the TCC reproduces itself through a complex hegemonic apparatus, namely the "profit-driven culture-ideology of consumerism." Once solidified, the TCC, operating in its own self-interest, can expect to work toward resolving two central global crises: the increasing gulf between rich and poor, and the ecologically unsustainable path of worldwide capitalism.[17] The TCC functions within four distinct but overlapping tiers—local, national, international (World Bank, IMF, WTO), and global corporations. There is presently so much at stake in the fruits of economic globalization, as Sklair observes, that elites presiding over it cannot simply allow it to unfold spontaneously, as if simple free-market logic prevailed; a grow-or-die system requires cohesive organizational structures and planning mechanisms if it hopes to survive long-term. Since the TCC cannot be expected to gain absolute power, it will need ancillary groupings such as bureaucrats, managers, politicians, various professional experts, and media operatives to carry out its historical ambitions.

Other writers have advanced similar projections. Thus William Robinson suggests that globalization has already reconfigured the whole character of class and power relations as capital expands with fluidity across every region of the globe, breaking down old territorial and institutional barriers while also laying the groundwork for a *transformed* network of political forms and processes. We know that globalization has already begun to erode national boundaries and reduce the independence of particular states, economies, social structures, and cultures. In Robinson's view, however, the nation-state does not wither away under the onslaught of global capital but in effect becomes *reconstituted* and internationalized as part of an emergent world ruling class. Supranational planning bodies—the WTO, IMF, World Bank, European Union (EU), even the UN—essentially collaborate with national structures and corporations to ensure growth and stability in the general economy. Thus national states retain power in a multilayered and pluralized system, but the power is built on symbiosis with and integration into the globalizing process, rather than separation from it. As territoriality recedes, the state systems (local, national, international) become a locus of the very class relations that permeate every other aspect of the global terrain. In this milieu national states wind up as little more than instruments for advancing the priorities of global capitalism, meaning neoliberal deregulation, fiscal austerity, social cutbacks, and economic privatization—priorities that local forces seem powerless to resist. Like Sklair, Robinson believes that the TCC, ever fearful of anarchy and breakdown but committed to an unfettered "free market," is forced to legitimate itself on a foundation of consumerism that serves above all to depoliticize mass publics.[18] Here politics, shorn of its democratic rhetoric, is reserved for global elites whose dilemma is that too little state control means possible chaos, while expanded state involvement potentially restricts their cherished freedom of action.

The idea of a transnational capitalist class that could stabilize the world system depends on a merging of different expressions of corporate power—economic and political, global and local. State autonomy is severely constrained, if not eviscerated altogether. One assumption underlying this thesis is that all nations are moving inexorably toward a neoliberal future in which effective national and local governance, not to mention antisystem social movements, will be essentially checkmated. An era of TCC rule, and with it some form of international planning, cannot logically be dismissed as an eventual possibility. At the start of the twenty-first century, however, prospects for such a globally unified system, presided over by a cohesive transnational elite, still appear remote. Tensions between national states and the imperatives of economic globalization are nowhere close to being resolved. Obstacles to transnational integration, both geopolitical and ideological, remain firmer than ever. Nation-states have long and complex histories that cannot be reduced to relations of production or class forces, and indeed competition among the most powerful of these states shows no signs of vanishing. Neoliberal ideology remains a fragile basis of unity and legitimacy at any level; consumerism might be viable for privileged countries like the United States, Japan, and Germany, but hardly for the global system as a whole. It is undeniably true that nation-states, viewed in terms of democratic leverage, have suffered considerable loss of power and autonomy. Yet the crucial fact remains that no international body has taken up specifically territorial, coercive, or military functions historically possessed by sovereign governments.

The vast majority of states in the world today still possess a monopoly over the deployment of "legitimate" violence and will continue to have it in the absence of any truly internationalized military force, which is nowhere on the horizon. (UN peacekeeping missions in the Balkans, Africa, and elsewhere, always patchwork and ad hoc, scarcely qualify as such a force.) This is notably the case with countries that have built strong militaries, above all the United States in its heightened role as world hegemon. Without a transnational state in control of its own military and police forces, it would be inaccurate to speak of a politically viable transnational capitalist *class,* even if some constituent elements of that class are already in place.

The persistence and growth of U.S. military power requires attention that it often does not receive at a time when globalization discourses seem so compelling. As we have seen, American economic, political, and military domination has actually increased throughout the international arena precisely in tandem with the processes of globalization identified by Sklair and Robinson, even as the *general* decline of nation-states proceeds without interruption. The United States presides over a reconstructed Empire as the lone superpower of the moment, a situation made possible by its controlling presence in global production and finance, its vast military strength, its central role in the spread of informational technology, and its capacity to disseminate the neoliberal American model. Using this awesome leverage, the United States easily prevails over weaker nations, over global structures, and over virtually the entire world environment as it pursues nationally defined strategic aims. This is what the concept New World Order means more than a decade after it was proclaimed by the first President Bush. Its prominence has been solidified by the ascendancy of Bush II, the impact of 9/11, the war on terrorism, and new aggressive U.S. military initiatives in the Middle East.

Arguments that emphasize a unilinear, homogenizing capitalist globalization have permeated the bulk of critical as well as mainstream thinking on world politics since the end of the cold war. The framework is designed to render more intelligible new configurations of corporate power, class forces, and social change appropriate to a new developmental phase. Sklair and Robinson are among the most lucid theorists of this tendency, and their perspective identifies far-reaching globalizing trends at work. Yet their work strangely ignores the role of military power in the world today, precisely at a time when U.S. imperial hegemony is greater than ever. Globalization theories usually downplay or ignore this expansion of American power on the premise that the nation-state has become obsolete, yielding its sovereignty to transnational firms and international structures like the WTO, World Bank, and IMF. There is much to this premise: globalization does in fact weaken the sovereignty of *most* nations. But "most nations" actually refers to those with the weakest economic and political leverage within the world system, that is, all but the leading G-8 powers. The few strongest nation-states, with the United States easily leading the way, have actually gotten more *powerful* with advancing globalization—a process fully dependent on the simultaneous *growth* of U.S. economic, political, and above all military domination, in a milieu where no effective countervailing forces exist. More than half of all TNCs (transnational corporations) and large banks are based in the United States, with most others located in Japan or Europe. American capacity to manipulate international agencies and regional bodies, including the UN, has met with only limited challenges. The determination of the United States to use its military power on behalf of both national and global interests is no longer debatable. Against this reality theorists like Sklair and Robinson can offer little supporting evidence for the prevalence of transnational classes or states that could effectively usurp American imperial power. Discursive silences regarding the facts of U.S. Empire and militarism merely weaken their case.

Few globalization theorists fully address the question of military power as a crucial factor in world politics, as if abstract market processes speak more loudly than the combined forces of corporate and military domination situated in one or a few countries. Many prefer to ignore the coercive, violent side of global power in favor of the impersonal, universal flow of markets and information that, in the end, seems to require little in the way of military intervention—perhaps even making such intervention obsolete. Where the stark reality of U.S. military force is taken into account, such force is regarded as benevolent, quite consistent with the official, stated aims of American foreign policy. This blindness to the actual record of U.S. intervention around the world—and above all to its great reliance on military might to achieve its imperial objectives—extends to presumed critics of American power. Thus Hardt and Negri have moved onto the public stage as mainstream media notables with the year 2000 publication of their book *Empire*, which promises a fresh approach to international class and power relations by drawing on a mixture of postmodern, neo-Marxist, and liberal motifs. They go to considerable lengths to distinguish between Empire, a general phenomenon tied to the globalization of markets, and imperialism, which is grounded in specific national interests. Like globalization, Empire supposedly renders familiar views of the nation-state obsolete, meaning that the use of political or military power on behalf of distinctly national interests no longer makes sense. Thus: "In contrast to imperialism, Empire establishes no territorial center of power and does not rely on fixed boundaries or barriers."[19] Here the ideas of Hardt and Negri, revolving around international flows of capital and technology, plural exchanges within the market system, and the blending of nations and cultures under a single (neoliberal) umbrella, differ little from standard globalization theories. Nor does their view of *American* global status depart significantly from these other approaches: "The U.S. does not, and indeed no nation-state can today, form the center of an imperialist project. Imperialism is over."[20] The supposedly old forms of international conflict have been superseded by a new paradigm, a new order characterized by a unifying world of markets, technology, and information flows.

Having established this framework, Hardt and Negri proceed to argue that the globalized world of postmodern capitalism still requires a powerful enforcing mechanism to defend Empire against its challengers—specifically U.S. political and military power. American enforcement is needed not in the service of *national* interests, however, but in defense of the integrity of the global system itself. Thus: "The U.S. was called to serve the role of guaranteeing and adding juridical efficacy to the complex process of the formation of a new supranational right."[21] Characteristic of the exposition throughout *Empire*, the reference to "supranational right" is obscure. In any case, it is clear that U.S. military interventions in the Persian Gulf and Balkans are best understood in this context. Despite their reputedly critical focus, the authors are emphatic about the benevolence of U.S. military power: "Even if it were reluctant, the U.S. military would have to answer the call in the name of peace and order." And: "The U.S. is the peace police." The extension of U.S. economic, political, and military force around the globe must be regarded as a "model of rearticulating open space" for the smooth functioning of Empire.[22] The authors are quick to add that "in this smooth space of Empire there is no *place* of power—it is both everywhere and nowhere."[23] This absence of self-interested coercive power, strange when applied to the most dominant nation in history, is compatible with the premise that a "universal notion of right" exists at the core of Empire.[24]

Enough has already been written above to refute this simplistic and crudely apologetic (for the United States) view of global politics. Like other globalization theorists, Hardt and Negri furnish no evidence in support of a universalizing, largely benign Empire or a peace-seeking U.S. foreign policy. There is nothing in recent history to sustain their obscurantist, postmodern view of power. True enough, the international scene has changed drastically over the past two decades, most significantly with the collapse of the Soviet bloc and concomitant growth of U.S. power—but the idea that globalization has somehow overtaken this development is sheer mysticism. Hardt and Negri do at least recognize the presence of a global U.S. military apparatus, but like so many others they must endow that apparatus with supremely benevolent, democratic, peace-making properties. The Pentagon system as locus of a war economy and rampant foreign interventions escapes from view. The "smooth world" of *Empire* ignores the close linkage between transnational corporate and U.S. military power; between globalization and the *expansion* of U.S. economic, political, and military domination; between regions of U.S. geopolitical interest and elite decisions to intervene with armed force. Hardt and Negri seem clueless about the role state power and national interests continue to play in both managing and preserving the "global market" that operates internationally but is institutionally based in the United States and other leading capitalist nations.

Fashioning arguments almost entirely at the level of concepts detached from the realm of class and power relations, Hardt and Negri conjure up a "postmodern," smoothly interactive world in which predatory social forces, narrow interests, and coercive designs are on the margins—in other words, outside the benign Empire presided over by the United States and its allies. This amounts to yet another convenient way to sidestep the historical implications of increasingly overt and arrogant U.S. designs for global domination. Despite its preposterous generalizations and overall lack of empirical validation, the schema advanced in *Empire* resonates with prevailing assumptions regarding the U.S. role in world politics—namely, that the United States is a benevolent, if often misunderstood and bumbling, superpower whose leaders seek a better, peaceful globe through free markets, liberal democracy, and humanitarian interventions. Such assumptions are eagerly seized hold of by a majority of progressives and liberals, as well as garden-variety neocons and right-wingers, a tribute to the seductions of patriotic ideology. The theme of globalization, focusing as it does on abstract historical processes, universal norms, and the devaluation of state power, is perfectly congruent with these assumptions and, moreover, easily coheres with a variety of theoretical perspectives. In the case of Hardt and Negri, their arguments underpinning the notion of a diffuse Empire are derived from a number of sources: neo-Marxism, anarchism, liberalism, postmodernism. An emphasis on the presumably smooth flow of global markets, shared in different ways by all these theories, coincides with a gaping silence about military power; the coercive side of U.S. imperialism in particular is absent, or is construed as benevolent. Such modes of thinking have become all the more seductive since 9/11.

Postmodern discourses—which figure centrally in *Empire* owing to its reliance on Michel Foucault's model of dispersed power relations—stress decentered forms of authority and social relations, diversity, and the fluidity of economic transactions. As such, these discourses converge nicely with globalization motifs. *Empire*'s almost mystical approach to social processes in effect conceals the self-interested, blatant, violent exercise of American power, as if such concerns were now rather out of fashion, irrelevant to a fully transformed world. The concept of Empire, vague enough in itself at the hands of Hardt and Negri, is meant to reinforce the idea that U.S. military action is undertaken only reluctantly, mainly for the sake of disinterested goals, on behalf of humanitarian and peaceful aims. Thus what we encounter in *Empire*, as in the bulk of leftist and mainstream discourses on globalization, is a profound retreat from the very realities we see before us: heightened U.S. global power; a resurgence of militarism, as seen in the war on terrorism and new armed interventions; growth of the Pentagon system; new aggressive strategies for world domination.

THE PERMANENT WAR ECONOMY

The steady expansion of U.S. imperialism has given rise to a military apparatus with global scope and power unparalleled in human history. While it
is customary to refer to this behemoth as a "permanent war economy," its
intricate and vast web of political, bureaucratic, social, and international, as
well as economic, institutions and processes suggests that perhaps another label, such as "Pentagon system," would be more appropriate. The economic
dimension, of course, calls attention to the multiple functions performed by
war and war making within the American economy: budgetary allocations,
stimulus to corporate power and profit making, impact on research and development, larger consequences for the domestic system of production,
work, and consumption. Yet, it is worth emphasizing, such functions converge with a variety of social, cultural, political, and international phenomena to sustain the larger matrix of Pentagon power.

The evolution of the Pentagon system over six decades, first given impetus in the aftermath of Pearl Harbor, has been fueled not only by war
itself, or by a chain of military interventions abroad, but by the perpetual
U.S. struggle for global domination, built on the extension of armed might
into every realm: land, seas and waterways, air, outer space, even cyberspace.
With World War II the Roosevelt administration moved to full-scale war
footing, which demanded vast increases in military spending, central planning, and the full-scale mobilization of resources over several years. The expected postwar demobilization, however, never occurred, as war footing
took on new dimensions: nuclear-weapons development, the Korean War,
the deepening of the cold war, the need to maintain a stimulus for industrial growth. The wartime threat posed by Nazis and Fascists was quickly
transferred to a new menace—international Communism—justifying continued massive Pentagon outlays. By the 1950s, as President Dwight D.
Eisenhower duly observed, the military-industrial complex had become a
durable feature of American society, holding together corporate interests,
political alliances, and the Pentagon labyrinth itself with contrived threats
presented as imminent dangers to national security. To improve its status as
the world's leading superpower—to widen its lead over the Soviet Union—
the United States incurred huge operational costs, the bulk of them paid by
taxpayers. By 1960 the U.S. military budget exceeded the entire gross domestic product of all but a few leading industrialized nations.

Deeply impacted by the Pentagon system, American society was already becoming progressively militarized. As a pillar of elite power, military
norms and priorities were beginning to influence the realms of education,
politics, science, technology, the media, even popular culture. Thus in the
late 1950s C. Wright Mills wrote, "It is not only within the higher political
and economic, scientific and educational circles that the military ascendancy

is apparent. The warlords, along with fellow travelers and spokesmen, are attempting to plant their metaphysics firmly among the population at large."[25] Anticipating future trends, he added: "American militarism in fully developed form, would mean the triumph in all areas of life of the military metaphysic, and hence the subordination to it of all other ways of life."[26]

Writing only a few years later, Fred Cook, in his seminal *The Warfare State*, analyzed this military trajectory with equal clarity, identifying a radical shift toward Pentagon domination that would forever reshape American politics, economic life, and culture—not to mention foreign policy. Said Cook:

> The crutch of the Warfare State is propaganda. We must be taught to fear and to hate or we will not agree to regiment our lives, to bear the enormous burdens of ever heavier taxation to pay for ever more costly military hardware—and to do this at the expense of domestic programs like medical care and education and healthy urban development.[27]

According to Cook, the 1946 elections marked the first real triumph of the military–industrial–government partnership that came to be shared more or less equally by Democrats and Republicans. It signaled a turning away from FDR's liberal emphasis (before the war) on social Keynesianism toward a military Keynesianism that would solidify throughout the cold war. As the Pentagon system became the "American way of life," cold war consensus meant that any dissent from military priorities would be regarded as un-American, even treasonous. This vast edifice thrived on a contrived arms race. Cook writes: "The picture that emerges is the picture of a nation whose entire economic welfare is tied to warfare."[28] Anticipating fearsome developments that would not fully unfold until decades later, Cook reflected: "The time has come when we can see clearly and unmistakably before us our chosen destiny. The Pied Pipers of the military and big business, who have been drumming into our ears the siren song of 'peace through strength,' can no longer quite conceal the brink toward which they lead us."[29]

The idea that postwar Pentagon expansion is grounded in Keynesian economics, a form of state capitalism, suggests a powerfully integrative process that is both structural and ideological, in which corporate, political, and military interests merge to drive the system. Military Keynesianism serves U.S. geopolitical designs as well as elite privilege, ensuring not only massive business profits domestically but also the freest possible terrain for global investments and the control of markets. Domestic *social* priorities are inevitably subordinated within this developmental model. It is a system that thrives on imminent external threats, whether real or manufactured, from the Nazis and Japanese of World War II to the Communists and USSR of the cold war to terrorists and rogue states since the early 1990s. The immense staying power of the war economy has depended on other factors: aggressive corporate lobbying, sheer bureaucratic power and inertia, scientific and technological agendas, armed services infighting over budgetary allocations, the entwined bipartisan interests of the two major parties. Every postwar American president, from Harry S. Truman to Bush II, has given his full, enthusiastic blessing to the Pentagon system.

In an otherwise largely unregulated capitalist economy that naturally veers toward planlessness, destabilization, and class polarization, military Keynesianism, by means of large-scale governmental intervention, works to infuse the system with elements of organization and planning, legitimated by appeals to national security and patriotism. Wartime mobilization or its equivalent promotes growth while restricting centrifugal tendencies—roughly the same functions that industrial policy performs for European and kindred welfare-state societies. From this standpoint, a powerful state apparatus is absolutely *essential* to corporate (and military) interests, even as both conservatives and liberals pretend to attack "big spending" and "big government."[30] We know that severe cuts in Pentagon spending since 1945 have been virtually unthinkable; proponents of even modest demobilization, or conversion, have been quickly marginalized by the propaganda network. The introduction of ambitious new military programs (e.g., nuclear arsenals, Star Wars, high-tech weapons systems, Stealth bombers, favored projects of the moment) is scarcely open to public input or even much legislative debate. The growth of a sprawling war economy, militarized society, and aggressive foreign policy reflect the same historical logic, transcending personality and party differences.

The Pentagon system constitutes a massive global network with more than a thousand military facilities spread across forty states and seventy nations around the world, from Latin America to Africa, Europe, the Middle East, Asia, and scattered islands in the Pacific and Atlantic oceans. Its sophisticated arms and intelligence web of power extends to the seas, land, air, and space. This virtual empire depends on the production and distribution apparatus of several thousand industrial firms and subsidiaries. It has intimate connections with such powerful institutions as the Central Intelligence Agency (CIA), Federal Bureau of Investigation (FBI), Bureau of Alcohol, Tobacco and Firearms (ATF), National Security Agency (NSA), National Aeronautics and Space Administration (NASA), and United States Information Agency (USIA). It exerts a pervasive ideological influence on the mass media, universities, popular culture, churches, and cyberspace, allowing it to become an integral part of the economic, political, and cultural life of the nation. The Pentagon structure itself, located in Washington, DC, lies at the hub of all this activity, the symbol of American imperial power since 1947, with 25,000 workers, 30 acres of offices and meeting rooms, and 17.5

miles of hallways. The Pentagon is a major center of communications, transportation, social life, and political activity. It is the site of the National Military Command Center, which processes enormous amounts of data collected from around the globe. It occupies the center of a network employing 1.6 million armed-services personnel, 800,000 reserves, and two million workers in the industrial sector. In providing far-flung support systems for troops, logistical operations, and employees, the Pentagon manages a multitude of information sites, entertainment centers, hospitals, schools, family apartments, officers' and enlisted clubs, churches, restaurants, sports facilities, and transportation systems.

By fiscal year 2003 Pentagon spending had reached $390 billion, though funding for all U.S. military operations was expected to be in the range of $500 billion, in excess of peak cold war years and nearly three times what all potential U.S. adversaries spent combined (Russian and China together spending less than $100 billion). The United States and its allies spent roughly 73 percent of total global military allocations in 2003. Pentagon outlays are conservatively expected to reach $500 billion for 2008 and close to $550 billion for 2010, according to the Pentagon's own estimates—a figure that would account for easily half the world's total. These amounts do not include money for intelligence agencies (nearly $70 billion in 2003), for homeland security (another $38 billion), or for the occupation and reconstruction of Iraq (untold billions)—numbers that could easily skyrocket beyond expected levels with just one more devastating terrorist attack. Such resource allocations, without parallel in history, are becoming the mark of something akin to a full-fledged garrison state.

The Pentagon stands at the center of a vast web of military, industrial, political, and global structures tied to complex bureaucracies, weapons systems, base facilities, communications networks, job and contract structures, and a labyrinthine network of armed-forces branches—all set in place during and immediately after World War II. Its allocation of resources, subsidized by taxpayers, goes well beyond the capacity of ordinary citizens to imagine. The system is routinely oiled by lobbies, friendly politicians, political action committees (PACs), think tanks, the media, universities, and big corporate contractors. Each year corporations donate several million dollars in campaign contributions: Lockheed-Martin, TRW, Raytheon, and Boeing together gave more than $6 million in the 2000 elections. Such corporations, naturally, in turn benefit greatly from new weapons contracts, as well as lucrative overseas arms sales. While the ideological apparatus creates awesome new enemies, profit-seeking businesses push for aggressive military policies to fight rogue states, terrorists, and drug traffickers. Leading military corporations were especially anxious to see NATO's expansion eastward, facilitated by the Balkans ventures, not only for geostrategic reasons but because it opened up vast new arms markets across Eastern Europe. Lockheed-

Martin CEO Norman Augustine was the most active on this front, and his efforts bore fruit: contracts for arms sales to Poland, Romania, Czechoslovakia, and Croatia, totaling $7 billion, were signed in 1999. Lockheed-Martin was able to peddle the most advanced fighter planes and transports, along with communications satellites, radar devices, and other high-tech equipment, often at discount prices. Vice President Richard Cheney, as CEO at Halliburton, also took an active role in arms profiteering before taking office.

To maintain dynamism, the war economy depends on a convergence of factors: its own deeply embedded culture, bureaucratic leverage, political conservatism, the fetishism of technology, a mass belief system saturated with national hubris. There might be some truth to Helen Caldicott's observation that "one could readily diagnose the attitudes of the Pentagon as clinically sick and suggest that all people who subscribe to these theories need urgent counseling and therapy."[31] Yet the seductive material and status rewards that come from an immense network of contracts and jobs could help reduce the need for psychological help. The Pentagon system thrives on an entrenched corporate oligopoly in which myths of free-market capitalism and its fierce competition and risks are scarcely operative; sales are to governments alone, and profitability is usually ensured. By 2000 the top military corporations had been reduced in number to just five: Lockheed-Martin, with $15 billion in contracts; Boeing, with $12 billion; Raytheon, with $6.3 billion; General Dynamics, with $4.1 billion; and Northrop-Grumman, with just over $3 billion. In 2003 the largest of these remained Lockheed-Martin, the product of 1990s mergers involving Lockheed and Martin Marietta, Loral Defense, General Dynamics, and scores of smaller companies to create a $36 billion empire that pushes for an extremely aggressive militarism. After 9/11 these corporations began to adapt their marketing strategies to accommodate new demands for space militarization, homeland security, and of course the war on terrorism. As the emphasis shifts increasingly toward high-tech items, allocations and contracts can be expected to balloon accordingly. In 2001 it cost more than a million dollars to dispatch a Tomahawk missile, about $2,000 an hour to operate a single M-12A tank, more than $2,500 an hour to fly an F-16, roughly $30,000 an hour to keep a navy destroyer active. The F-16 alone costs more than $50 million to build. Any escalation of the Star Wars commitment, which has had Bush's full backing from the outset, will entail allocations in the hundreds of billions.

A crucial linchpin in sustaining military Keynesianism has been technology: since World War II upwards of 70 percent of all resources devoted to research and development, combining efforts of the armed forces, corporations, and higher education, has come under the auspices of the Pentagon. The military sector has been and remains a growth catalyst for science and technology. With its emphasis on remote aerial warfare and sophisticated communications systems, technowar has been a durable feature of U.S. military operations at least since the Vietnam era. By the 1990s, however, Pentagon technology, enhanced by computerized systems, was making even greater leaps forward, characterized as a paradigm shift often labeled a "revolution in military affairs," or RMA. Increasing resources were being poured into the new "paradigm"—high-tech weapons systems, Star Wars, surveillance, information networks, and lighter, more mobile combat units for all branches of the military. A high-tech military would presumably enable the United States to achieve global domination more efficiently, wedding flexibility, mobility, and computerized response to a terrifying arsenal. As one of the main champions of RMA, Secretary of Defense Donald Rumsfeld, as expected, became a catalyst for this new phase in U.S. military evolution once Bush II took office. As outlined in the 2001 Pentagon *Quadrennial Report*, the United States was now prepared to move beyond established military conventions and open up a new era in warfare, a shift hastened along by 9/11 and the war on terrorism. In reality RMA had already been set in motion at the time of Desert Storm, when the U.S. military started relying on high-tech communications and information systems, including space-based satellites and precision-guided bombs and missiles, within an integrated electronic battlefield.

It was already clear from the first Gulf War that RMA would mean a more fully integrated military combining a wide range of combat operations through multiple communications systems: screens displaying information fed digitally from sensors and cameras on aircraft, ships, ground stations, and space satellites, all linked by sophisticated computer networks. An integrated command and field system obviously permits quicker, more flexible, more efficient armed responses; it is also far more expensive. Among the many RMA innovations can be found pilotless aircraft like the Global Hawk, made by Teledyne Ryan, which can hover over an area for twenty-four hours at sixty-five thousand feet, well outside the range of missiles. The Global Hawk and the unmanned Predator fall under the rubric of uninhabited combat aircraft vehicles (UCAVs), which can be piloted from the ground via computers—a method destined to gain currency in the future. UCAVs, like technowar in general, are designed to maximize battlefield firepower while minimizing (American) casualties. Unmanned aircraft, along with the rest of the RMA repertoire, were introduced during U.S. operations in Afghanistan and Iraq at the time of the second Gulf War. Indeed these operations gave the Pentagon its first opportunities to adopt RMA full tilt, allowing for quicker decision making and greater use of precision-guided bombs, missiles, and artillery shells.

The new military technology was put on display at a huge Pentagon electronics show in San Diego just weeks before the onset of the second war against Iraq. The exhibition presented a larger-than-life, 3-D, aerial image of

Baghdad, an obvious imminent target of a computerized U.S. aerial barrage—yet another oversized video-game extravaganza made possible by RMA. According to the exhibits, every phase of the new war would be thoroughly integrated and rationalized digitally, by means of a complex network of supercomputers, permitting a system of Internet-like mechanisms to instantly bring together the movements of planes, ships, tanks, ground troops, and communications centers within a hypermodernized technowar framework. Tens of billions of dollars were earmarked for RMA in 2002–2003 alone, with hundreds of billions more anticipated in future Pentagon budgets.

The war economy is reproduced through a convergence of state and private, military and corporate, global and domestic interests having no precedence in any modern society; it is a system sui generis. Thus the so-called privatization of military functions has turned out to be perfectly compatible with statist administration of the production system and security apparatus. Corporate involvement in the military is, of course, nothing new. Since the early 1980s, however, an increasing proportion of Pentagon operations has been farmed out to private firms, staffed by retired armed-services personnel who help carry out U.S. foreign-policy objectives. Many enterprises, such as Military Professional Resources, Inc. (MPRI), have been hired by the Pentagon to provide training and assistance to military and law-enforcement agencies in countries deemed friendly to American interests. Such "private" contractors engage in many tasks—planning, engineering, furnishing expertise, general infrastructure rebuilding—almost completely beyond the purview of public or legislative oversight. Ken Silverstein writes: "These Private Warriors have a financial and career interest in war and conflict, as well as the power and connections to promote continued hard-line policies. Their collective influence is one reason that the United States seems incapable of making the transition to the post-Cold War world."[32]

MPRI, founded in 1987 by retired Army General Vernon Lewis, has been deeply involved in keeping the Saudi Arabian regime in power, working beneath the radar to buttress its coercive military and police organs. MPRI's involvement has been crucial to protecting U.S. oil interests in the region. The company received more than $500 million in the 1990s to train similar forces in Bosnia and Croatia under repressive right wing governments. Indeed, just a few weeks after MPRI performed its tasks in Croatia (mid-1995) the Tudjman regime initiated its bloody assault on Serbs in the Kraijina region, resulting in hundreds of killings and tens of thousands being forced out of their homes. Corporations like MPRI and Vinnell have received billions in taxpayers' largesse over the past two decades to provide aid and training to dictatorial regimes in Central America, Indonesia, Malaysia, South Korea, Kuwait, and Saudi Arabia, along with right wing elements in the Balkans and the Persian Gulf. Joint Pentagon-corporate programs fund and train tens of thousands of troops yearly, at a variety of military schools and training camps, and these troops carry out U.S. objectives in countries spread across the globe. Meanwhile, the military and big business work together in the most ambitious arms export program in history, sending around the world more than $10 billion in weapons annually. Private military companies along with huge arms contractors reap more than $100 billion all told each year, all of course subsidized by citizen taxpayers.[33] Such "privatization" of war functions allows the Pentagon (also relying on covert CIA, FBI, and NSA operations) to escape close scrutiny.

This dimension of American foreign policy takes on new meaning in the context of Iraq following the second Gulf War, as the United States desperately seeks to solidify its occupation of a nation roughly the size of California. For 2003 and beyond the Bush administration has awarded billions of dollars in contracts to such firms as Halliburton, Bechtel, and Fluor to rebuild the Iraqi infrastructure destroyed by two United States–initiated wars and more than a decade of United States–sponsored economic sanctions. In the immediate aftermath of the invasion Bechtel, for example, received $680 million in contracts for domestic reconstruction, surely facilitated by the company's long, intimate relationship with Bush and his cronies. Take, for instance, former Bechtel president George Schultz: the secretary of state under Reagan is now both a Bechtel board member and chair of the neocon Committee for the Liberation of Iraq. Jack Sheehan is simultaneously a Bechtel vice president and a member of the Pentagon's key Defense Policy Board. And Riley Bechtel, chair and CEO of the corporation, was appointed by Bush to the President's Export Council only weeks before the war started. Among its numerous charges, Bechtel was chosen to protect and rebuild the Iraqi petroleum infrastructure, clearly the number one U.S. priority. In fact Bechtel had for many years been angling to gain access to Iraq for purposes of building an extensive oil pipeline system (rejected in the late 1980s despite Rumsfeld's pleas to Hussein). The Bechtel contract, like those awarded to Halliburton, WorldCom, and others, came in the absence of genuine competitive bidding, a common practice where global privatization is concerned. WorldCom had already been accused of massive accounting fraud but was nonetheless given a $45 million contract to build a wireless phone network in Iraq. Hundreds of smaller U.S. corporations were scrambling in the midst of war, destruction, and occupation to obtain major pieces of the rebuilding action. Not surprisingly, companies like Halliburton, Bechtel, and WorldCom were significant donors to Bush's 2000 presidential campaign.

As mentioned, Pentagon spending for the fiscal year 2004 is expected to reach nearly $500 billion when all expenses are taken into account. Bush asked Congress in late 2003 to finance the U.S. occupation of Iraq, having already spent several tens of billions on military preparation and invasion. In Iraq, as in the Balkans and Afghanistan, private companies make up a substantial portion of the military infrastructure. It hardly needs to be emphasized that all of these programs, highly profitable to every contractor involved, are fully insulated from the vagaries of the market economy and proceed with no open bidding procedures. The costs of rebuilding Iraq could well exceed $500 billion—by far the biggest such reconstruction project ever undertaken. The boondoggles for corporations like Halliburton and Bechtel have gone off the charts, but these are simply the most visible of some twenty thousand foreign companies joining the rackets made possible an open investment policy decreed by the occupation authority. In late 2003 Dynacorp received a $480 million contract to restore the Iraqi police force, while Bechtel won $1.8 billion in early 2004 to help rebuild airports, roads, the water system, and power networks. Meanwhile, the Iraqi economy was fully privatized while the United States seized nearly $2 billion in national funds to help finance reconstruction.

U.S. militarism as both structure and ideology is a function of several converging factors: bureaucratic power, corporate leverage, military Keynesianism, resource objectives, the struggle for geopolitical advantage, politicians' efforts to deflect public attention away from domestic crises. The ideology and practice of war making is central to the push for global domination, for Empire. Conservative presidents like Nixon, Reagan, and the two Bushes, rhetorically committed to free-market capitalism and minimal government, have for reasons of Empire turned out to be even more statist than their supposedly liberal "tax and spend" opponents.

Expanded Pentagon control of resources, justified by recurrent military interventions, the war on terrorism, homeland security initiatives, and costly programs like Star Wars and RMA, both legitimates and reinforces state power on a grand scale. With few exceptions, elites across the political spectrum remain wedded to this costly, bureaucratic, destructive system; politicians rarely have the audacity to oppose it, or even to argue for its scaling down. For many Americans, too, including those who champion the blessings of free enterprise, a sprawling Pentagon structure stands as a great symbol of American status and power. For leaders ruling a nation that consumes up to 40 percent of the world's energy supplies, resource wars will continue to drive the mechanisms of statist political and economic organization. An increasingly large chorus of Bush critics on the right, generally supportive of his specific policies, have actually raised questions about the vast gulf separating conservative theory and practice: how can the celebration of bureaucratic, statist, highly centralized military-industrial complex be squared with traditional Republican values of minimal government? Bush elites, comfortably perched atop the imperial bureaucracy, have frequently sought to crack down on vocal criticism of their support for broadened state power, calling attention to the requisites of a militarized Empire. Opponents like Pat Buchanan have accused Bush of selling out genuine conservative free-market principles for the sake of a militant globalism that, inevitably, requires heightened state power. But the statism of Republicans and Democrats alike remains more deeply entrenched than the free-market ideology would have us believe. It turns out to be one of the enduring legacies of the war economy—a seeming fixture of contemporary American life.

While the Pentagon system functions as a stimulus to economic growth, such growth has been increasingly detrimental to the social infrastructure. The American developmental model favors the military sector and global priorities over a wide range of civilian programs and services. Fred Cook's description, cited earlier, of "a nation whose entire economic welfare is tied to warfare"[34] takes on added meaning decades later, when the cumulative Pentagon budget has reached a staggering $20 trillion. It takes little imagination to perceive that enormous material, human, and technological resources have been devoted mainly to waste and destruction. In other words, military products (spin-offs notwithstanding) are devoid of use-value insofar as they never contribute to ordinary patterns of production and consumption, or to the welfare of the general population. On the contrary, they lead to a profound deformation of the economy.[35]

This point can be pushed further: the war economy, as part of its very logic, reproduces material decay, inequality, and social disruption at the very moment it helps sustain a technologically advanced industrial order. As we have seen, U.S. military spending since World War II has been greater than that of all other leading nations combined. During the period when the cold war was ending the Pentagon budget stood at roughly $300 billion, followed by a modest and brief decline in the Clinton years. Government and military leaders then fashionably spoke of armed-services reductions, troop demobilizations, and base closings, in keeping with a much-celebrated "peace dividend." A limited shift in this direction did in fact occur, but the operative change was toward modernization: fewer domestic bases and personnel along with a phasing out of earlier weapons systems in favor of a high-tech military. The newer weaponry had much greater firepower and efficiency than what it replaced. The Pentagon itself went along with most of these reductions, often against the strenuous objections of politicians hoping to keep military facilities in their own districts and states. Since 9/11, of course, the idea of even such modest reductions has been scrapped from the political agenda.

It is an iron law of post–World War II American economic development that as the Pentagon system expands, the domestic infrastructure correspondingly deteriorates. In 2003, as before, we find an inverse relationship between the scope of U.S. imperial power and indices of social and material well-being for the vast majority of the population. According to the 2003 discretionary budget, total military spending (including veterans' benefits) amounted to 56 percent of the federal budget, compared with 6 percent for health care and education alike, 5 percent for community development (including transportation), and 3 percent for miscellaneous social services. Such lopsided priorities are unheard of in other major industrialized societies. At the same time, Bush unveiled a plan to cut taxes (mainly for corporations and the most affluent sectors) by $350 billion over ten years, further exacerbating the decline, more accurately *crisis*, in domestic programs and services. In the richest country in the world, the job structure has weakened, with civilian deindustrialization proceeding at an alarming rate: there were ten million people unemployed in 2002, along with eight or nine million in extremely low-paying, dead-end, seasonal or temporary jobs. The poverty rate had reached 23 percent. More than forty million Americans lacked health-care insurance. State budget crises forced massive cuts in an educational system that was already poorly serving the needs of students. Environmental problems were veering out of control, with no countervailing mechanism in sight. Public child-care programs were virtually nonexistent. The nationwide prison population stood at 2.1 million—easily the largest prison population in the world—with nearly half the inmates incarcerated for drug-related offences. Family life was deteriorating, as a variety of mental and physical health problems (including substance abuse) worsened with each passing year. Meanwhile, less than 5 percent of the American population controlled fully 70 percent of its resources, while the Pentagon devours more than half of all discretionary spending.

Confronting the vast dysfunctions and tragedies—indeed horrors—of a U.S. Empire that has become more robust and expansionary, more fiercely militarist, at the start of the twenty-first century, Cook's observation from the early 1960s seems more prescient than ever: We have reached a point in history where American leaders, having constructed a global military machine on a rationale of peace through incessant armed mobilization, can no longer obscure their true imperial ambitions or conceal the enormous costs and risks of such ambitions.

2

THE U.S. STRUGGLE
FOR GLOBAL DOMINATION

The post-9/11 world has given new impetus, and to some degree new legitimacy, to the long-standing U.S. pursuit of global domination, carrying forward in a new context the perpetual growth of American economic, political, and military power. Among other things, the discourses and practices associated with the phenomenon of Empire that were previously kept sotto voce have by the end of the twentieth century come into the open, with a vengeance. The horrific events of 9/11 brought unprecedented levels of worldwide sympathy for what was already a global hegemon, owing in no small measure to the influence of United States–controlled systems of international communication. This control guaranteed widespread attention to the supposedly unique American experiences of suffering and victimhood—attention usually denied the far greater suffering produced by a long series of U.S. armed interventions throughout the twentieth century.[1] Even while the terrorist blow was clearly directed against the heart of the U.S. Empire—the World Trade Center and Pentagon—Americans were typically seen as fully justified in striking back at perpetrators in Afghanistan and elsewhere. From this standpoint 9/11 can be understood as a kind of worldwide spectacle that, in effect, revealed the scope of Western power to shape beliefs, attitudes, and responses. At the same time, it helped validate more aggressive geostrategic moves by American elites as they moved to further consolidate their hold over the world system. As at the end of World War II, the United States now defines itself as an indispensable nation committed to universal ideals of democracy, peace, human rights, and lawful behavior among nations.

Of course these images and discourses turned out to be highly misleading, ephemeral, in many ways false as U.S. preparation for war against Iraq was in full swing by fall 2002. U.S. ambitions for a global Pax Americana had become more transparent, increasingly freed by the 9/11 aftermath, which licensed an aggressive militarized war on terrorism. Yet 9/11

35

performed another function: it reinforced the idea, long held in elite circles, of a Hobbesian universe filled with manifestations of evil and danger. This nightmarish image benefits the militaristic impulses of U.S. leaders increasingly prepared to combat those threats with maximum force. Indeed the imperialist strategy, bent on establishing and maintaining a New World Order under U.S. neoliberal auspices, thrives on perceptions of a chaotic jungle in which international relations are turned into a *Blade Runner* culture devoid of moral or political cohesion aside from what can be provided by the all-inclusive Leviathan (read: the military-industrial complex). As the one remaining superpower with unrivalled military power, and with an elite seemingly anxious to use that power, it would presumably fall on the United States as an indispensable nation to carry out the burdensome task of imposing the requisite global "order." Any challenge to that order, to the self-appointed rights and powers of the hegemon, are sure to be met with awesome displays of military force, as in Yugoslavia, Afghanistan, and Iraq—carried out, to be sure, in the name of various benevolent ideals. In such a Hobbesian world, it is much easier to frame conflict, diversity, and challenge in Manichaeistic terms, as expressions of a historic struggle between forces of good and evil, between a benign status quo and the diabolical terrorists and dictators who challenge it. Seen thusly, we have a replay of familiar World War II scenarios in which virtuous and triumphant allies, fighting the good war, were able to defeat the wicked Fascists and Nazis, punishing them for their monstrous aggressions and crimes. It is out of such mythology that present-day American moral narcissism and political arrogance, mixed with a might-is-right sense of *Machtpolitik*, have been nurtured, reinforced by the (surely temporary) victim status conferred by the events of 9/11. It is precisely here that the United States seeks to extend, possibly reinvent, traditional forms of imperial domination by means of unsurpassed military force, including the threat and conceivable use of nuclear weapons.

AN IMPERIAL STRATEGY

For many decades U.S. governing circles have wanted to organize the entire planet according to their own neoliberal, corporate principles, ensuring conditions that would broaden and strengthen their economic and geopolitical domination. Only with the eclipse of Soviet power and the end of the cold war, however, was the way paved for all-out pursuit of these goals. For the first time the very idea of U.S. Empire was openly and to some extent even proudly trumpeted by government and corporate elites, politicians, the media, and a surprising number of academics. Of course *this* empire would be different from those of the past, far more benevolent and peace seeking than the Roman, British, Spanish, Japanese, and Soviet empires, for example. U.S. imperialism throughout the twentieth century rested on an ensemble of myths: free markets, democracy, human rights, peaceful intentions, a variety of humanitarian concerns. It follows that at the start of the new century Empire as discourse and reality has become incorporated into American political culture in ways somewhat novel and yet more strident and monolithic than in the past century. What I refer to in this book as "the new militarism" is grounded precisely in this altered historical conjuncture; it is part of President George W. Bush's expansionary initiatives but simultaneously located in long decades of continuity.

The post-9/11 world has seen not only armed interventions to achieve "regime change" but an ongoing expansion of U.S. military deployments worldwide—on the seas, in the air, in outer space, and on the land, where American bases sprawl across more than 130 countries, the most ambitious and far-reaching military presence in history. Bush's famous "axis of evil" rhetoric has targeted three nations for imminent possible military action, while a series of Pentagon documents identified an even longer list of prospective enemies as part of the war on terrorism: Syria, Yemen, Libya, Cuba, Sudan. By 2003 the Bush administration had secured regime overthrow in Afghanistan and Iraq, with intimations that Syria and Iran (supposed havens of terrorists) might be next. The United States has advertised its long-held ambition to create permanent bases in the Middle East and Central Asia, to which end it has built facilities in Saudi Arabia, Kuwait, Qatar, Pakistan, Uzbekistan, Georgia, Turkey, and Kyrgyzstan, as well as the Balkans, Afghanistan, and Iraq. This fits a well-designed imperial project intended to nullify the power of Russia and China, solidify U.S. geopolitical control of the region, and exploit the region's massive resources, all in the name of halting weapons of mass destruction, fighting terrorism, and bringing democracy to subjected populations.

In this historical context Bush and his neoconservative "cabal" have scarcely been shy about their grandiose objectives, which after 9/11 took a harshly aggressive turn: unrestrained military action, contempt for international law and the UN, an overtly militaristic ideology, willingness to attack sovereign nations and occupy their populations, a move to forcibly colonize local resources. As the United States undertakes to consolidate its global military preeminence, the material benefits to the U.S. economy and transnational corporations become more starkly obvious—enhanced Pentagon spending for warfare, multibillion-dollar contracts for the reconstruction of areas devastated by military action, profits from oil and other resources, a clearing out of the terrain for "free trade" and general corporate expansion. Moreover, U.S. military facilities themselves offer promising economic boondoggles for corporations like Raytheon, Northrop-Grumman, Lockheed-Martin, General Electric, Bechtel, and Halliburton, insofar as these bases require large infrastructures.

A more expansionist imperial strategy—one reliant on the primacy of military power around the globe—actually surfaced right after the collapse of the Soviet bloc and ensuing frustrations related to an incomplete victory during Desert Storm. This epic turn reflected the inroads of a neocon ideology carved out by a small nucleus of defense intellectuals associated with the Council on Foreign Relations (CFR), American Enterprise Institute (AEI), Hudson Institute, and the journals *Foreign Affairs* and *Weekly Standard*, with strong participation by a group of pro-Israeli hawks. Many were eventually affiliated with the Project for a New American Century (PNAC), formed in 1997 by neocons who had served in the upper echelons of the Pentagon or State Department in the first and then second Bush administrations, with some (including Secretary of Defense Donald Rumsfeld) going back as far as the Nixon administration. The PNAC elites included Cheney, Rumsfeld, Paul Wolfowitz, Richard Perle, Douglas Feith, Elliott Abrams, and Scooter Libby, along with such writers as William Kristol, Kenneth Pollack, and Robert Kagan. The editor of the *Weekly Standard*, Kristol emerged as a prime mover in galvanizing this shift, which took shape with the ascendancy of Bush II, the role assumed by Vice President Cheney in the transition team, and of course the events of 9/11. A tiny group of erstwhile outsiders, PNAC achieved intellectual and political influence far beyond its numbers, owing to its ideological coherence, its take-no-prisoners style, its close proximity to Pentagon culture, and its historical association with Israeli interests and lobbying power. The group was able to coalesce around several overriding goals: a massive buildup of Pentagon strength, the global expansion of the U.S. military, a willingness to intervene anywhere to protect American interests and send messages, the notion of preemptive war giving the United States license to act militarily as it pleases, a dismissive attitude toward the UN, a desire to junk arms control and other international treaties deemed at variance with U.S. strategic aims, fervent support of the Israeli right. PNAC also embraced Star Wars, with a keen orientation toward the militarization of space. The extraordinary influence of this "cabal" (as its members jokingly referred to themselves) on mainstream media—the Fox and CNN television networks, book publishing, op-ed pages, talk radio—ensured a critical mass audience. The mounting consensus around launching a war against Iraq in late 2002 and early 2003 grew out of this milieu.

A PNAC statement drawn up in September 2000, titled "Rebuilding America's Defenses: Strategy, Forces, and Resources for a New American Century," had elaborated these ideas even before Bush took office and the terrorists carried out their attacks. The statement begins with the observation that "at present the United States faces no global rival. America's grand strategy should aim to preserve this advantageous position as far into the future as possible." The idea is to maintain U.S. global domination indefinitely, denying any and all challengers, by using maximum force wherever it is necessary. Toward this end U.S. military forces ought to be seen as *permanently* deployed in vital strategic regions, dispensing with the (liberal) rhetoric of temporary commitments of bases, troops, and resources. The nation should be committed to an ongoing struggle intended to cut short the proliferation of WMD, with Iraq presumably the first object lesson. Heightened U.S. military power is made necessary by drastically altered conditions stemming from end of the cold war. Thus:

> The military's job during the Cold War was to deter Soviet expansionism. Today its task is to secure and expand the "zones of democratic peace"; to deter the rise of a new great-power competitor; defend key regions of Europe, East Asia, and the Middle East; and to preserve American preeminence through the coming transformation of war made possible by new technologies.[2]

Crucial to this imperial agenda were two related aims—a more flexible, usable nuclear force and a space-oriented military presence involving a "layered system of land, sea, air, and space-based components." The PNAC recipe for U.S. world domination permeates succeeding pronouncements and documents emanating from the Bush administration and its neocon supporters.

Secretary of Defense Rumsfeld's 2001 Pentagon report, the *Quadrennial Defense Review*, amounts to perhaps the most comprehensive statement of this neocon-inspired shift in foreign and military policy. Predictably, the report begins with the premise that the events of 9/11 changed everything, bringing the United States into a "new and more dangerous period" requiring some fundamentally new outlooks and methods for the twenty-first century. Since the geographical position of the United States no longer guarantees immunity from attack owing to the global dispersion of terrorist groups, a more aggressive strategy is now in order, demanding an all-out rebuilding of Pentagon strength, stepped-up worldwide deployment of U.S. forces, a more refined nuclear posture, more technological flexibility, renewed emphasis on communications networks in warfare, and unhindered access to space. Within this bold modus operandi, strong elements of unilateralism are spelled out: "Wars are best fought by coalitions of the willing—but they should not be fought by committee. The mission must determine the coalition. The coalition must not determine the mission."[3] The continuous spread and further refinement of weapons of mass destruction, and the likelihood that terrorists will gain possession of such weapons, justifies not only unilateralism—the United States remains, after all, the primary global target because of its imperial status—but also preemptive strikes ostensibly designed to destroy WMD programs in various rogue nations even in cases where they are not yet operational.

Rumsfeld's lengthy report outlines in stark detail a nuclear posture that moves toward a more "flexible," open-ended policy grounded in specific "contingencies" that might permit first use of nuclear weapons. According to the Pentagon's revised strategy, nuclear weapons will be made smaller and more mobile to allow for a variety of *tactical* options, moving away from a *strategic* focus that governed the cold war period. Contingencies include a quick response to an immediate (now vaguely defined) threat, such as the acquisition of WMD by hostile groups; attempts to combat a "peer competitor" or menacing coalition that might challenge U.S. interests and security; a rapid change of circumstances, such as a regime change bringing to power a military antagonist. Here the entire network of space operations and weaponry, often misleadingly called a "missile defense system," is vital to both U.S. nuclear and overall military direction for the coming decades. This naturally means that American leaders will pour vast resources into the nuclear and space programs for the indefinite future and resolutely oppose test-ban treaties, but they will simultaneously oppose similar weapons for other nations. U.S. nuclear options, supposedly unthinkable during the cold war balance of terror, will now be taken as simply one of many alternatives for any particular combat challenge. Thus, while the United States rails against WMD possessed by "rogue states" as some kind of moral outrage, its own nuclear politics has come more brazenly into the open.

U.S. global military preparedness, referred to in the Pentagon report as "global situational awareness," requires a vast, sophisticated space monopoly that incorporates full-scale weapons deployment, total surveillance capabilities, communications networks, and various nuclear devices. Thus: "A key objective of the Department's space surveillance and control mission is to ensure freedom of action in space for the United States and its allies and, when directed, to deny such freedom to adversaries." Space colonization is therefore absolutely central to the U.S. drive for global domination, all part of a manifestly *offensive* posture that contradicts the mythology of a Star Wars network geared strictly to *defensive* purposes.[4] Most importantly, a space-based military network will permit the immediate, flexible, and accurate targeting of objects on the ground anywhere across the globe. A revitalized nuclear and space program, spurred along by rapid technological and cyberspace developments, involves unprecedented levels of *integration* among the different armed-forces branches, relying less on manpower than on technology. For Rumsfeld as for the ideologues of PNAC, the American Enterprise Institute, *Foreign Affairs,* and elsewhere, space-based technological rationalization takes the United States, virtually alone among nations, into the era of technowar grounded in new capacities made possible by RMA.

The Pentagon's new militarism derives considerable academic justification and theoretical articulation from the stratum of neocon intellectuals who stand unabashedly in favor of Empire. Kenneth Pollack's treatises on the historical necessity of U.S. military action against Iraq are well known, including his *The Threatening Storm: The Case for Invading Iraq* (2002). In a similar vein, Robert Kagan, in his aforementioned and widely praised *Of Paradise and Power* (2003), lays out the intellectual and political foundations for continued buildup of American global power. He argues that the time has come to get beyond liberal skittishness regarding the use of armed force. With the dramatic shift in power relations, and with the U.S. ascendancy to global domination, a growing reliance on military capacity along with a strategic readiness (and flexibility) to intervene makes perfectly good sense—American imperial power is, after all, benevolent in its protection of democracy, human rights, and free markets. Armed force in defense of good values, after all, can only produce good outcomes. Heightened military preparedness is necessary given that the United States "remains mired in history, exercising power in an anarchic Hobbesian world where international laws and rules are unreliable, and where true security and the defense and promotion of a liberal order still depend on the possession and use of military might."[5] Such a global imperative separates the United States from, for example, Europe, where diplomacy, agreements, and peaceful means are instinctively preferred to military action, owing to the relative decline of European power, along with the protection those nations enjoy by virtue of the U.S. military-nuclear umbrella. Since the end of World War II, Europeans, already victimized by two bloody conflagrations, have been anxious to establish social over military priorities, just the reverse of the American model, with its permanent war economy.

For Kagan and the neocons, European preoccupation with diplomatic and legal solutions and with domestic programs is a clear sign of *weakness,* of unwillingness to assume global obligations. Like Rumsfeld, he sees a chaotic, menacing world—reflected above all in the events of 9/11—that can be kept under control only by a military behemoth, that is, the Pentagon. The Europeans now live in a "postmodern" setting that transcends concerns with the old international balance of forces, that rejects military solutions as outmoded and dangerous. European idealism relies more on regional or global treaties and international bodies like the UN, dismissing unilateral armed intervention as a relic of the past, associated with the "crimes against peace" that the Nuremberg Tribunal so severely punished. Through all this, however, the European "paradise" lacks the capacity to keep itself from being subverted or overrun; it fails to recognize the risks and dangers endemic to life in the international jungle.[6] This is where American "strategic and economic generosity" enters the picture: a vast global system of armed might is needed to carry out the ugly but indispensable tasks of fighting evil in the real world, to subdue the ethnic cleansers, genocidal maniacs, terrorists, and wicked dictators whom Europeans either want to ignore or lack the will to confront. Such an imperial mission is "deeply rooted in the American character," according to Kagan. Moreover, as the United States advances its own interests it is not doing so selfishly, as a matter of realpolitik, but is simultaneously "advancing the interests of humanity."[7] The emergence of a new geopolitical logic means that at the start of the twenty-first century the United States is in a position to assert its global supremacy by whatever means it chooses, as it upholds a "liberal world order" against all challengers.[8] These basic differences, in Kagan's view, help explain why most Europeans were reluctant to initiate war against Saddam Hussein's Iraq. In the final analysis, since their actions (by definition) benefit the entire "civilized world," U.S. leaders are more enlightened once they recognize a new paradigm in which domestic and international restraints on military action are stripped away.

The new militarism can now be loosely associated with what might be called the "Bush Doctrine"—an aggressive global strategy revolving around the idea of preemptive strikes on nations (or groups within nations) deemed hostile to the United States. The notion of deploying military power to contain or eliminate WMD, though not only hypocritical but counterproductive at its core, is a corollary of this supposedly novel doctrine. It is a modus operandi largely devoid of ethical, legal, and political limits, sidestepping (as in Iraq) the UN Charter and international law in pursuit of higher ends justified by the war on terrorism. The rules of behavior created on a foundation of postwar international arrangements have been overturned, with diplomacy ultimately subordinated to, or placed in the service of, American nationalism. As global hegemon, the United States now more than ever adheres to the "right" of military intervention on its own terms. The Bush Doctrine corresponds to a renewed moral fervor and self-righteousness that comes naturally to elites bent on making the world safe for corporate expansion and U.S. global hegemony. It is nothing less than a virulent ideological fundamentalism tied to neoliberal globalization with its mixture of economic, political, military, and cultural domination.[9] In such a world a good many familiar agendas become outdated: playing by the rules, global treaties, diplomatic engagement, collaborative action, response to world public opinion. True enough, the United States already has a long history of ignoring or subverting these agendas, but the new militarism has now brought this Darwinian ethos more brazenly to the forefront. The reality is that U.S. leaders not only seek world domination but want to fully reconstruct all material and social relations in their own image.

Under the Bush Doctrine, Pentagon buildup and expansion coincides with efforts to rejuvenate the United States–based arms industry, to develop more sophisticated high-tech weaponry, to deploy armed forces with increased mobility, and to utilize new combat situations so as to test high-tech weapons. All this requires high levels of patriotic mobilization, more easily achieved in a context of widespread fears of terrorism and a propagandistic mass media. U.S. strategy accordingly goes far beyond the war on terrorism, strictly understood, to include hegemonic aspirations throughout the world. As the neocons emphasize, a major goal of Pentagon strategy is to prevent any serious counterforce to American power, above all in the Middle East, with its vital geopolitical significance and it concentration of natural resources.

As of the year 2000 the United States consumed more than 25 percent of total world oil supplies, with the Pentagon alone devouring nearly 2 percent. With domestic sources in severe decline, the Middle East possesses 65 percent of *known* resources—Iraq itself accounting for as much as 15 percent of the total. American control of sprawling petroleum fields in Saudi Arabia, Kuwait, and Iraq would ensure a steady flow of oil under the auspices of Western corporations, the power to decisively influence international prices, and strong long-term U.S. leverage against European, Russian, Chinese, and Japanese interests in the region. U.S. bases in Turkey, Saudi Arabia, Kuwait, the Balkans, and Central Asian republics, as well as Iraq, combined with the Israeli presence, help solidify U.S. supremacy. This dimension of the Bush Doctrine, part of an intensified U.S. dedication to pursue resource wars, cannot be stressed enough. Yet this pattern is much larger than a neocon coup or right-wing diktat, grounded as it is in deeper historical trends.[10] From this standpoint, the U.S. fear of Iraqi regional domination—or its rejection of Washington agendas—in the Middle East is hardly a new phenomenon. Hence the Bush schema of a more aggressive, militaristic Pax Americana is nothing but a recognition of strategic and economic interests now driving U.S. foreign and military policy with a mounting sense of urgency. Such interests and outlooks figure to loom larger in the years ahead.

After 1945 the U.S. struggle for global preeminence, in many ways partial and uneven, relied extensively on economic, political, and cultural forms of domination; systemic integration depended on a global stability allowing American leaders to manage their affairs with minimal armed intervention. By the 1990s, despite its status as the only superpower, the U.S. found itself confronting a more unwieldy universe marked by growing civil wars, challenges from other powers, increasing resource pressures, and blowback in the form of terrorism. At this point the exercise of military power took on new meaning, both in theory and practice, reflecting a declining capacity of the United States to manage and contain conflict. Elites were troubled by challenges from Russia, China, Europe, and Japan, fearful of losing resource competitions in the Middle East and Central Asia and then, following the events of 9/11, preoccupied with the terrorist threat. From this standpoint, the seemingly new imperialism was no radical departure from a previously benevolent foreign policy but signified rather a *continuation* and *deepening* of trends already at work. The main difference was that, by the start of the new century, Empire had congealed into a more durable, systemic reality, becoming a powerful element of daily American life. While the neocons obviously took advantage of new openings, the new militarism was in no measure simply a reflection of extreme right-wing misadventures, much less some kind of Washington coup. The military actions in Afghanistan and Iraq were neither an aberration from earlier foreign-policy contours nor the doings of a single political leader or elite grouping. The proof of this can be readily detected in the overwhelming consensus behind U.S. imperial ambitions and global agendas shared fully by elites of both major parties.

Riding the crest of this momentum, an expansionary U.S. hegemon, theorized and given political girth as the neocons rose to influence under Bush and Cheney, is increasingly viewed by most of the world's population as a fearsome development. Fundamentalist in defense of corporate interests and neoliberal agendas, U.S. rulers are widely perceived as ruthless, arrogant, and brutal, willing more than ever to unleash their "shock and awe" methods of armed intervention on targeted nations. A provincial, heavy-handed approach to other cultures, religions, and countries has become an integral part of a globalist strategy oriented toward a simple unipolarity.

MILITARISM AND
TERRORISM: THE DEADLY CYCLE

The catastrophic terrorist attacks of 9/11 set in motion a series of responses and counterresponses destined to shape world politics well into the twenty-first century. The cliché that everything seems to have been recast is nonetheless true: U.S. foreign policy, the global economic situation, the character of political alliances, ideological discourses, above all the scope and potency of military power in a world already overrun by deadly weapons and veering toward breakdown and destruction. The scenario can be understood as a deadly cycle involving the dialectical interaction of militarism and terrorism—twin expressions of the same New World Order—comprising a historical logic sure to deepen as elements of U.S. superpower hegemony become more visible. Whatever the phenomenon of terrorism calls to mind (and it is a slippery concept at best), 9/11 constitutes a series of violent attacks on an Empire held together in the final instance by U.S. military power. The overriding goal of American leaders has been to make the world accessible to corporate penetration, open trade, and unfettered capital investment while closing off alternatives to the neoliberal order those leaders hope to further solidify. Here terrorism amounts to both a visceral striking back at Empire and the unintended relegitimation of that same Empire. Hence the endless war against terrorism promised by Bush after 9/11, when coupled with jihadic tendencies in the Arab world, serves as a kind of Hobbesian self-fulfilling prophesy—a recipe for continued violence and warfare with no obvious political solution on the horizon.

In the difficult aftermath of 9/11 a new global set of relations seemed to emerge, shaped by heightened public fears and insecurities—although this was not so much new as simply an intensification of already existing trends. Forces of destruction now appeared more ominous, more random, more threatening to the smooth functioning of Empire itself, and those fears and insecurities spread into the very citadel of global power. The United States has forever been deprived of its taken-for-granted sense of invulnerability, its long-standing exceptionalism born of geographical separation, affluence, technological superiority, and the largest military machine in history. These conditions no longer seemed capable of protecting Americans from military invasion, owing in part to the more pervasive incursions of Empire itself (creating blowback), in part to the growth and sophistication of dispersed terrorist networks. At the same time, as Gilbert Achcar points out, 9/11 took on the character of a world spectacle in which international attention was riveted on the attacks and their victims, far out of proportion to media play given disasters elsewhere—for example, the Bhopal catastrophe in India, which killed more people. One immediate consequence of this hyperrealistic event was that U.S. global policies enjoyed a certain immunity to criticism; another was its legitimation of military action in the war on terrorism.[11]

The new terrorist challenge can be seen as an expression of blowback, which, as Chalmers Johnson argues, can take on the character of a virulent reaction against U.S. imperial domination, fueled by a sense of powerlessness (both elite and mass) where alternatives to the status quo are blocked. Johnson writes that the attacks "are all portents of a twenty-first century crisis in America's informal empire, an empire based on the projection of military power to every corner of the world and on the use of American capital and markets to force global economic integration on [U.S.] terms, at whatever costs to others." He adds: "There is a logic to empire that differs from the logic of a nation, and acts committed in service to an empire but never acknowledged as such have a tendency to haunt the future."[12] In the case of al Qaeda, it would be impossible to view its actions as anything but payback for stepped-up U.S. military operations in the Middle East: U.S. support for the Israeli occupation of Palestine, bombings and sanctions against Iraq, military bases spread across the Eurasian region, massive weapons sales to repressive regimes, covert actions going back many decades, and the general machinations of oil politics. It is hardly a coincidence that Middle East–inspired terrorist attacks—including the 1993 World Trade Center bombing, the 1996 assaults on U.S. military bases in Saudi Arabia, the 1998 destruction of U.S. embassies in East Africa, and the 2000 bombing of the USS *Cole* at anchor in Aden harbor—were launched in the aftermath of the first Gulf War. Such blowback was in fact widely predicted at the time of Desert Storm, even if the massive scale of 9/11 was never anticipated by even the most astute observers.

After 9/11 it had become abundantly clear that blowback was a predictable outgrowth of U.S. interventions in the Middle East and elsewhere. Whereas terrorism was previously isolated or localized, on the whole limited, today it has become more organized, dispersed across dozens of countries, and far more adequately funded. Although terrorism spreads as a reaction against imperial power, in the U.S. references to al Qaeda and kindred groups as anything but demonic monsters who hate America, ostensibly because of its prosperity and wonderful ideals, remain quite rare. Osama bin Laden, like Saddam Hussein, has emerged in the public discourse as another incarnation of Hitler, a diabolical enemy, easy to hate, in whom the menace of rogue states and global terrorism is easily personified. Moral outrage is an emotion that tends to obliterate any rational search for explanations that might help us understand *motives*. Terrorism is defined as an evil act pure and simple, while *any* U.S. military operation is unquestionably accepted as vital, necessary, defensive. It is one thing for Bush, in his speech of October 11, 2001, to say, "I'm amazed that there's such misunderstanding of what our country is about that people would hate us," adding that it is just the awesome presence of American wealth, freedom, and democracy that makes people around the world insanely jealous to the point of carrying out violent assaults. It is something else again for such simplistic, self-serving platitudes to find resonance throughout American intellectual, cultural, and political life. To even consider the possibility of blowback—that is, to explore the social and historical context of terrorist actions—is taboo within the existing public sphere, taken as a sign of treachery or even complicity with those evildoers who hate the United States. Such thinking constituted the basis of ideological consensus behind the 2003 U.S. military attack on Iraq.

This ultrapatriotic, in many ways paranoid milieu recalls the darkest moments of cold war hysteria, xenophobia, and ethnocentrism: the levels of arrogance, denial, and contempt for other nations replicates the ideological atmosphere of the 1950s, the heyday of McCarthyism. Informed observers in Europe and elsewhere quickly grasp the dialectic linking militarism and terrorism, connecting U.S. intervention and blowback; few are surprised that the imperial center has come under violent attack, and fewer yet are swayed by myths suggesting that terrorism is motivated by hatred of American freedom and democracy. After decades of nuclear swagger, funding of right-wing dictators and death squads, support for bloody proxy wars, military interventions, and arms sales to anyone willing to pay—not to mention the routine predations of the New World Order—it should be easy to see why the United States—notably its centers of economic and military power—might be targeted. There is in fact little that is new in the American denial. As Michael Fischback writes, U.S. leaders have consistently dodged the issue of motivations underlying terrorism since the 1968 assassination of Robert Kennedy, killed by Sirhan Sirhan, a Palestinian who detested the senator for his fervent support of Israel. Thus: "Today, as in 1968, Americans seem to obfuscate this political motivation by focusing on what our leaders insist are broader cultural reasons for the [9/11] attacks," giving rise to the same popular delusions. The roots of terrorism, according to Fischback, lie not in Arab or Muslim envy but in generalized anger directed at the U.S. imperial presence.[13]

Perhaps the most tragic aspect of the militarism/terrorism dialectic is that this refusal to consider motives, causes, and contexts for 9/11 has the effect of reinforcing those very conditions sure to generate future blowback. If the United States continues to behave as a rogue superpower in world politics, terrorist retaliation ahead is all but guaranteed, whatever the scope of Bush's immediate military successes in Afghanistan and Iraq. If victory over the Taliban in Afghanistan came relatively easy, with few American casualties, the larger war has just begun, with an entire global landscape still to be purged of anti–United States political forces and terrorist cells. U.S. military operations in Afghanistan have not come close to destroying al Qaeda, which, by all accounts, remains as strong as before 9/11. Bush stated the case for endless war in his "axis of evil" 2002 State of the Union address, when he stressed that the new military campaign was being directed not only at dispersed terrorist networks but at such incorrigible enemies as Iran, Iraq, and North Korea. For the Bush administration, in fact, the axis of evil is far more widespread, permeating a world in which anger toward the United States presumably has nothing to do with the specific policies and actions of a superpower. The national refusal to think about the origins and consequences of blowback indicates a mode of political retreat (reinforced by the daily media propaganda barrages) from the fearsome realities of world affairs. As Johnson writes:

> What we have freed ourselves of . . . is any genuine consciousness of how we might look to others on this globe. Most Americans are probably unaware of how Washington exercises its global hegemony since so much of this activity takes place either in relative secrecy or under comforting rubrics. Many may, as a start, find it hard to believe that our place in the world even adds up to an empire.

Despite intensified secrecy, deceit, and media manipulation, however, it is easy for a careful observer today to see how the groundwork is being laid for future blowback, while "blowback itself can lead to more blowback, in a destructive spiral of behavior,"[14] further reinforcing the cycle of militarism and terrorism.

Since 9/11 a new paradigm for interpreting terrorism has emerged, corresponding to a new phase in global anti–United States forms of blowback; strategies, weapons, targets, indeed the entire modus operandi has significantly changed. The new terrorism is emphatically more international in character, dispersed across small cells and larger networks of cells within dozens of countries, comprised of dedicated, mobile fighters capable of hitting many different targets, including of course the United States. Sophisticated technology available to these networks adds a new dimension to terrorism, especially given the strong possibility that WMD will someday enter into the arsenal. As Walter Laqueur observes, "The conjunction of technology and terrorism makes for an uncertain and frightening future."[15] Finally, lending new meaning to the famous "strategy of tension," developed by European groups, global terrorism today is more amorphous, suggesting that any "war" directed against it will be very protracted and frustrating indeed—a long struggle likely to generate new economic and legitimation crises in the United States, perhaps beyond.

This highly dystopian image of the future has been taken up by Bush, who has warned that "our war against terror is only in the beginning," that the Afghan operations were nothing more than an initial skirmish, with "thousands of dangerous killers still at large." However the U.S. campaign unfolds—and it has been superseded by the obsession with Iraq—it could easily veer out of control as it extends to new regions deemed to possess WMD or harbor terrorists, with Iraq seen as just one phase in protracted global warfare. The dispersed, secretive, international nature of al Qaeda and its collaborating groups (in 2003 estimated to number thirty-six in all) makes it difficult to locate and destroy even part of an apparatus that has no organizational center, requiring vast resources and intelligence capabilities. According to intelligence data in mid-2002, perhaps fifteen thousand al Qaeda fighters remained deployed in such far-flung areas as Indonesia, Pakisatan, the Philippines, Malaysia, and Somalia, not to mention Afghanistan, many European nations, and the United States itself, all organized in local, decentralized, hard-to-infiltrate cells. This presence continues to be a serious threat to U.S. and other Western interests around the globe: military installations, embassies and consulates, businesses, nuclear plants, water-treatment facilities, and so forth. As we have seen, the brief legacy of 9/11 has produced record increases in Pentagon spending, along with close to $40 billion yearly earmarked for homeland security—although measures to strengthen national security have fallen considerably short of needs. Even the most casual mention of terrorism has been enough to guarantee easy passage of appropriation bills, with both Republicans and Democrats anxious to show their patriotic mettle. Bush has deftly used the war against terrorism as a catalyst for advancing related military agendas—Star Wars, nuclear modernization, Plan Colombia, intelligence operations, mobile units for global deployment, military action against Iraq. This escalation of certain U.S. foreign and military agendas—a frightening turn for the prospect of world peace—brings new vitality, something of a new trajectory, to the permanent war economy.

The antiterrorist campaign, in Bush's scheme of things, knows few limits of time and space, as the United States escalates its military and nonmilitary interventions, augmented by proxy regimes and subregime groups across the globe and reinforced by space-based surveillance. Intelligence networks are expanding far more rapidly than at the height of the cold war. It might be argued that the cold war finally ended on September 11, 2001, as U.S. preoccupation with established national powers like Russia and China ebbed in favor of more dispersed operations against rogue states and terrorist networks, at least for the time being; in fact the *restraints* on military power appear to be at an all-time low. In an ironic twist, the "strategy of tension" developed as a familiar terrorist methodology today permeates the entire global theater, with the United States itself an integral part of the escalating cycle of destruction.

Insofar as this new phase of terrorism is a manifestation of blowback, it can be seen as rational in this context—yet it is hardly "ideological" in any generally accepted sense of the term. It is more an expression of outrage centered in the Islamic/Arab world, where the mechanisms of political-interest representation are weak. The hulking U.S. presence, stronger economically and military today than ever, is much too strong to be jettisoned through the vehicle of normal politics, and indeed al Qaeda and related groups know no political platforms, no alternative vision of social life, no strategy beyond violent removal of the infidel Western cancer (which itself is only vaguely specified). Here Islamic radicalism and the Salafi tradition define U.S. power as the pinnacle of all evil, as the "Satan who rules the world" and must be fought until utterly destroyed.[16] Islamic terrorism constitutes a militant but nonetheless extremely diffuse anti-imperialist struggle, suggesting a mood of political impotence that, fixated on the mythological value of armed violence, lacks any transformative ethic or strategy. Thus a strategy of tension can have no progressive resolution, as history has amply demonstrated. Michael Doran writes that Salafi-influenced terrorists "have precious little to offer in response to mundane problems that people and governments face in the modern world."[17] While international in scope and strategy, Salafi militants exude powerlessness, an abandonment of politics—in contrast to more coherent, politicized organizations like Hamas and Hezbollah.

The post-9/11 Pentagon buildup is conceived as part of a long-range plan to mobilize U.S. security personnel and military forces throughout the Islamic world and Asia, spurred by the war on terrorism and by the invasion and occupation of Iraq. Worldwide military deployments give the appearance of awesome strength, resolve, and flexibility, but actually widen the field of vulnerability owing to the proliferation of inviting targets, military actions that breed popular anger and hostility, the sharpening of cultural and political tensions, prospects for new outrages over incidents like those in Okinawa, South Korea, Afghanistan, and Iraq under U.S. occupation. Such armed buildup is guaranteed to produce even more blowback. At the same time, the terrorist groupings are far-flung and mobile enough to resist superpower efforts at military annihilation. Conventional large-scale military strategies overlook the great adaptability and elusive character of terrorist networks, as well as the increasingly porous character of national borders. As the legacy of guerrilla warfare has shown, local units are more flexible and adaptable than larger, hierarchical, rationalized military structures. This familiar superpower predicament is worsened by the strongly bureaucratic, tradition-bound, hunkered-down modern armed forces, perhaps none more so than the American—though Rumsfeld has taken steps to shake up the Pentagon both structurally and technologically. It was in recognition of this stubborn reality that one U.S. counterterrorism officer said: "We are, in fact, our own prisoners of war." The burden of living under a continuous state of heightened alert—an inescapable feature of American political and military life abroad since 9/11—inevitably gives rise to additional material and psychological quagmires associated with imperial buildup. This impasse is reflected in the recurrent assaults on U.S. facilities in such countries as Saudi Arabia, the Philippines, Afghanistan, Morocco, and (on a daily, more explosive basis) Iraq.

As U.S. militarism expands to meet the requirements of Empire, terrorist networks can be expected to develop beyond their 9/11 level. Simplistic references to jihadic "holy war" and a "conflict of civilizations," to deranged madmen carrying out evil agendas, therefore make little sense, useful largely as propaganda for U.S. home consumption. A large percentage of Islamic terrorists are educated, middle class, cosmopolitan, on the surface often secular, fully immersed in the routines of daily life—a profile contradicting what we have come to think about people who join gangs, cults, militias, bandit groups, and terrorist cells. Members for the most part do not visibly stand apart in their lifestyles, ideology, or even religious practices. Complicating this situation further is the fact (downplayed in the media) that it is *European* countries—mainly Germany, France, England, and Spain—that have become havens for Salafi education, recruitment, and mobilization. What those involved generally share in common is a profound rage against the United States and its client state Israel.

During late 2002 and early 2003, Bush was fond of saying that al Qaeda had been broken, its leadership and organizational structure in disarray; the war on terrorism was already a resounding success, though it would have to continue into the indefinite future. U.S. and British intelligence reports, however, did not concur with this wildly exaggerated claim, concluding (in spring 2003), that the terrorist challenge was probably greater than ever.[18] In May 2003 al Qaeda did strike again, with three simultaneous attacks in Saudi Arabia—at al Hamsa Oasis Village, the Jadwel complex, and the Vinnell compound—killing more than thirty people and wounding hundreds. Vinnell was chosen as a target because of its role in training the Saudi national guard. The attacks were brilliantly executed with skilled use of high explosives, involving perfect timing and coordination. They were meant to shock and destabilize the United States–client Saudi regime, and they reverberated deeply throughout the country, which had been tense after the U.S. invasion of Iraq. A few days later five more well-coordinated terrorist bombings were carried out in Morocco, yet another Arab government friendly to the United States. In Casablanca the attacks left more than forty dead and roughly one hundred injured, producing in their wake another terrified population. Other Arab or Muslim nations were considered imminent targets, including Egypt, Jordan, Pakistan, Yemen, and Turkey. Whatever their immediate successes, these well-planned, deadly terrorist onslaughts seemed to validate intelligence assessments that al Qaeda had absorbed blows against it and was back stronger than ever, with its organizational resources and funding seemingly intact.

As Laqueur has observed, radical Islam—for better or worse—entered into an ideological void created when enduring political traditions (Communism, Fascism, liberalism, nationalism) had lost their relevance.[19] Of course religion is one belief system that readily fills this void, but it does not by itself furnish a coherent political strategy addressing economic and global problems, much less inspire social transformation; it can be anti-imperialist without posing an alternative to Empire. As for Islamic militancy, its assaults on American power have probably done more to reinforce than to undermine that power. Yet radical Islam appeals to tens of millions of people around the world, and here it is necessary to refuse the impulse that locates terrorism in specific geographical zones like Palestine, Afghanistan, and the Persian Gulf. Jihadism is widely dispersed, following serpentine journeys across the European continent, Africa, the Balkans, Central Asia, Russia, the Far East, and the United States. It flourishes in networks throughout Germany, England, France, and Spain, where thousands of Muslims pass through radicalized mosques, schools, and cells. Much of the planning for 9/11 took place in Germany. While nearly all the hijackers were Saudi citizens, they mostly spent their formative years in Europe. All were drawn to militancy by protracted fighting in Afghanistan, Palestine, Chechnya, and the Balkans, and were driven to further outrage by the U.S. military presence close to holy lands in Saudi Arabia, the war on and sanctions against Iraq, and the long years of Palestinian-Israeli conflict.

Considerable attention has been devoted to what are said to be debilitating intelligence failures leading up to 9/11. No doubt the FBI and CIA, not to mention several other government agencies, lacked full awareness of the expanded threat of international terrorism, which should have been obvious (especially to them) by the late 1990s. Repeated warnings of imminent large-scale actions were downplayed or ignored. Coordination between agencies was lacking. Right-wing commentators saddled President Clinton with this default, but, as Laqueur and others have noted, President Bush received abundant warning of forthcoming al Qaeda attacks using hijacked planes as late as August 2001. During an interview former secretary of state Madeleine Albright commented that the incoming Bush officials expressed little interest in the problem of terrorism in general or al Qaeda in particular during lengthy briefings. In any event, it has become clear that the audacious maneuvers of 9/11 caught all U.S. leaders off guard, partly because the attacks so dramatically upended the familiar pattern of more limited, localized terrorist actions.

To explain this epic failure commentators have referred to several factors: a lack of skilled FBI and CIA agents who could penetrate Islamic networks; an intelligence obsession with *states* as the locus of major threats; a tendency to view terrorists as mere thugs, psychopaths, and criminals; and of course simple incompetence. The deeper problem, however, is far more embarrassing. Terrorism as an Islamic challenge was largely downplayed by the entire political establishment—not just intelligence agencies—because the United States in the early 1980s entered into a fateful partnership with Islamic fundamentalism to aid the cold war struggle against the Soviet Union and Communism. The Afghan wars of the 1980s and early 1990s, largely instigated by the United States to give Soviet leaders their "own Vietnam," was a crucial turning point, insofar as radical Islam and the terrorist movement received a crucial impetus from the war in Afghanistan.[20] Bin Laden and al Qaeda were in large part creatures of America's own jihad. Not only the FBI and CIA, but more tellingly the NSA (as James Bamford shows in his 2002 book *Body of Secrets*) were completely unprepared for anything on the scale of 9/11, although there should have been warning enough with the World Trade Center bombing in 1993. The elites were still caught up in cold war thinking, the bulk of resources going to investigate (mostly nonexisting) threats from Russia and China. At the same time both the Clinton and Bush administrations were sidetracked by the costly, ill-conceived, and counterproductive war on drugs. As for the CIA, it was always far more an organization devoted to international covert action and intrigue than to intelligence gathering as such, as former operatives like Ralph McGeehee[21] have been telling the public for years. Most intelligence amassed in the Middle East and elsewhere was regularly tailored to fit existing U.S. agendas and policies—not the other way around. This perverse dynamic surfaced again at the time of Bush's cynical efforts to shape intelligence data leading up to the invasion of Iraq. So 9/11 illuminated not only a catastrophic flaw in the intelligence apparatus but a more telling *political* blindness across the entire power structure. It was a disaster born of outmoded priorities combined with exceptional hubris and ideological rigidity.

The situation in the Balkans deserves special mention here. As both Laqueur and Diana Johnstone show,[22] United States–organized and -funded Islamic radicalism played a vital role in Bosnia and Kosovo as the United States and its NATO allies moved against Slobodan Milosevic and the Serbs—a point taken up more fully in chapter 5. Many Afghan veterans fought in the Balkans during the 1990s, fully encouraged by the United States, and in Chechnya. The mujahideen groups fighting in Bosnia, Kosovo, and Chechnya had little interest in the ideological rationalizations of Western elites: democracy, multiculturalism, a secular state. Well after the Taliban took control of Afghanistan, it was possible to speak of the "Talibanization" of Bosnia and Kosovo, as these regions came under the influence of the same fundamentalist elements that define al Qaeda. Though largely ignored by Western media and politicians, the Balkans remain something of a base area for Islamic jihad. As with the mujahideen in Afghanistan, former military partners in the Balkans no longer respond to the entreaties of U.S. Empire; on the contrary, many have become sworn enemies of that same Empire.

In this historical milieu the failure of U.S efforts to turn the tide against Islamic militancy reveals some basic contradictions in the war against terrorism. First, a highly decentralized, mobile system like al Qaeda will be less vulnerable to the Pentagon's conventional tactics and weapons: the United States easily destroyed the Taliban government in Afghanistan, but the wreckage merely sent local operatives scurrying for cover in the mountains, Pakistan, and elsewhere, where they could eventually renew their fighting capabilities. Second, American political and military elites grossly misunderstood the degree to which al Qaeda could quickly rebuild its debilitated leadership. Third, the new round of attacks in May 2003 and later illustrated a certain poverty of U.S. intelligence work—the combined efforts of the CIA, FBI, and NSA, along with those of the Pentagon, being woefully inadequate to the task of locating and destroying groups that pose a threat to U.S. national security. Finally, the Bush administration's obsession with the war against Iraq demonstrated its own naïveté about blowback, about the extent to which terrorism is bound to flourish in a milieu of popular Arab/Muslim anger directed at continuing episodes of U.S. militarism. On this point a former Pakistani intelligence officer, Khalid Khawaja, comments as follows:

> Your government's actions are breeding our homicidal bombers at such a
> fast rate that we cannot cope, what with the meager resources we have to
> counter the threat you pose to us. Your government proposes [later carries

out] a course of action against Iraq and beyond that will lead only to one thing: the breeding of tens of thousands of baby Osamas who will be ever more desperate to tear you down, just as your leaders today seek to destroy the Iraqi regime and next, the one in North Korea or Iran or maybe one day my country.[23]

Of course terrorism has been a recurrent fact of political life throughout the nineteenth and twentieth centuries, often the expression of a rational strategy incorporated within broader popular struggles against repression or for national independence—examples being Land and Freedom in Russia, the FLN in Algeria, the IRA in Ireland, the ETA in Spain, Hamas in Palestine. One might even say that the political landscape was permeated with leftist terrorist groups in the 1960s and 1970s, including the Red Army Faction in Japan, Baader-Meinhof in Germany, the Red Brigades in Italy, the Tupamaros in Uruguay, and the Weather Underground in the United States. Today, however, terrorist organizations like al Qaeda have built a legacy of armed rebellion detached from popular movements, national objectives, or even specific designs on state power. One result is that the strategy of tension, at times effective in destabilizing or overthrowing regimes under conditions that prevailed earlier in Russia, Algeria, and Ireland, has now given rise to an altogether different outcome—namely, a dramatic *strengthening* of the central governmental apparatus, with the security and military side of the state gaining new power over civil society. In the existing global circumstances, moreover, the distinction between local terrorism and the routine exercise of state power (always blurred in any case) has broken down to the point of invisibility. At the same time, "local" terrorism has, in the case of Islamic radicalism, metamorphosed into a largely international phenomenon, evolving from previously isolated and limited threats to the power structure—more of a nuisance factor in Western societies—into a large-scale, well-financed, sustained global challenge that lends the cycle of violence an entirely new meaning, but one still devoid of ideological content.[24]

The global reach of terrorism has led to a significant reshaping of the rules of engagement, for both nation-states and subnational groups, calling into question a wide range of international norms and conventions. While this development is scarcely new, over the past few decades the very existence of binding universal standards of military behavior has been so compromised as to be meaningless. We long ago reached the point at which war crimes are committed almost routinely, on all sides of most conflicts, but such crimes generally go unrecognized and unpunished even where civilian death tolls might be enormous, as in Vietnam, the Persian Gulf, Central America, Chechnya, and Palestine. Put differently, the discourse of human rights and international law is increasingly shrouded in hypocrisy, double standards, and the insistence that some parties (such as the United States) be exempted from the rules. Entire civilian infrastructures have been annihilated, provoking little if any moral outrage among world politicians, UN officials, media pundits, and academics. Viewed from this angle, the new terrorism has simply contributed its part to reshaping global rules of engagement. We have entered an era of indiscriminate warfare in which barbarism seems to have become something close to the norm: all that human beings have constructed seems worthy of devastation in a world that recognizes fewer and fewer ethical or political constraints.

As the war against terrorism unfolds against a larger backdrop of U.S. militarism, we encounter a basic question: What precisely *is* terrorism and who are its main perpetrators on the world scene? A definition involving simply the use of violence for political (or religious) ends is not too useful, since its application then becomes universal. Focusing on the actions of individuals and small groups narrows the frame of reference but ignores the role of states that carry out or sponsor the very same atrocities as those individuals and small groups—the main difference being that the violence of states has the imprimatur of governmental legitimacy, is carried out by formal military organizations, and is usually more horrendous. Missiles sent into the heart of cities from great distances are generally *more* destructive than the work of suicide bombers. If we turn to violent actions targeting specifically civilian objects, we arrive at a more coherent approximation of what terrorism is today, although such a definition is summarily rejected by leaders and apologists of powerful states, for obvious reasons. As modern warfare increasingly blurs the distinction between military and civilian targets, this last definition may still lack clarity, but it is probably the best we have. Horrific as the 9/11 terrorist attacks were, therefore, they do not logically or morally stand apart from most of what has passed for conventional or guerrilla warfare since World War II. Military action, whether carried out by states or by other actors, has involved a massive loss of civilian life—much of it the result of deliberate, planned, ruthless strategies. Aerial bombardment in particular has had devastating effects, but artillery, infantry, armor, and government-sponsored death squads have also taken an unspeakable toll.

A New World Order dominated by U.S. economic and political interests, and policed by the largest war machine in history, is destined to generate more episodes of local terrorist violence. Such episodes will gather a degree of popular support in many countries, especially in the Middle East, where the Israeli occupation of the West Bank and Gaza contributes mightily to regional anti-imperialist sentiment. Lacking ideological focus, militant groups will nonetheless be driven to oppose corporate globalization, which, as Laqueur argues, furnishes a kind of axis around which dispersed movements can mobilize. Thus: "Antiglobalism means opposition to capitalism, neoliberalism, and corporate power. It regards globalization as a synonym for the Westernization or the Americanization of the world. It believes that globalization perpetuates social injustices or even aggravates them." Yet there is no ideology that goes beyond this. As Laqueur adds: "If there is an Islamic theory of imperialism, it resembles less Lenin's or Rosa Luxemburg's but more the ideas developed at the beginning of the twentieth century by some of Mussolini's predecessors. . . . For radical Islam, the West—and above all America—is the great threat, and their aim was and remains to weaken it politically, militarily, and economically."[25]

As the war on terrorism builds, therefore, U.S. superpower hegemony is destined to aggravate the existing Hobbesian state of nature, in which chaos, fear, despair, and violence rule as daily features of social life around the world, particularly in the great megacities shaped by the dynamics of globalization. Such a volatile situation means that ethical principles are thrown onto the periphery, that political and legal methods for containing the spread of militarism and terrorism will be checkmated in an atmosphere of mounting conflict, disorder, and blowback. Thus globalization could readily turn into a nightmarish reality of worldwide civic crisis, social polarization, and local wars in which progressive outcomes—requiring a strong countervailing power against Empire—will be increasingly difficult to imagine.

WARS IN THE NEW WORLD ORDER

U.S. military interventions since the end of the cold war, always tied to pursuit of global domination, have taken on new meaning with the rise of the New World Order. In little more than a decade American forces have invaded Panama, launched the Persian Gulf War, bombed and occupied parts of both Yugoslavia and Afghanistan, and then invaded Iraq with the idea of converting that nation into a U.S. colony. Further intervention against rogue states or countries placed on the Pentagon's enemies list (Iran, Syria, North Korea, Libya, Somalia, etc.) can be expected so long as the Bush circles remain in power and perhaps beyond that. Everything fits into Washington's evolving strategy for maximum global power to be achieved by a mixture of economic, political, and military instruments, with renewed emphasis now on the military side. Since 9/11, of course, the war on terrorism has served to further legitimate foreign interventions, each of which leaves in its wake an ever-broadening (but still fragile and uneven) sphere of American control. Over the past decade U.S. base deployment has been strongly augmented in the Persian Gulf, across the Middle East, in Central Asia, and the Balkans, all strategically vital zones. At the beginning of the twenty-first century what has become a ruthless U.S. imperial strategy has run roughshod over the UN, international law, a series of multilateral treaties, and the interests of several other nations, including some of America's own allies.

The U.S./NATO operation in the Balkans—economically and politically throughout the 1990s, militarily in spring 1999—will probably be remembered as the first war to secure and expand the New World Order. Earlier attacks on Panama and Iraq, though merciless and costly, were less geopolitically ambitious, more "surgical," more limited in their rationale. In the case of the Balkans, military action was justified as a humanitarian move to put an end to massive war crimes and human-rights violations, to carry out regime change with the aim of creating democracy, free markets, and regional stability. Pursuing only the most bogus diplomatic initiatives, the action was in fact a brazen form of military aggression that was carried out in violation of well-established norms of international law, the UN Charter (prohibiting armed intervention except in cases of self-defense), and the much-cherished tradition of national sovereignty. Demonizing the Serbs and their elected leader, Slobodan Milosevic, Western powers (the United States, Britain, Germany) sought to extend their hegemony into the region, where the Serbs remained virtually the lone holdout against Western corporate penetration, resisting NATO efforts to recolonize the area through its push eastward. U.S. leaders in particular were anxious to engineer a complete triumph of the neoliberal corporate order, which had begun with previous attempts to encourage secessionist and centrifugal tendencies within the Federal Republic of Yugoslavia.

NATO's seventy-nine-day offensive was intended to achieve these historic goals by force, in the process sending a message to the world that war had become a more integral, perhaps even celebrated, instrument of American foreign policy. The end of the cold war and disintegration of the Soviet bloc had cleared the path. As Diana Johnstone writes: "The bombing of Yugoslavia marked a turning point in the expansion of U.S. military hegemony."[26] This model of intervention would be further embellished in Afghanistan and Iraq.

The Serbs became the target of severe ideological attacks despite the long, complex, multifaceted nature of the Yugoslav civil wars, involving years of violence on all sides—Serbs, Croatians, Bosnians, Kosovar Albanians, the Western powers themselves that were interested in breaking up the Federal Republic of Yugoslavia (FRY). The reality is that the Serbs were specifically isolated not because of regime-sponsored terrorism (much less genocide) but simply because they constituted the largest, most influential nationality grouping in the FRY, with by far the largest percentage of socialists and Communist Party members in the country.[27] Add here the stridently independent character of the Milosevic regime and the ethical double standards applied to the Serbs begin to make sense within the larger U.S./NATO strategic picture.

NATO in fact wanted the FRY fully integrated into the regional and larger capitalist world economy, with the famous Rambouillet conference serving as pretext for escalating the conflict and justifying the bombing campaign. The result is well known: under U.S. instigation, NATO forces pounded the FRY into submission with deadly, around-the-clock aerial bombardments spanning the period of March 24 to June 10, 1999, leaving in their wake more carnage, deaths, injuries, and homeless refugees than anything credibly attributed to the Serbs. The operation was essentially a terror bombing that destroyed large parts of the Serb infrastructure, with civilian casualties outnumbering military ones; densely populated urban areas, mostly lacking air defenses, were systematically bombed, leading to more than two thousand deaths in Belgrade alone. The kind of technowar conducted against Serbia can be described only as criminally punitive, in stark opposition to its supposed humanitarian goals.

The road to U.S./NATO military intervention was smoothed by a massive propaganda campaign waged by the government and media and supported by portions of the liberal intelligentsia, branding Milosevic as Hitler and the Serbs as recycled Nazis bent on armed conquest, ethnic cleansing, genocide, virtually every atrocity imaginable, all for the goal of a Greater Serbia. Within this scenario only the Serbs were singled out in this fashion, against the preponderance of evidence showing that *all* sides were guilty of excessive armed violence. Serbs were pilloried for their "extreme nationalism" and grandiose ambitions, but their nationalism was, if anything, less virulent than that of the fascistic Croatians, Bosnian Muslims, and Kosavar Albanians—all supported and financed by the United States. One searches in vain for statements, documents, or concrete policies indicating any drive toward ethnic cleansing or a Greater Serbia, much less genocide. Johnstone argues that this was basically a well-financed advertising campaign riddled with lies and myths, not too far removed from the narrative in *Wag the Dog*.[28] Further, as Johnstone notes, the war was the first in several decades to revive the European colonial legacy of the "white man's burden," at this point directed against the much-despised Slavs of Eastern Europe. Horrible crimes committed by mad Serb leaders compelled the (benevolent, democratic) West to carry out its moral and political obligations to rectify the situation. Thus: "The focus on 'evil dictators' conveys the message that they can be stopped, judged, and punished by the benevolent outside intervention of the 'international community.' [Such an outlook] enforces a dualistic view of the essentially good Western imperial condominium obliged to punish 'bad' men who trouble the moral order."[29] A moral imperative resulting from the Balkans conflicts therefore must supersede everything else: global norms of behavior, the UN Charter, national sovereignty, the safety of those very civilian populations deemed threatened.

The U.S./NATO "liberation" of Kosovo and the FRY turned quickly enough into a political nightmare: Kosovo itself was largely abandoned, permitted to degenerate into an economic and social wasteland characterized by widespread poverty, unemployment levels reaching fifty percent, impoverished public services, corruption, and pervasive mafia influence. The gift of "democracy" and "free markets" bequeathed by military attack has brought to Serbia (in 2003) an even more authoritarian government, replete with ongoing mass arrests, crackdowns, corruption, even the forced removal of Serbs from areas of Kosovo. Within only a few years the country as a whole has seen its public security, social planning, and political freedoms decline, even as the post-Milosevic regimes have received generous U.S. economic aid. The huge U.S. military base near Prishtina, Camp Bondsteel, is itself surrounded by poverty, crime, prostitution, and mafia corruption—some of the familiar consequences of U.S. intervention around the world. The long-term Western strategy to destabilize, dismantle, and privatize Yugoslavia through a combination of economic, political, and military methods has worked, with sadly predictable results.

In Afghanistan, U.S. intervention goes back to the early 1980s, when the CIA began anti-Soviet, promujahideen operations that would eventually cost $3.5 billion. Having funded and armed right-wing Islamic fundamentalists in Afghanistan (as in Bosnia), the United States readily developed a cozy relationship with the Taliban government that would rule the country during the late 1990s—reversing course only in the circumstances of 9/11, long after the Taliban and al Qaeda had turned against American interests in the region. The new war on terrorism was designed to get rid of the Taliban, as well as dozens of al Qaeda base camps across Afghanistan; it succeeded after weeks of intense bombing and Special Ops ground campaigns that sent tens of thousands of militant fighters into remote areas, retreating into the normalcy of civilian life, or scurrying for cover in Pakistan. U.S. military forces were able to establish in Kabul a new friendly government, the Northern Alliance, with a political outlook nearly identical to that of the Taliban. In the process U.S. air and ground operations killed an estimated four thousand Afghan civilians, wounded tens of thousands, and left up to a half-million homeless and dislocated. Meanwhile, American troops achieved political control over Kabul and one or two other urban areas, enabling them to set up a puppet regime led by handpicked Hamid Karzai, a former paid consultant for the oil giant Unocal.

In the weeks and months following 9/11, Bush referred to military actions in Afghanistan as "defensive" in nature, part of "the first battle in the wars of the twenty-first century." No UN permission would be necessary. Bush was correct insofar as this was clearly the first sustained armed intervention to be carried out under the auspices of the war on terrorism. As in the case of Yugoslavia, however, the action ultimately makes greater sense as a stratagem behind resource wars and geopolitical interests in a region where the United States has long coveted a hegemonic presence. From this standpoint, such aims as democracy, women's rights, and national reconstruction were rather meaningless, largely a cloak for the American grand strategy.

From the outset the Bush administration emphasized the *military* side of operations in Afghanistan, including high-altitude bombing raids, helicopter gunship attacks, and Special Ops commando raids that continued throughout 2003. U.S. high-tech warfare, potentially efficient in tactical situations, relied on faulty or outdated local intelligence. More problematic yet, since the Taliban had deep roots in Afghan society, distinctions between fighters and civilians were difficult to make in actual combat circumstances. The bombing of roads, bridges, public buildings, electric power stations, and other parts of the infrastructure became a routine occurrence. Hundreds of towns and villages were struck, typically from high altitude, often indiscriminately. In such "warfare" large numbers of people, vehicles, and structures wound up as potential targets. As of late 2003, with the Karzai government lacking genuine legitimacy and Taliban/al Qaeda forces still scattered across the country, skirmishes continued almost daily as war persisted as a dominant feature of Afghan life. The countryside was increasingly taken over by warlords, local militias, armed gangs, and remnants of the previous regime.

The stubborn chaos of Afghan society meant not only continued shock, hardship, and dislocation for the general population but also major obstacles to reconstruction. All rhetoric aside, the United States placed few resources in the service of rebuilding the war-torn country, consistent with Bush's earlier dismissive attitude toward "nation building." As the United States remained attached to military priorities, it was left to the UN and some NGOs (nongovernmental organizations) to tackle the social agenda—with precious few results, as of early 2004. By early 2003 public infrastructures had been fully restored for only three of a total of thirty-two provinces. The refugee problem festered. And the United States, owing largely to its own strategic concerns, discouraged any major UN or other international role in the country. Despite the chaos—and U.S. failure to apprehend either bin Laden or Taliban leader Mullah Omar—the Pentagon was able to consolidate its presence not only in Afghanistan but in neighboring zones: Pakistan, Iraq, Tajikistan, Uzbekistan, Kyrgyzstan.

The war against Iraq was on the Pentagon agenda as early as 1991, following the Iraqi incursion into Kuwait, Desert Storm, and the decision of the first Bush administration to stop short of overthrowing the Hussein regime. Neocons, especially frustrated by this retreat and anxious to extend U.S. power across the Middle East, began to agitate for regime change, even as the Gulf War and economic sanctions had already severely undermined the Baghdad government while further impoverishing Iraqi society as a whole. A strong nucleus of ardently pro-Israel figures, led by Paul Wolfowitz, Richard Perle, Douglas Feith, and Robert Kaplan, along with Dick Cheney, most of them affiliated with the American Enterprise Institute, had begun to see Iraq as a threat to U.S. national interests for several reasons: its supposedly aggressive foreign policy making it a danger to Israel, its possession and use of WMD, its harboring of terrorists, its general challenge to American domination in the region. These claims were supplemented by a widely held critique of the Hussein regime as totalitarian and barbaric, a candidate for "humanitarian" intervention. The propaganda apparatus catalyzed by the Pentagon, mass media, advertising firms, PACs, and think tanks worked overtime throughout the 1990s to instill these notions—mostly outright lies, distortions, and half-truths—in leading sectors of the population, with enough success that by the ascension of Bush II and the events of 9/11 a "preemptive" war against Iraq could win majority consensus. Aside from literally hundreds of op-ed pieces, position statements, pamphlets, interviews, and talk radio shows championing prowar attitudes, the work of Kenneth Pollack stands out as notably critical to the framing of an aggressive military stance toward Iraq. In his 2002 seminal book *The Threatening Storm: The Case for Invading Iraq*, Pollack assembled the above contentions and more as the basis for regime change. Preemptive war was envisioned as a crucial step in the revitalization of U.S. foreign policy, protection of Israel, and strengthening of American global hegemony.

By early 2003 most of the U.S. public seemed to have bought the underlying motif of these arguments—namely, that Iraq was an imminent threat to Americans even after a decade of sanctions, more bombings, and UN inspections, even as the Iraqis were spending just $1 billion yearly on their military forces (compared to $400 billion for the United States). Democrats and Republicans alike seemed comfortable with these distortions and falsehoods, along with the imperial agenda undergirding them; indeed within Congress the murmurs of dissent were rare. Bush's hour-long State of the Union speech to Congress in January 2003, dwelling on the Iraqi menace and the need for immediate war to repel it, was interrupted no less than seventy-three times by raucous applause from both sides of the floor. In his call to war Bush compared Hussein to Hitler and Stalin as an evil dictator obsessed with taking over the world. Thus: "Throughout the twentieth century, small groups of men seized control of great nations, built arms and arsenals, and set out to dominate the weak and intimidate the world. In each case, their ambitions of cruelty and murder had no limit."[30] It was up to the United States, of course, to mobilize its own armed might to defend the civilized world from the deeds and threats of a horrible tyrant.

On March 19, 2003, the United States did indeed launch the anticipated second Gulf War, a massive attack several months in preparation—despite its failure to win UN endorsement, the lack of evidence supporting claims of Iraqi WMD or ties with al Qaeda, and widespread antiwar opposition around the globe, including large militant protests in the United States itself. The goals set forth for public edification were to "liberate" Iraq from an oppressive dictator, establish democracy, locate and remove WMD, and stabilize the region. Waging "shock and awe" aerial and ground operations against a weakened Iraqi military that by now possessed no air force and little air defense capability, the United States was able to conquer an oil-rich nation of twenty-three million in little more than three weeks, averting prolonged, bloody urban warfare in Baghdad and possibly other Iraqi cities. The Pentagon carried out its promised technowar, unleashing thirty thousand high-explosive bombs and missiles, some tipped with depleted uranium, in the first few days. On the eve of invasion the U.S. military had marshaled over two hundred thousand combat troops, along with a massive armada of tanks, humvees, artillery pieces, ships, planes, and missile launchers, surrounding a nearly defenseless country from the eastern Mediterranean to the borders with Kuwait, Saudi Arabia, and Turkey. In contrast with the 1991 Gulf War, this campaign stressed lighter vehicles, a mobile force, more sophisticated high-tech weaponry, and more workable satellites, along with the famous "shock and awe" strategy—all part of the Pentagon's integrated electronic battlefield. If the initial phases of invasion brought seemingly easy "victory," the larger U.S. objective would be considerably more multifaceted: to secure territorial control over Iraq, test new military weapons and operational methods, justify further increases in Pentagon spending, advertise to the Middle East and the world the awesome features of U.S. military supremacy, and provide Americans with the illusion of a resoundingly successful campaign against terrorism.

The second Gulf War involved one of the grossest inequalities in firepower capability between two combatants in the history of warfare. In the first three or four days of combat the U.S. military exploded more than $3 billion in ordnance, roughly triple the entire Iraqi military budget for one year. Baghdad itself was taken in five days of relatively moderate fighting, made easier by the collapse of the Baath leadership. Casualty rates in this early phase were more than one hundred to one in favor of the U.S./Coalition forces. As we have seen, the "war" was launched not only to advance U.S. geopolitical objectives but to send a clear message to the rest of the world. As John Berger writes: "The primary aim of the war, launched in defiance of the United Nations, was to demonstrate what is likely to happen to any leader, nation, community, or people who persist in refusing to comply with U.S. interests."[31]

For the United States, regime change in spring 2003 was the culmination of more than a decade of economic, political, diplomatic, and military ferment, a strategy that clearly predated 9/11 or even the ascension of Bush II. The real goals—oil, geopolitical domination, bolstering Israel, war profiteering, weapons testing—were shrouded in a torrent of rhetoric about liberation, democracy, human rights, and valiant efforts to curb WMD and terrorism. Like the Balkans intervention before it, the recycled Gulf War was based on systematic deceit: lies about WMD, forged documents showing purported nuclear capabilities, false reports regarding al Qaeda in Iraq, fear mongering over Hussein's ability to harm the United States, manipulation of intelligence data, and so forth. These phony pretexts became all the more visible in the months following the attack, as shown by a rich abundance of postinvasion sources: James Bamford's book *A Pretext for War*, Richard Clark's book *Against All Enemies*, Robert Greenwald's film *Uncovered: The Truth about Iraq*, Michael Moore's film *Fahrenheit 9/11*, and Bob Woodward's book *Plan of Attack* (all appearing in 2004). In his 2003 State of the Union speech Bush claimed with great passion that war was an urgent imperative owing to Iraq's development of dangerous weapons, including "a growing fleet of manned and unmanned aerial vehicles capable of dispersing vast chemical and biological weapons through missions targeting the U.S." Bush stated this bogus case despite the failure of UN inspectors to locate any WMD after years of searching and the scant evidence of such weapons uncovered by both British and U.S. intelligence. We know after the U.S. invasion that no WMD were ever used by Iraq—nor were any such weapons found after months of meticulous searches throughout the country. In the same address Bush said that intelligence sources revealed that Iraq was seeking large amounts of uranium from Africa to stoke its nuclear-weapon program. This too was a complete lie: it turned out the documents in question were signed by an official who had given up his post ten years earlier, information, the CIA had already apparently given the White House.

Crucial to the media and government propaganda barrage were a variety of key *omissions*—the most obvious, and most often ignored, being the U.S. quest for new sources of petroleum. White House and Pentagon officials steadfastly denied that oil reserves (more than 120 million *known* barrels worth in Iraq) had anything to do with the push for regime change; Bush, Rumsfeld, and Wolfowitz insisted repeatedly that the oil "belongs to the Iraqi people." The media, for its part, simply indulged this fraudulent discourse, refusing to press officials for the real motives for invasion. The first order of business for U.S. troops upon entering Iraq was to secure the extensive oil fields and refineries, making sure the infrastructure went directly into American hands. American corporations (e.g., Bechtel, Halliburton) would be in the forefront of rebuilding, protecting, and exploiting the Iraqi oil fields. This would be the spoils of war—the most lucrative heist in history, assuming the United States could solidify its hold over the country. The United States has vowed to keep other nations (excepting Britain) away from the petroleum supply, which it intends to privatize, breaking up the

National Oil Company, no doubt as soon as international vigilance begins to wane. Transnational oil corporations have plans to explore, develop, and tap new oil fields that could produce in exess of two hundred billion barrels, an output that would make Iraq the largest known source in the world. Previous oil contracts signed between the Hussein regime and such nations as Russia, France, and China have become null and void. The United States, according to this scenario, will end up in a splendid position to subvert OPEC and more decisively influence the conditions of oil production and consumption well into the twenty-first century.

Wartime propaganda was aided and abetted by the major media outlets, notably the five largest TV networks (ABC, CBS, NBC, Fox, CNN). More even than during the first Gulf War, the media were transformed into superpatriotic cheerleaders for Pentagon war and U.S. invasion, blocking any genuine debate or questioning. This was true not only of the big networks but also the cable stations, talk radio, and print outlets. More than five hundred reporters became "embedded" within the full scope of military planning and operations, dependent on the Pentagon for access, resources, equipment, and perhaps above all psychological support. Journalists covering the war operated out of a sprawling, modern, $1.5 million media center located in Qatar. Naturally everything was relayed to the American public through the prism of a fast-moving, high-tech, intimidating military structure, capturing each phase of U.S. combat advance as part of a glittery media spectacle. As war predictably ended up a one-sided contest, it also became aestheticized in the manner of an exciting sports event, the carnage mostly left out of the picture, as it had been during Desert Storm and the Balkans war. The devastating effects of war on the Iraqi population were rendered largely invisible or, where visible, diminished within a framework of triumphal, superpatriotic representations.

The parade of TV and radio experts moving before the American public offered a monotonous diet of proadministration military, ex-military, governmental, and academic guests who dwelled almost exclusively on the logistics and tactics of U.S. combat operations. Larger strategic, political, moral, and historical questions were ignored or dismissed as the rantings of squeamish liberals and peaceniks. The few antiwar spokespeople allowed on the airwaves were castigated as misfits, unpatriotic, even sympathizers of terrorists. In late April the Pentagon voiced its pleasure at the "professionalism" displayed by members of the embedded press corps. Commenting on the Pentagon's "media-friendly 'reality' war," Robin Anderson writes: "Empowered by riding shotgun with these road warriors, journalists barely contained their excitement. They wore goggles, flack jackets, and even reported through gas masks as they adopted military jargon. . . . They interviewed Top Gun pilots and crawled along the ground with gunfire in the distance, pressing microphones into soldiers' faces as they pointed their weapons." When one embedded journalist was asked about taking pictures of civilian casualties, the response was: "We're telling the U.S. military's story, that will be up to other journalists."[32] As for freewheeling discussion in a vibrant democracy back home, a Fairness and Accuracy in Reporting (FAIR) study found that of 1,617 on-camera sources appearing on TV networks from March 3 to April 9, 2003, only 3 percent of the American sources had even moderate antiwar views. Among appearances by current or former government and military officials, only *four* contained significant antiwar opinions—two by Representative Dennis Kucinich (D-Ohio) and one each by Representative Pete Stark (D-California) and Senator Robert Byrd (D-West Virginia).

The closure of the public sphere—most emphatically in foreign relations, and especially since 9/11—was nowhere more telling than in what has become an ossified two-party system. As Bush pursued his preemptive invasion, Democrats with few exceptions simply followed along, refusing the imperatives of healthy debate and declining to probe outlandish claims about the Iraqi threat. As will be explored more fully in chapter 3, the major parties have converged ideologically around strategic global aims, with dissent feeble and marginalized. The march to war against Iraq could not have gone more smoothly through the entire political apparatus, despite reports of policy divisions within the Bush administration itself. A lonely holdout in the Senate, Robert Byrd (D-West Virginia) reacted bitterly to the conformism of Washington, wondering in amazement how the nation could be moving toward a potentially horrific, costly, self-destructive war while "this chamber [U.S. Senate] is silent—ominously, dreadfully silent. There is no debate, no discussion, no attempt to lay out for the nation the pros and cons of this particular war. There is nothing. We stand passively mute in the Senate." Byrd added: "In the space of two short years this reckless and arrogant administration has initiated policies which may reap disastrous consequences for years. . . . It is business as usual in the U.S. Senate."[33]

The U.S. military aggression against Iraq might be divided into five distinct but overlapping phases: buildup for war, invasion, occupation to establish control, reconstruction, exploitation of resources and geopolitical position. No one can doubt that the first two phases were carried out brilliantly, if also deceitfully, even after the U.S./British failure to win over the UN. Media-led public relations campaigns helped immensely. Military conquest went more quickly and smoothly than even the Pentagon optimists had anticipated. It is the third phase—military occupation—that has already turned out to be the most intractable, owing to basic contradictions inherent in the struggle of a foreign nation to rule a population by force, especially where such vast cultural differences come into play. Where occupation becomes a protracted and costly burden, the phases of reconstruction and exploitation (expected to bring enormous profits to Western corporations) will inevitably be placed in jeopardy. The U.S. commitment to rebuilding a society it has helped so much to destroy since 1991 has nothing to do with humanitarian or democratic goals but rather with the self-interested drive toward social and economic order essential to phase five.

Despite far greater roadblocks than ever imagined, the Bush administration—with Britain as junior partner—seeks full political and military control over Iraq well into the future; occupation has no fixed time frame, nor could it, owing to the imperatives of both reconstruction and control over resources. Any transfer of "sovereignty" is bound to be purely fictional. So long as military occupation signifies coercive rule, the issue of popular *consent*—that is, legitimacy—immediately comes to the forefront. The overriding question here is: How can a legitimate Iraqi state, possessing genuine sovereignty, emerge under conditions of foreign military domination? If the United States was able to win quickly on the battlefield, it does not follow that subsequent efforts to impose (its own) order on a defeated, angry, recalcitrant population will similarly work. Judging from history, the task before American elites would seem to be hopeless. The result is more likely to be social and political breakdown, ethnic/religious strife, chaos, and large-scale resistance. As of early summer 2004 this was precisely the scenario, with Saddam Hussein's authoritarian order supplanted by the *disorder* of an occupation regime that, from every piece of evidence, militates against prospects for a stable, legitimate governance. Those who believe occupation can serve as a basis of revitalized economic and political life are fond of citing the post–World War II U.S. experience with Germany, Japan, and Italy. Such comparisons are false, however, insofar as those countries were relatively advanced industrial societies and were never targets of preemptive war or resource exploitation; nor in fact did the United States quickly relinquish its political and military control.

With the onset of summer 2003, the U.S./British occupation was already settling in to a bloody, costly, quagmire with no end in sight; throughout the following year the situation only worsened. Iraq had become a society where turbulence was the everyday reality, including disintegration of the system of law and security, impoverishment of the population, an infrastructure in shambles, the virtual absence of social governance, and of course intensifying violent conflict across the terrain. Such chaos was the product of three wars, a decade of economic sanctions, and finally protacted foreign occupation. The U.S. military victory, celebrated as another great achievement of Pentagon technowar, turned increasingly precarious as Iraqi resistance stiffened in Baghdad, Falluja, and other parts of the country, with scattered local forces fighting by means of sniper attacks, ambushes, suicide bombings, kidnappings, and full-scale assaults mixed with periodic mass uprisings and demonstrations. Urban combat fed into harsh military crackdowns that in turn bred further anger and resistance. Following the invasion, combined U.S. and British troops numbered almost 200,000 but urgent calls for reinforcements had boosted the total to 240,000 by spring 2004—still obviously not adequate to the hopeless task of solidifying the occupation. While the United States was ready to leave resource-poor Yugoslavia and Afghanistan largely to their own devices once military action was completed—abandoning even the pretense of reconstruction and democracy—that kind of outcome in the case of Iraq is unthinkable given the overriding economic and geopolitical interests at stake.

Imperial expectations (hopes?) were that the invaders would be welcomed as liberators, thanked profusely for getting rid of Hussein, and treated as friends. Whatever local acceptance the invaders might have initially encountered soon evaporated as the brutal occupation took its hold over the population. Military rule was set up and enforced by armored vehicles, planes, heavy weapons, and thousands of troops on the ground, by daily searches of persons, autos, trucks, homes, and offices leading to arrests and killings that have become routine. U.S. troops charge through neighborhoods, looking for pockets of resistance, for remnants of the Baath regime. Local customs and traditions have been trampled on, for example by stationing troops near mosques, by violating the sanctity of religious institutions, by failure to respect domestic privacy, and most egregiously by brutal, sexually degrading treatment of prisoners. Occupation authorities say they want to secure the "consent" of Iraqis, to win the "hearts and minds" of ordinary people, but the logic of occupation dictates behavior destined to intensify popular hostility. Thousands of Iraqis have been arrested and detained, criminalized as outlaws and terrorists, and abused once in prison. According to one U.S. soldier, as reported in the *Los Angeles Times* (June 13, 2003): "If you ask these people nicely to do something, they won't do it until you yell at them. The way the culture is here, they don't have any social skills." Commented another: "I have been here for two months. I am sick of this. I have no sympathy for these people." In June 2003 Lieutenant General David McKiernan, commander of the Coalition ground forces in Iraq, said that refusal to go along with occupation was nothing but the dying gasp of small pockets of Hussein loyalists—a theme repeated endlessly by other military figures. The fact that foreign occupation itself *inescapably* breeds resistance seems far beyond the arrogant mindset of the imperial managers.

The contradictions of U.S. military rule have surfaced in the political realm too, where the propaganda of liberation, of bringing the gift of democracy and freedom to a downtrodden people, has been revealed as fraudulent. Movement toward a stable governing system has been marked at various turns by U.S. schemes to maintain dictatorial control. The Coalition Provisional Authority quickly asserted itself as sole legal power bent on destroying all vestiges of the previous government, all forms of opposition to the foreign occupation. People hoping to work for the government in any capacity were forced to accept conditions laid down by civilian administrator L. Paul Bremer III. A major affront to Iraqis was contained in a document all public workers were required to sign, reading in part: "I will obey the laws of Iraq and all proclamations, orders, and instructions of the Coalition Provisional Government." Despite massive protests in July 2003, Bremer refused to budge, insisting on full, unqualified control over the state apparatus—a governing arrangement likely to continue even past the celebrated "transfer of sovereignty" in July 2004. In another show of brazen arrogance, occupation managers scoffed at the notion that the Iraqi people were prepared to have a say in their own fate; local participation in governing structures would be checkmated by Coalition power over police and military functions. One U.S. official stated in summer 2003: "The mentality doesn't exist. They need us. They know it is up to us." In response, one Iraqi professional was quoted as saying: "According to what the U.S. government said, this was a liberation. Now that they say American law should be implemented, it means this is an occupation. They didn't say anything about Iraqi law. This is a full occupation."[34]

In the context of U.S. military rule, with its attendant repression, chaos, and violence, the very idea of democracy seems rather pointless, absurd even, although it has been championed by the Pentagon throughout the occupation regimen. The economic situation has drastically worsened: jobless rates skyrocketed after the invasion, when thousands of laid-off workers around the country went into the streets to protest. Bremer, previously known in Washington as a terrorism expert, vetoed plans to have Iraqi citizens select their own interim government; most important decisions, including the formation and composition of new governing bodies, were to be the prerogative of U.S. authorities. In mid-May 2003 Bremer banned tens of thousands of Baath Party officials from public employment, then dissolved the military and information ministries, putting more than four hundred thousand people out of work. He moved to privatize the entire Iraqi public sector along lines favored by the IMF, raising the specter of a "shock therapy" that did so much harm to countries of the former Soviet bloc. On questions of state policy and development, privatization has become the guiding mantra, resulting in further erosion of already dilapidated social programs and public services. The long-range goal, of course, is to open the system to Western corporate penetration. Even before the war, Bush and Rumsfeld insisted that all decisions pertaining to Iraq should favor "market priorities," seen as the basis of reversing the nation's downward economic and political spiral.

The cost of rebuilding Iraq, assuming it can be done under foreign occupation, is predicted to run minimally $200 billion—part of an enormous largesse to be reaped by dozens of mostly U.S. companies. Even before the invasion had run its course U.S. and other Western corporations were lining up at the trough to get the fruits of war profiteering. Bechtel, a San Francisco–based global engineering firm with close ties to the Bush administration, was set up as the prime contractor to renovate the Iraqi infrastructure—a project (to Bechtel) worth nearly $700 million but that could easily reach $1 billion or more. The Kellogg Brown and Root subsidiary of Halliburton, an oil services company once headed by Cheney, took control of Iraqi oil fields under a no-bid contract from the Army Corps of Engineers. The Pentagon awarded MCI a $45 million contract to establish a wireless network throughout the country. DynCorp International, a military contractor charged with streamlining law enforcement, received a State Department contract worth $50 million. Health-care and pharmaceutical corporations were also lining up for their share.[35] As for Bechtel's gargantuan project to restore economic order to Iraq, no fewer than seventy-two hundred (about five thousand from the United States and Britain) registered with the engineering giant, hoping to win lucrative subcontracting deals. These companies are expected to carry out virtually every conceivable task: oil facilities repair, electronics, port development, sanitation, road construction, manpower supply, medical technology. As was widely reported, "the corporate gold rush to Iraq has begun" (as of May 2003). According to Mark Baxter, director of a U.S. energy institute: "Companies see a huge pie in Iraq, one with a special flavor they like: oil [which is] the commodity that ensures the companies will be paid."[36] Whether such companies will be able to operate freely in a context of guerrilla insurgency is another matter, but quite clearly Iraqis are expected to play a minimal role, at best, in reconstructing their own country.

As war and occupation left Iraq open for Western business operations, the United States (joined by Britain) steadfastly rejected any major role for the UN, international agencies, NGOs, or nations like Russia and France that had a long-standing involvement in the Gulf region. (Once Iraqi resistance started to build, the Bush administration did make some overtures to the UN, but indicated that the United States would not relinquish its power.) Put crudely, the United States was able to bomb its way into a vital new zone of free enterprise, free trade, and open investment for transnational corporations—again, assuming a stable military environment. Sadly, this process was accompanied by no congressional oversights, no legislative debates, no popular input from either Americans or Iraqis, and was met (at least in its early stages) with scarcely any journalistic investigation. Everything was set in motion by a small cabal, by authoritarian diktat, even while democracy remained the preferred rhetoric of the day. The ultimate rewards for global business interests—given long-term economic and political stability—will run into the hundreds of billions, perhaps trillions, of dollars.

The U.S. rationale for this war had been the Iraqi threat posed by its arsenal of WMD along with supposed connections with al Qaeda, but as these pretexts were thoroughly discredited the Bush administration turned to the familiar myth of democratization: the world was being told that the United States was in the Persian Gulf to bring liberation in the form of pluralist democracy, humanitarian ideals, and regional stability. Opponents and supporters of preemptive war alike referred to this as the "new imperialism," a form of intervention already visible in Panama and Yugoslavia. The United States was dedicated to punishing transgressors against peace, democracy, and human rights, standing tall against the forces of international gangsterism, terrorism, and ethnic cleansing. This is yet another meaning of the United States–engineered New World Order, replete with generous offers of nation building and reconstruction under the auspices of the Pentagon and multinational corporations.

Whether it is the epic struggle for democracy and human rights or the militarized war on terrorism, the United States has been ready to trumpet the great achievements of post–cold war interventions—in the Balkans, Afghanistan, and the Persian Gulf. Anyone who believes these claims has apparently paid less attention to actual developments on the ground than to White House and Pentagon public-relations statements. In Kosovo, the NATO bombings left a demolished, broken society now ruled by a Taliban-style government, with escalating poverty and joblessness, civic violence, and renewed ethnic conflict the daily fare of a dispirited population. Islamic militants operate out of Kosovo and Bosnia, not too far from the sprawling Bondsteel U.S. army base that blights the Yugoslav landscape but remains as a guarantor of crucial American geostrategic interests in the area. If democracy exists there, it is only in the minds of U.S. military enthusiasts who gather for conferences at the American Enterprise Institute, the Hoover Institute, and other hawkish neocon think tanks. In Afghanistan, lacking any viable central government and overrun by warlords and militias, all armed with abundant sophisticated weapons, the situation has steadily deteriorated since U.S. military operations began in late 2001, leaving the country in economic and political ruins, a continuing haven for terrorist actions. Here too democracy amounts to nothing more than a tragic fraud.

As for regime change in Iraq, circumstances have turned even more dire than in the Balkans and Afghanistan. By spring 2004 the violence and chaos had worsened as the Iraqi resistance intensified and spread across the country, with mounting casualties on both sides. Guerrilla insurgency was flourishing, with attacks numbering *on average* more than thirty daily (as of June 2004). Raging gun battles involving large forces were taking place in scattered urban areas. Acts of sabotage were routine, directed not only against occupation forces but against political targets and oil pipelines and refineries. The capture of Hussein in December 2003 produced no downturn in the insurgency.

By early summer 2004, with the much-ballyhooed transition to an "interim" Iraqi government, popular insurgency was at its peak, galvanized by a resurgent nationalism that spread as the occupation grew more repressive, more violent. Resistance forces drew from an ever-broadening opposition: Sunni and Shiite, urban and rural, secular and religious, ex-Baathists and those who had no involvement with the Hussein regime. Dispersed around the country, the daily uprisings and firefights followed no simple command and control structure, no easily identifiable leadership, indeed no cohesive ideology or strategy beyond eviction of the occupiers. Recruitment of insurgents was no problem owing to conditions of occupation—high levels of unemployment, collapse of public services, lack of security, the jailing of thousands of people in prisons like Abu Ghraib where cruelty and torture became the norm. Access to popular support, intelligence, funding, technology, and sophisticated weapons posed no difficulty. As in Vietnam, the development of such an efficient guerrilla resistance could not be subdued by anything short of a brutal, lengthy war of attrition. But with much fewer than two hundred thousand troops in the field, the occupation authority—poorly trained in counterinsurgency methods—was woefully inadequate to this task. The morale of U.S. and British soldiers, moreover, was collapsing under the mounting violence, chaos, political failures, and simple absence of purpose.

The move toward an interim government in July 2004 was unlikely to alter this downward spiral. A major problem is that, given nearly exclusive reliance on *coercive* power—above all the lurking force of the U.S. military—any new regime could never hope to establish political *legitimacy*; it would lack widespread consent. Having invaded Iraq for its own economic and geopolitical ends, the United States did not appear ready to relinquish its military hold over Iraq. Further, the interim apparatus is nothing but a quisling government, its leaders handpicked and controlled by the United States and Britian, much like what the Nazis set up during World War II and what the United States had previously established in Afghanistan. The *symbols* of national sovereignty do not represent true independence or even a viable governing structure— much less anything that gives empowerment to local constituencies. The interim prime minister, Iyad Allawi, is a former member of the Baath Party who later conducted anti-Hussein terrorist operations in Iraq on behalf of the CIA. Under these circumstances, any reference to "democracy" makes little sense. Indeed the new Iraqi regime is entirely prohibited from changing existing (i.e., occupation-determined) laws or making new legislation. This new state is a product of U.S. imperial design and geopolitical strategy, and nothing more.

WEAPONS OF MASS DESTRUCTION

In the wake of 9/11, the Bush administration became obsessed with the threat of weapons of mass destruction, using that "threat" as its major pretext for war against Iraq. Other nations said to be developing WMD, including

Iran and North Korea, were placed on a target list for possible future pre-emptive attacks. At the same time, however, the United States was moving to upgrade and rationalize its own WMD programs, above all its nuclear capability—a decision clearly spelled out in the 2001 Pentagon *Quadrennial Defense Review.* This particular form of hypocrisy seemed endemic not just to the Bush circle but to the larger perquisites of Empire—a special privilege that comes with the world's largest military apparatus. U.S. exceptionalism of this sort, while nothing new, ultimately works against prospects for global arms control. The Bush-Rumsfeld regime looked toward a sweeping trans-formation of U.S. military policy, with greater attention devoted to WMD fueled by technological innovations, the need for global flexibility, and the weaponization of space. Key to this strategy, well beyond the parameters of the war on terrorism, is the American capacity to intimidate or repel any challenger that might appear on the world scene.

The WMD strategy turns out to be more diversified and complex than is generally believed. Contrary to popular myth, the phenomenon of WMD not only includes nuclear, chemical, and biological weaponry but extends to conventional arms (for example, saturation bombing) and economic sanc-tions, which have become an integral part of the U.S. modus operandi. These instruments of war have awesome destructive power in at least three respects: the boundary separating combatants and civilians is *by definition* obliterated, the potential for casualties is typically massive, and the environmental impact can be unimaginably catastrophic. Of these five types only chemical and bi-ological warfare have been explicitly outlawed; the use of nuclear and con-ventional weaponry, as well as sanctions, violates international law only in the sense that it can be deemed "wanton destruction," where civilians might be directly targeted. The United States alone among nations has employed *all* these weapons of mass destruction and, since 1945, is the only country to de-velop and use them in ways fitting the category of war crimes. As for satu-ration or "strategic" bombardment, it has been a cornerstone of U.S. military policy at least since the final months of World War II, when American planes destroyed no less than sixty-six Japanese cities using incendiary bombs from high altitudes. Since then area bombing has been an accepted instrument of United States Air Force (USAF) operations in such theaters as Korea, In-dochina, the Persian Gulf, and the Balkans, leaving a death toll of several mil-lion (mostly civilians) in the postwar years. In the case of economic sanctions, Cuba, Iraq, and other nations have been victims of cruel policies initiated by the United States and sometimes carried out under UN auspices. The Iraqi situation is well known: between 1990 and 2003 sanctions blocked much-needed imports such as medical supplies, water-treatment technology, even certain foodstuffs, leading to the deaths of at least five hundred thousand peo-ple (again, mostly civilians).[37] This program was a deliberate extension of warfare that was first conducted during Desert Storm.

In the realm of chemical weapons, the United States has been the world leader by far in the production, dissemination, and use of highly toxic liquids, sprays, incendiary devices, powders, and explosives. The American military first experimented with napalm in World War II, refined its usage in Korea, employed it on a massive scale in Vietnam, and has kept it as part of its arsenal ever since; incendiary bombs, designed to burn large urban areas, follow a similar pattern. It is well known that the United States sprayed tens of thousands of tons of herbicides over three million acres in Vietnam from 1965 to 1971, with the intent of wiping out jungle foliage and crops. The use of Agent Orange polluted Vietnam with five hundred pounds of the deadly chemical dioxin, impacting several million Vietnamese along with tens of thousands of U.S. troops. There have been reports of high levels of cancer and birth defects in regions saturated with Agent Orange. The U.S. Army also deployed such toxic chemicals as CS, DM, and CN gases, designated by the Pentagon as "riot control" agents.[38] According to the *Hatfield Report*, the legacy of chemical warfare left behind by the United States in Indochina would have health and ecological consequences for many decades. For all this the United States never offered any apologies or reparations, nothing for cleanup or health services. The United States has not shrunk from later use of chemical agents, including their widespread adoption in Plan Colombia to defoliate coca plantations—nor has it been reluctant to share its scientific knowledge and resources with other nations. In Colombia the United States has begun spraying a new Monsanto-produced fungus, glyphosate, an herbicide that causes lethal infections in humans. In its lengthy discussion of chemical weapons use in violation of international law, the text *Crimes of War*[39] scandalously omits any reference to the extensive history of U.S. chemical warfare. The main culprit identified is Iraq, with Russia getting honorable mention. The volume does report that 111 states (including the United States) signed the Chemical Weapons Convention in Paris in 1993, with the convention taking legal force in 1997, but fails to mention U.S. efforts to subvert the treaty by denying inspection provisions to any external body.

In January 1998 President Clinton said that the world must "confront the new hazards of chemical and biological weapons, and the outlaw states, terrorists, and organized criminals seeking to acquire them." Anticipating Bush's later rhetoric, he particularly castigated Iraq for acquiring "weapons of mass destruction." Yet it was U.S. corporations that initially furnished the Iraqis with a wide variety of chemical and biological agents, exported and licensed through the Department of Commerce—an arrangement going back to at least 1985. Shipments included materials related to anthrax and botulinum toxin, vital to whatever programs Iraq was able to develop.[40] It was recently learned that the U.S. military tested a variety of bioweapons in and near local civilian populations, off the coast of such states as California,

Florida, Maryland, and Hawaii, exposing millions of people unknowingly to deadly agents between 1962 and 1973. The report makes clear that such weapons tests (including of sarin nerve gas) were held to experiment with both offensive and defensive weaponry.[41]

Earlier reports of widespread U.S. military deployment of biological weapons in Korea have been recently documented with some degree of certainty.[42] Bioweapons were in fact an officially sanctioned part of Pentagon strategy in the early 1950s and surely much later. Both Koreans and Chinese complained about significant death tolls resulting from plague, smallpox, anthrax, scarlet fever, encephalitis, and other diseases unleashed by bombs and artillery shells from U.S. military operations. We know that the U.S. Medical General Lab, Far East, had become a center for researching insect vectors for such lethal diseases as smallpox, cholera, and encephalitis.[43]

The general U.S. strategy in Korea was to wear down and ultimately annihilate the enemy. Under such circumstances, any "rules of engagement" were fully jettisoned. Atrocities were routinely committed from the air and on the ground. The USAF bombing campaigns, as earlier in Japan, were nothing short of barbaric. Prisoners of war were killed en masse. Stephen Endicott and Edward Hagerman write: "These acts in Korea indicated again that the U.S. subscription to laws of war and treatment of prisoners was no check on its political and military leaders' use of whatever methods and weapons were considered necessary to achieve their goals." Faced with a seemingly endless stalemate on the battlefield through 1951 and 1952, the United States looked desperately for new solutions. One answer was to expand the war further into civilian population centers, to which end the USAF demolished eleven hydroelectric plants along the Yalu River in June 1952. Another response was President Eisenhower's resurrection of Truman's earlier threat to use atomic bombs in order to break the impasse. A third response, evidently carried out with vigor, was biological warfare. In the words of Endicott and Hagerman:

> The U.S. had substantial stocks of biological weapons on hand. Moral qualms about using biological or atomic weapons had been brushed aside by top leaders, and biological warfare might dodge the political bullet of adverse public and world opinion if it were kept secret enough to make a plausible denial of its use. If it were uncovered, a last resort could be to fall back on the fact the U.S. had not signed the 1925 Geneva Protocol on biological warfare.[44]

Evidence of U.S. biowarfare came not only from Korean and Chinese government archives but from the testimony of American flyers (later forced to recant under pressure) and eventually from independent scholarly research. In the end, however, the resort to bioweaponry achieved only limited results: thousands of people were hospitalized and scores killed during 1951 and 1952, but the overall impact on Korean-Chinese military efforts was negligible.

Within the international arsenal of WMD, the most awesome and planet-threatening are nuclear weapons, first used in 1945 and continuously refined ever since. We know that the United States dropped two atomic bombs on Japan at the end of World War II, just days before capitulation, causing unnecessary wanton destruction of civilian targets. With the onset of the cold war the United States rushed to further develop its nuclear capability and laid out a strategic doctrine tied to first-strike potential.[45] By the 1950s the Pentagon was on perpetual ready alert, prepared to rain more than eight hundred Hiroshima-type bombs on the USSR, developing further its power to destroy human civilization on the earth several times over. In Sven Lindqvist's view, U.S. embellishment of the threat of nuclear annihilation could be explained partly as a product of certain white-male ruling-class fantasies with roots in Wild West mythology.[46] In any event, the Armageddon-style policies established during the cold war remained in force throughout the succeeding decades, backed by increasingly massive and flexibly deployed nuclear power. There is evidence that the United States has *threatened* to use nuclear weapons on several occasions in the postwar years. In 1968, nations of the world signed the Nonproliferation Treaty, but this did not stop the United States from augmenting its warhead total from forty-five hundred to nearly ten thousand within a decade, an arsenal that has been regularly modernized since. Far from renouncing nuclear warfare as inherently barbaric, the United States (under all presidents) has been dedicated to absolute domination in this area, which is one reason it rejects antiballistic and other arms-control treaties and is moving full speed toward the weaponization of space.[47] As of 2003, the United States had manufactured and deployed more nuclear weapons than all other nations combined.

In 2002, President Bush and Russian leader Vladimir Putin signed the Moscow Treaty, ostensibly to control the production and deployment of nuclear weapons by the two powers. The treaty, however, was essentially a fraud from the outset: as part of the arrangements the United States wound up scrapping all *binding* agreements, involving strict limits and regular inspections, in favor of one that is largely unilateral and *voluntary*. With the new accords all categories of nuclear warheads and delivery systems are left uncontrolled—precisely what the United States, and especially the Bush administration, had wanted all along. Meanwhile, Bush had already turned away from the Comprehensive Test Ban Treaty and had withdrawn from the 1972 Anti-Ballistic Missile Treaty.

In the realm of WMD, nuclear warfare stands alone in its awesome destructive power—at present it is the only form of attack that could place the entire globe in peril. The U.S. nuclear posture in the age of Bush II has already signaled a dramatic escalation in the worldwide nuclear danger: the United States and Russia possess nearly thirteen thousand atomic weapons combined, most of them pointed at each other, while the threat of proliferation (surely helped along by Bush's policies) has no doubt reached its most fearsome point. Since 9/11 Bush has deftly used the war on terrorism and the menace of rogue states to expand the Pentagon's general strategic (including nuclear) capabilities. The existing American stockpile has been modernized, funding for new programs has been sharply increased, new targets have been identified (some three thousand all told), and long-standing first-strike options have been reaffirmed. Most crucially, the Bush-Rumsfeld circle has moved to thoroughly integrate nuclear weaponry into the larger strategic framework, looking to create a new generation of tactical, lower-yield, more "usable" nukes adaptable to ordinary combat situations. One example is the B6-11 earth-penetrating bunker buster, with yields between three hundred tons and three hundred kilotons, for deployment against underground and other remote targets. Such nuclear flexibility lies at the basis of a more aggressive, integrated global military strategy. As Helen Caldicott writes: "A huge conventional and nuclear arsenal allows America to do what it will around the world with impunity—it is the iron hand in the velvet glove of U.S. corporate globalization."[48]

To further advance U.S. military supremacy, nuclear weapons labs at Los Alamos and Sandia in New Mexico and Lawrence Livermore in California have embarked on the largest scientific-military project ever, called Manhattan II, set up presumably to ensure the safety and proper functioning of the post–cold war strategic military machinery. In reality scientists are designing and testing new nuclear devices at a yearly cost of nearly $10 billion projected over at least the coming decade. There is an inherent violation of the Comprehensive Test Ban Treaty (CTBT) agreements within this program, but the violation has been ignored. Ironically, the United States in 2002 spent more on nuclear weapons design and testing than at any point during the cold war; moreover, as we have seen, it also spent far more for these purposes than Iraq spent on its entire military.

Recognizing the limits of a nuclear strategy grounded in the postwar balance of terror, with its overwhelming focus on long-range delivery systems, Bush looked toward a more flexible, balanced approach mixing strategic and tactical, fixed and maneuverable, offensive and defensive nukes within a paradigm of more "thinkable" nuclear options appropriate to a more "modernized" defense of Empire. This was the essence of Rumsfeld's 2001 *Quadrennial Defense Review* and the subsequent *Nuclear Posture Review*, which outlined new strategic and tactical departures given the added impetus of 9/11. Not only did the *Nuclear Posture Review* stipulate a greater variety of nuclear alternatives, it laid out conditions under which such alternatives might come into play. These were defined by military planners as three "contingencies" that could appear at any moment—*immediate*, where the WMD of another nation would have to be destroyed; *potential*, requiring a response to some imminent threat to U.S. security; and *unexpected*, where regime change somewhere in the world might demand quick military reaction.[49] It is clear from this schema that the U.S. nuclear outlook adheres to few if any universally fixed limits or boundaries. A loosened policy of this sort, combined with the general renewal of U.S. militarism and imperial ambitions, has the effect of encouraging other nuclear powers to further modernize their own arsenals and, even more ominously, helps trigger "lateral proliferation" by pushing weaker states, above all those potentially targeted by the United States, to accelerate their nuclear programs. It no doubt sends a comparable message to terrorist groups.

The new "flexibility" of U.S. nuclear strategy has already made itself visible in two wars since 9/11—in Afghanistan and Iraq—where contingencies for nuclear options were openly discussed by the Pentagon and even reported in the media, reducing the threshold to its lowest point since World War II. Both countries were regarded as havens of terrorism, both regimes (Taliban and Baathist) were seen as dire threats to the United States, and both combat settings could easily have presented the American military with nightmare scenarios in which conventional weaponry reached an impasse. Iraq, moreover, was said to be in possession of huge stores of WMD, implicitly justifying a (preemptive) response in kind. Tactical bunker-buster nukes were thought to be a quick way out of any protracted military quagmire—fighting the Taliban and al Qaeda in the mountains and caves of Afghanistan, fighting Iraqis in difficult, endless, bloody urban warfare across a sprawling city like Baghdad. It was precisely such fears and calculations that prompted Truman to drop atomic bombs on Hiroshima and Nagasaki, and to consider the same thing in Korea. While the United States never used nuclear weapons in Afghanistan or Iraq, such weapons were surely an integral part of contingency plans; the dividing line between nuclear and conventional warfare had broken down in theory, if not yet in practice.

Despite its proclaimed holy crusade against WMD, therefore, the United States has established a military posture bound to create just the opposite—*proliferation* of such weapons. While hostile to states designated "rogues" that might want their own WMD, the Bush administration shows no interest in setting up international arms-control agreements binding on *all* states. The United States fully reserves for itself the right to manufacture, distribute, and use WMD. Washington has come to accept large WMD programs for friendly nations such as Israel, Pakistan, and India. For its tentative and meager assistance in the war on terrorism, Pakistan was rewarded with a $3 billion aid package in 2002 and was indirectly given a green light to build its nuclear capacity, even as Bush and Rumsfeld issued dire warnings to Iran and North Korea regarding nuclear intentions. Actually Pakistan, like India and Israel, has never signed the 1968 Nonproliferation Treaty (NPT) or the 1996 CTBT, which would have inhibited its testing in 1998. (The NPT was signed by Iraq, Iran, and North Korea.) The fact that Pakistan and India have been able to avoid UN-sponsored inspections—the very same inspections that were demanded of Iraq—has drawn nary a protest from the United States. This has been the case despite historic tensions between India and Pakistan over Kashmir, not to mention the highly explosive situation within Pakistan itself, which could easily give rise to a Taliban-style Islamic regime.

The United States wants maximum freedom for itself and a few favored allies to expand and modernize nuclear arsenals. Interwoven with this strategy is the Star Wars project—more accurately, the militarization of space—that goes back to the Reagan presidency but that has gained new currency under Bush II. According to the Rumsfeld report, the Pentagon envisions a high-capacity, integrated, full-spectrum, global armed network coordinated through space, combining both offensive and defensive instruments. This entails nothing less than the full extension of U.S. Empire into space, a Manifest Destiny for the twenty-first century. The report states: "A key objective of the Department's [Pentagon's] space surveillance and control mission is to ensure freedom of action in space for the United States and its allies and, when directed, to deny such freedom of action to adversaries." To the degree that new forms of warfare will require the most sophisticated technology, information, surveillance, and global flexibility, along with heightened nuclear capability, the space program emerges as a cornerstone of future U.S. military strategy, meaning that criticism of Star Wars for its presumed *defensive* inadequacies misses the central point. The space dimension of armed deployment furnishes the Pentagon with a quality "networked environment" facilitated by space-based satellites, military platforms, radar, and infrared systems of the sort already found valuable in the Balkans, Afghanistan, and Iraq.

The U.S. colonization of space ensures a qualitatively improved global strategic capacity in which ground, sea, and air operations can be fully coordinated from above. In flagrant violation of the 1967 Outer Space Treaty prohibiting weapons in space, the Bush administration has committed tens of billions of dollars to streamline Star Wars, a cost that over coming decades can be expected to reach into the hundreds of billions. As Karl Grossman puts it, the United States desires nothing less than to become the sole "master of space,"[50] thereby gaining qualitative military advantages over any and all world powers—one inevitable result of which is a strengthening of U.S. militarism. Indeed, the mastery of space represents a crucial signpost of the new militarism. A space empire will involve hundreds of nuclear-armed satellites orbiting the earth in many directions. Seeing both geopolitical and economic value in this, the Council on Foreign Relations—backed by the Heritage Foundation, the American Enterprise Institute, and several university think tanks—is strongly pushing the more expansive definition of Star Wars. Corporations such as General Electric, TRW, Lockheed-Martin, and Raytheon have powerful vested interests in Star Wars, as do many academic research and development programs. Seen from this vantage point, United States–engineered globalization combines the future trajectories of the corporations, government, and military.[51] Weapons planned for development within the Star Wars framework include laser-beam devices, particle-beam devices, and other systems tied to orbiting nuclear reactors for sources of power. The colonization of space means not only military weapons in orbit but also *nuclear* devices existing side by side with them. This trend has so alarmed many observers around the world that in November 1999 a UN resolution aimed at preventing an arms race in outer space was signed by 138 nations intent on reserving this realm for peaceful uses. Only the United States and Israel refused to sign it. Regarding prospects for an arms race in space, the Bush administration has moved to short-circuit this possibility by means of solidifying its own (unilateral) domination of outer space.

Yet another dimension of nuclear militarism deserves mention: over the past decade and more the United States has been the only country to use depleted uranium (DU) in its bombs, missiles, and artillery shells. The Pentagon had more than one billion pounds of nuclear waste available, much of it converted to reinforce conventional weaponry in the Gulf and the Balkans, with predictably deadly results. Tens of thousands of DU-enhanced rounds were released in these theaters, producing radioactive effects upon explosion that will have long-term consequences for people, crops, animals, and the general ecology. It is believed that widespread use of DU in the first Gulf War gave rise in part to Gulf War syndrome among both Iraqis and U.S. troops.[52] Upon impact with a target, DU disintegrates into a widening mist of particles which, once inhaled or ingested, can produce cancer, kidney disease, and genetic defects. By 1995 Iraqi health officials were reporting alarming increases in rare diseases, especially among children.[53] Such weapons inevitably cause wanton destruction, despite Pentagon claims to the contrary, and therefore must be considered criminal. In 1996 a UN subcommission passed a resolution condemning DU, but the United States simply ignored it, refusing any legal or moral restraints on its conduct of warfare.

For several decades the U.S. war machine, swollen through perpetual quests for unfettered imperial domination, has built its strategic force around weapons of mass destruction—nuclear, conventional, and economic (sanctions) above all. Chemical weapons have been used widely in counterinsurgency, while biological weapons, ostensibly retired from the arsenal in the 1950s, have not been a desired option in the wake of the Korean fiasco. In 1972 the United States, along with 140 other nations, signed the Biological

Weapons Convention treaty outlawing the production, development, and use of germ warfare agents. There were still, however, provisions needed for compliance and verification. Discussions aimed at strengthening the treaty continued throughout the 1990s, with the United States dead set against inspections that it considered an infringement on commercial rights of American chemical and pharmaceutical companies. Finally, even the watered-down draft favored by the United States was rejected by Bush in July 2002, leaving the world without any effective biological weapons prohibitions. Here too the United States insisted on concessions from all other parties but steadfastly refused to accept any for itself.

Given their strategic centrality to the logic of Empire—their very *threat* constitutes an intimidating military fact—WMD today would appear to represent a fully *nonnegotiable* part of the U.S. arsenal. This helps explain why American leaders (both Democrats and Republicans) have strongly opposed most far-reaching efforts by nations of the world to establish treaties and conventions limiting or outlawing the production and deployment of WMD. Because of its extraordinary superiority in this area, moreover, the United States possesses greater flexibility than ever to pursue its aggressive militarism worldwide, and this only reinforces a Hobbesian global anarchy in which brute military and economic power obliterate any prospect for binding laws, treaties, ethics, or rules of engagement.

3

THE MILITARY
AND SUBVERSION
OF DEMOCRATIC POLITICS

One of the great casualties of an expanding security state, of the militarization of American society in general, is democratic politics, generally considered to be the centerpiece of the U.S. historical experience. Empire, the war economy, a national security apparatus, militarism in the service of corporate and geopolitical interests—all of these have had a powerfully corrosive impact on domestic politics since the onset of the cold war. The events of 9/11 and their aftermath, including the war on terrorism and new military adventures abroad, have only deepened this trend. A shrinking public sphere, marked by increasing xenophobia, jingoism, celebrations of armed violence, and narrowing political debates, has become a seemingly durable feature of American society: not only in politics but in mass media, popular culture, professional life, and academia.

Despite troop and base reductions here and there over the past few decades, the U.S. military has steadily extended its *power* across both the international and domestic terrain. As we have seen, the Pentagon system functions to protect Empire, which, since the fall of the USSR and end of the cold war, has risen to unchallenged hegemony. The military and security network presided over by the United States requires patriotic mobilization that in turn depends on an efficient propaganda system operating largely in the service of government agendas. Where such mobilization is highly effective, as in the case of the two Gulf Wars, the result is a strong authoritarianism marked by ideological conformism, institutional narrowing, a regime of surveillance, media manipulation, secrecy in government decision making, the growing concentration of power in a few hands. If Empire signifies an increasingly militarized politics and society, where "national security" priorities shape elite agendas, then democracy winds up as something of a charade where lies, myths, distortions, and cover-ups that shape public life are embraced and passed on by Republican and Democratic politicians alike. This is probably more true of international affairs than of

81

any other realm. The maintenance of Empire, always costly and destructive, requires ongoing legitimation, which it receives from politicians, officials, the media, and intellectuals who exercise their influence within reputedly free and open public forums. With the disappearance of any semblance of a Soviet challenge by the early 1990s, global terrorism soon furnished the perfect demonized enemy, joined by a few "rogue states" led by modern-day Hitlers. Public support for U.S. militarism was of course much easier to galvanize after 9/11, patriotism reaching its highest point since World War II as the fear of new terrorist episodes lent a sense of national urgency to crucial state functions: surveillance, intelligence, law enforcement, military preparedness. In such a setting, new weapons systems were much easier to justify and sell. In his 2002 State of the Union address Bush argued for a military budget reaching nearly $400 billion, including new requests for high-tech weaponry, mobile antiterror units, space militarization, nuclear modernization, and expanded worldwide military deployments.

EMPIRE AND POLITICAL DECAY

The corrosive effects of the permanent war economy, along with the process of corporate colonization in general, have been increasingly obvious since the 1970s. By the turn of the century American society had become probably more depoliticized than at any time in many decades, which is ironic given worsening social problems as well as the rapid growth of higher education and spread of the informational revolution. The vast majority of Americans felt alienated from politics, disempowered, cut off from hopes for remedies to pressing challenges: corporate downsizing, poverty, crises in education and health care, civic violence, environmental decay. Such disenfranchisement meant a decline of citizenship, a profound erosion of civic culture that transformed democratic values and practices into something of a facade. As E. J. Dionne comments:

> Americans hate politics as it is now practiced because we have lost all sense of the public good. Over the last thirty years . . . politics has stopped being a deliberative process through which people resolved disputes, found remedies, and moved forward. When Americans watch politics now . . . they understand instinctively that politics these days is not about finding solutions. It is about discovering postures that offer short-term political benefits.[1]

The American political system had severely atrophied, involving greatly reduced levels of citizen participation, whether at the ballot box, in formal party activities, in the corridors of power, or in local community life. This deepening antipolitical culture is not simply a matter of failed or corrupt leaders, weak parties and movements, or flawed structures; it reflects long-term historical processes shaping every facet of daily life. Seen in this way, the depoliticization of American society is in many ways a predictable mass response to a governing system designed to control public opinion, marginalize dissent, privatize social relations, and reduce the intensity of popular involvement. As William Greider writes: "If citizens sometimes behave irresponsibly in politics, it is the role assigned them. They have lost any other way to act, any means for influencing the governing process in positive or broad-minded terms."[2] The political, economic, and cultural impact of an oversized Pentagon system on all this cannot be overstated.

In this transformed setting—corporate, globalized, militarized—politics has degenerated into a mix of narrow interest-group maneuvers, bureaucratic intrigues, and electoral rituals, even while corporate and military priorities remain largely unchecked in a context where Empire takes on a logic of its own. While there is little that is novel about such developments, taken together they have produced a truncated party system, passive citizenry, and trivialized public discourse that does little justice to the historic norms of liberal democracy. In American society "politics" now constitutes the domain of corporate and governmental elites whose overriding ambition is to perpetuate their own oligarchical power and wealth. Nowhere has this phenomenon become more visible than in the sphere of foreign and military policy.

Political dialogue in the United States has degenerated into rhetorical flourishes tied to abstract platitudes like "free market," "family values," "personal responsibility," "economic progress," and "peace" that in the end have little do with either material welfare or public policy. In place of an active, engaged citizenry once associated with populism, the civil rights movement, and feminism, for example, we find an atomized population increasingly devoid of civic trust, enmeshed in private life (TV, computers, shopping malls, autos) that runs counter to a vibrant public sphere. The revival of social movements—antiglobalization struggles begun in late 1999, a large and diverse antiwar movement in late 2002 and early 2003—seems to have broken the consensual stillness, but the durability of these movements has yet to be established. Meanwhile, the corporations, state, and military reinforce their hold over public life as their interests meet little in the way of sustained challenges within or outside of electoral campaigns. If the system reproduces all the external trappings of democracy, legality, and citizenship, it has become more repressive and antidemocratic in practice, more emphatically so in the aftermath of 9/11. It works efficiently to subvert potentially significant expressions of political agency at the mass level. Owing in part to the workings of the permanent war economy, the most imposing crisis in American society today is no doubt the crisis of *citizenship*, since without its resolution the destructive path of American society is extremely unlikely to be reversed.

The narrowing public sphere is easy enough to identify—lower voter turnouts, a decreased sense of political efficacy, a waning popular trust in government, a declining knowledge of issues, the erosion of the party system, the ideological convergence of elites. Predictably, major social problems wind up suppressed or trivialized within what passes for public debate. This state of affairs is marked by nothing short of the banality of politics itself: corruption, deceit, propaganda, false promises, empty rituals, the power of money dominate the landscape. Enshrouded in the great myths of American democracy is a political system that responds far more to wealth, bureaucratic power, and influence peddling than to local citizen initiative. While the procedural elements of liberal democracy remain intact, vital areas of decision making (finance, corporate agendas, foreign policy) remain the preserve of a small stratum of elites. The more that political activities like voting, candidate debates, and legislative activity wind up detached from everyday social life, the more they seem to be trumpeted as necessary features of democracy—and thus the more they obscure genuine popular concerns.

In the recent trajectory of American politics, differences between Republicans and Democrats have shriveled—or, more accurately, Democrats have gravitated toward the ideological orbit of Republicans. From the 1930s through most of the postwar years Democrats pushed for a Keynesian liberal agenda with a broad commitment to the redistribution of wealth, public welfare, economic regulations, and expanded social investment. The New Deal coalition was rooted in a mixture of progressive constituencies (labor, minorities, the poor) galvanized by an ethos of political reform within capitalist boundaries. By the 1990s this synthesis had broken down, having yielded to a congeries of narrow, sectoral interests working to push the party toward the middle and away from its New Deal legacy. Today the Democrats have adopted a procorporate outlook that meshes with the antipolitical mood of the times, invoking a mixture of conservative ideas and symbols: free market, free trade, law and order, traditional values, deregulation, a strong globalized military. Beneath the contrasting rhetoric one can detect an imposing common agenda: Democrats, like Republicans, are enmeshed in the all-consuming interests of Wall Street, multinational corporations, and the New World Order, part of what might be called a Republicrat consensus. After his 1996 victory, Clinton outlined a new Democratic program geared to the "vital center," freeing his energies to "prepare America for the twenty-first century." Clinton's departure was little more than a thinly disguised conservatism—balanced budget, free trade, reduced government spending, stronger crime initiatives, aggressive U.S. intervention abroad—under the old Democratic label. Clinton's "alternative"—and that of an entire generation of "new" Democrats—was neither liberalism nor even centrism but simply a formula for capitulation to Republican agendas which themselves have taken a more conservative turn.

This historic convergence reflects a progressive weakening of the two-party system itself—a narrow set of political arrangements that, rather unique among nations, has been a defining feature of American politics since the mid-nineteenth century. As Democrats and Republicans monopolize public discourse, elections, and legislative activity, their organizations perform less and less the functions usually associated with parties: offering real policy choices, framing identifiable issues and programs, articulating social interests, providing forums for genuine debate, mobilizing popular constituencies. The modus operandi of these parties, diffuse as it is, fits comfortably within a corporate structure that possesses a coherence the parties lack. The single-member electoral arrangement further ensures the parties will be drawn toward the "center," especially during presidential contests. Moreover, party structures have been taken over by professional campaign staffs, media and technical experts, pollsters, and fund-raisers—groups scornful of ideology and dedicated to the idea of politics as a marketing enterprise.[3] The primary role of parties is to aggregate millions of atomized voters whose involvement ends at the ballot box. The results are predictable: surely nowhere is the poverty of discourse more visible than in the greatest spectacle of American politics—presidential campaigns and debates. Minor issue or style differences between the two contenders get blown out of proportion. As crucial economic and global problems get largely ignored, packaged images inevitably define the spectacle. The complexities of political life are overwhelmed by a cacophony of shrill, repetitive, often debasing platitudes. The rivals argue for tax reductions, free trade, getting tough on law and order, the war on drugs, reducing big government, and a modernized, more efficient Pentagon. In foreign and military policies, the last time genuine differences could be detected in a presidential campaign was during the 1972 contest between Richard Nixon and George McGovern.

This depressing state of affairs should hardly be surprising, given the overriding influence of money, corporations, political action committees, and mass media in American politics. The TV presidential debates, for example, have been sponsored by the Commission on Presidential Debates, comprised of an array of big business interests: Philip Morris, Dow Corning, AT&T, Prudential, IBM, Ford, and General Motors, among others. Such a commission is naturally averse to seeing the corporate system and war economy challenged. The Clinton-Dole exchanges in 1996 and the Gore-Bush debates in 2000 will be remembered for their general failure to address issues, for the candidates' refusal to say anything about foreign policy beyond simplistic platitudes endorsing peace and U.S. military strength. They will also be remembered for their patently unfair exclusion of strong third-party candidates—Ross Perot in 1996 and Ralph Nader in 2000, despite the latter's inspiring Green Party campaign. In 2000 the more aggressive military stance was actually embraced up by the Democrats, with Gore arguing for an even larger increase in Pentagon spending, continued U.S. international troop presence, and a readiness to undertake "humanitarian" interventions, while Bush, oddly, stressed the importance of "humility" in world politics and wariness about "nation building."

What passes for debate in foreign and military policy fits the pattern of "bipartisan consensus" typical of the postwar years, except for the final years of the Vietnam War era, when a sector of elites grew disillusioned with the costly military quagmire. Democrats and Republicans have fought mainly over nuances of policy—timing, logistics, spending, and so forth. From the late 1940s on, military action was justified by the need to fight Communism, with dissent effectively marginalized as treasonous, un-American. The long-term buildup of global Pentagon power was championed by all major politicians, with Democrats often taking the lead. During the period of U.S.–Soviet nuclear standoff elites across the political spectrum vigorously supported high levels of military spending, because they shared President Kennedy's assessment of Communism as a "monolithic and ruthless conspiracy" that could be stopped only by massive armed force. The Communist threat, magnified over the years (well after the McCarthy witch hunts), served as the perfect cold war tool of patriotic mobilization, until it was replaced by other demons such as rogue states, terrorists, and drug traffickers.

A menacing world filled with subversive enemies, of course, necessitated ever-increasing levels of Pentagon spending, which the elites heartily endorsed, simultaneously pushing for a weakening of "big government," the welfare state, and public regulations—a refrain shared by all presidents after Lyndon Johnson. What set military Keynesianism apart, of course, was its vital role in catalyzing the economy and legitimating enormous outlays for high-tech research and development; its role in fighting Communism and advancing U.S. global interests scarcely needed restating. Cold war liberalism rested on a certain ideological closure: a fervent sense of historical mission, xenophobic attitudes, a willingness to deploy military forces anywhere on the globe, a fear of genuine political debates.

The end of cold war politics in the early 1990s might have led to far-reaching reductions in military spending, with some demobilization of troops and perhaps a conversion to civilian production (the famous "peace dividend"). But such a dividend never arrived, nor was it seriously contemplated within the power structure; local groups pressing for a shift in resources were dismissed as naive, utopian, unaware of the continuing evil potential lurking in such regions as China and Russia. Public input into major investment decisions had no more leverage than it did at the height of the anti-Communist frenzy. "Conversion" was indeed ultimately taken up, but meant nothing more than job retraining for some workers laid off in the aerospace sector, along with modest budget cutbacks that made little dent in the overall military apparatus. Public discourse turned out to be even more bipartisan than during the 1950s. No politician from either major party ran on a platform advocating significant cutbacks in Pentagon spending.

Clinton's foreign and military policy departed little from that of his Republican predecessors, as indeed Clinton himself often repeated. In his celebrated effort to take American politics to the "center," he pressed for conservative agendas: free trade, a downsized welfare state, draconian crime and drug measures, the Telecommunications Act of 1996, economic deregulation, a heightened U.S. military presence required for global supremacy. (To be sure, Clinton's global strategy was more two-pronged than Bush's, focusing on the combined ends of corporate globalization and military power in contrast to Bush's stronger military emphasis.) Clinton called for a Pentagon capability that would enable the United States to fight two or more wars simultaneously, supported the first Bush's Gulf War along with continued bombing campaigns and sanctions against Iraq, instigated NATO military aggression against Serbia in the name of "humanitarian intervention," gave support to regimes (Israel, Colombia, Indonesia, Turkey) with egregious human-rights records, and pushed for high levels of military spending even with the eclipse of Soviet power. Zinn writes: "Clinton's foreign economic policy was in keeping with the nation's history, in which both major parties were more concerned for corporate interests than for the rights of working people, here or abroad, and saw foreign aid as a political and economic tool."[4] This rigid adherence to old military (and corporate) patterns at a time of historic new opportunities in world politics was a major source of increased voter disenchantment throughout the 1990s.

If any single event could further eviscerate the public sphere, especially in foreign affairs, that would be the terrorist attacks of 9/11. One might argue that terrorism in general tends to favor a mood of antipolitics in which security concerns, authoritarian politics, and conservative agendas come to the fore . The depoliticizing impact of the Red Brigades in Italy and Baader-Meinhof in Germany during the 1970s offers two excellent cases in point. The "strategy of tension" adopted by terrorist groups hoping that dramatic acts of political violence will bring chaos and instability, creating new space for insurgency, has usually brought just the opposite: new levels of legitimacy and heightened coercive powers to security states long dependent on heavy doses of patriotic mobilization, intelligence gathering, surveillance, police controls, and militarism. After 9/11 a nominally liberal-democratic system began moving ever faster along the road to corporatism, undemocratic practices, and narrowing public discourses. If the terrorist methodology of al Qaeda and kindred groups is designed to generate crisis and an opening for change, its actual consequences have run counter to that aim—that is, toward a diminution of public life endemic to psychological retreat, collective fear, and social conservatism. In the United States, such trends were at least partly reversed during Bush's buildup to the second Iraq war.

Terrorism as both political act and imminent possibility is usually accompanied by fear, despair, and paranoia—emotional responses hardly conducive to open discourses and democratic politics. People find themselves isolated, atomized, and thus more vulnerable to governmental controls. Dissent and protest are stigmatized and marginalized, negated or crowded out within an atmosphere of superpatriotism, demonization of enemies, and scapegoating; political complexities and nuances quickly vanish. In the United States after 9/11, differences between Republicans and Democrats, Bush supporters and loyal opposition—already narrowed after decades of bipartisan foreign policy—became hard to distinguish. The terrorist attacks generated a united patriotic response that continued into the second Gulf War. Congressional action was hurriedly taken without the distractions and impediments of debate: both the nearly carte-blanche war powers delivered to Bush and the Patriot Act, for example, won quick passage in both Houses, over minimal and easily discredited opposition. Bush's military option, starting with the bombing of Afghanistan in October 2001, short-circuited discussion of possible alternative courses of action. The jingoism and ethnocentrism that came to define patriotic unity seemed to repeat the popular mood of the Desert Storm period, again legitimating many of the symbols and rituals vital to militarism and Empire.

If 9/11 reinforced the convergence of elite opinion around Bush's presidential agenda, the result was nothing short of a historic retreat from the increasingly complex demands of global politics on entering the new century. Reflections on the tremendous risks, costs, and consequences of U.S. Empire had little resonance within the political culture. U.S. intervention had been catastrophic for Central America, Indochina, the Persian Gulf, and Asia, but contemporary recognition of such realities among American politicians and media pundits, even academics, has been rare. Military operations abroad, with a few exceptions, are more often celebrated than criticized or protested, especially where U.S. casualties are kept to a minimum. The mass media and popular culture are filled with cartoonlike images of Muslims and Arabs, of demonized others said to be standing in the way of progress, modernity, democracy, and peace. Callous attitudes regarding foreign victims of U.S. military operations have become disturbingly common. When General Norman Schwarzkopf was asked, at the end of Desert Storm, about severe Iraqi casualties from U.S. bombings and sanctions, he blandly replied: "We need not get into the body count business." Former secretary of state Madeleine Albright's cavalier stance toward a possible half million Iraqi civilian deaths is well known.

Ideological conformism still marks American politics at the beginning of the twenty-first century: examples in the Bush II era are plentiful. Representative Barbara Lee (D-California) was the lone dissenting voice when Congress gave Bush unlimited military power to fight terrorism. She called for open debate on what she regarded a life-and-death issue, stating: "As we act let us not become the evil we deplore." Lee was quickly denounced as a traitor, Communist, and terrorist sympathizer by outraged citizens, some even issuing death threats. In October 2001 the Berkeley, California, City Council passed a resolution asking the federal government to halt the bombing of Afghanistan, affirming the council's desire to minimize casualties on both sides while calling for a national campaign to reduce U.S. dependency on foreign oil sources. The nationwide response was immediate and fierce, with hundreds of boycotts directed at businesses in Berkeley, threats made against council members, and a website urging a national effort to "Boycott the City of Cowards." TV networks like Fox, CNN, and MSNBC dwelled on the treasonous Berkeley initiative for weeks, while talk radio hosts feasted on this (and other) supposedly un-American displays of callousness toward the U.S. military and the victims of terrorism. University faculty participating in teach-ins across the country found that even the mildest criticisms of U.S. foreign policy were met with unthinking hostility and a willingness to condemn any discourse placing terrorism in a historical context. Hundreds of dissident faculty were recipients of harsh rebukes, hostile e-mails, hate calls, and threats of disciplinary action, including firing. A conservative organization, the American Council of Trustees and Alumni, founded by Lynne Cheney, built a strong presence on many campuses—a major goal being the stifling of alternative views on world politics. Faculty and students were attacked for the sin of being "insufficiently patriotic," with teach-ins monitored for appropriate boundaries of debate. Many academics were upbraided for not preaching the virtues of American history and culture, or for allowing discourses of multiculturalism to get out of hand. Ideals of academic freedom, intellectual tolerance, and citizen engagement were more fragile in the post-9/11 milieu than at any time since the early days of the cold war.

Attorney General John Ashcroft contributed his part to the political shrinkage, insisting that anyone criticizing Bush's policies at a time of national crisis was guilty of "aiding terrorists." The government spent nearly $4 million for Super Bowl TV advertisements linking the war against terrorism to the already failed war on drugs, on the assumption that these two practices—committing terrorist acts and taking drugs—have a common linkage with the plague of violence. As Bush intoned: "If you quit drugs, you join the fight against terror in America." The ultrapatriotic atmosphere also infected the book-publishing industry. Michael Moore's book *Stupid White Men* was ready to be distributed by HarperCollins at the very moment of the terrorist attacks. It contains a searing critique of the conservative, white, male culture that shapes the corporate, government, and military establishment. The book was suddenly deemed too controversial by the editors and publisher, who finally agreed to release the book (eventually to become a best seller) only after several months of intense arm twisting by Moore, his legion of supporters, and his lawyers.

Yet another case was that of Janis Besler Heaphy, publisher of the *Sacramento Bee*, whose commencement speech at Sacramento State College in June 2002 was repeatedly interrupted and then finally terminated when graduating students and their relatives unceremoniously booed her off stage. Heaphy's offense was that she worried that the war on terrorism might wind up compromising civil liberties as the nation became preoccupied with issues of security—a concern she framed in hypothetical terms, and one that turned out to be entirely legitimate. A few days later Heaphy wrote an essay in the *Bee* lamenting the sorry state of academic freedom and intellectual tolerance in American institutions of higher learning after 9/11. What she never mentioned was the role of the war economy and security state in helping reproduce this kind of political culture.

The 9/11 attacks not only gave rise to a war on terrorism and U.S. military operations in Afghanistan, but helped reinforce Bush's aggressive stance toward Iraq as one pillar in the axis of evil. We know that the Bush administration was already determined to launch its war *before* 9/11. It is also true that politicians of both parties shared equally in the building war mood. In December 2001 the House voted 393 to 12 to brand any Iraqi rejection of new arms inspections an "increasing threat" to U.S. security, reflecting a bipartisan consensus in the lead-up to the second Gulf War. The United States and Britain had been waging aerial warfare against Iraq since the time of Desert Storm, so this was no qualitative shift in policy. War on Iraq had been the strategic option of a small grouping of right-wing hawks in and close to the Pentagon, and elites of both parties (along with the media) soon bought in to this agenda. By late 2002 the idea of regime change in Iraq had developed into something of an obsession among the elites and media pundits. The earlier PNAC statement, as just one example, made it clear that no evidence of terrorist links or WMD was needed to justify military action; only later, for public edification, did the propaganda machine give forth such flimsy pretexts. In the midst of an economic downturn, corporate scandals, and an already compromised war on terrorism—not to mention the Bush/Ashcroft assault on the Bill of Rights—a national preoccupation with Iraq would obviously pay huge political dividends. And the Democrats, for their part, allowed this scenario to play out with no complications.

By mid-2002, as the war drums picked up momentum, Saddam Hussein had emerged as a demonic figure more threatening even than bin Laden, the presumed mastermind of al Qaeda and the terrorist attacks. During the fall 2002 congressional elections Democrats and Republicans strove to outdo each other in their readiness to conduct war. In fact, Bush's foreign policy hardly surfaced during the 2000 presidential campaign; his ideas were vague, for the most part not very well formed or salient to his electoral strategy. It is enough to say that each candidate wanted to be viewed as the strongest champion of U.S. military power. In November Congress voted overwhelmingly in favor of military force against Iraq—the Senate by 77 to 23, the House by 296 to 133. As before, debates were limited, confined to matters of timing, strategy, and logistics. Leading Democratic senators, including John Kerry, Joseph Biden, Joseph Lieberman, Tom Daschle, and Christopher Dodd supported Bush to the hilt, while House minority leader Richard Gephart of Missouri worked closely with the president to finesse his legislative agenda. Lieberman, at the time a hawkish presidential hopeful, collaborated with Bush at all stages of the congressional war-making process. By the end of 2002, despite rapidly growing antiwar opposition across the country, the Democrats had given the idea of loyal opposition an entirely new definition: total capitulation to Republican politics.

Even Nancy Pelosi (D-California), selected House minority leader in fall 2002 and expected to create a strong liberal presence, quickly yielded to the war hysteria. In her first interview after taking up the new position, Pelosi mentioned the need to establish a "political middle" and a "common ground with the administration," basically ceding the entire terrain of foreign and military policy to the right. One of the few Democrats to voice opposition to Bush at this time was Al Gore, now freed from the constraints of political office. Shortly after his speech denouncing Bush in December 2002, he decided to relinquish any presidential ambitions, realizing he had run up against an overwhelming bipartisan wall. The defeat of Representative Cynthia McKinney (D-Georgia), perhaps the most outspoken antiwar politician in the House, further demonstrated the vast power of prowar lobbies associated with corporate, Middle Eastern, and especially Israeli interests. The message was that no candidate for either major party could afford to depart from the official line: regime change in Iraq had become the hegemonic discourse in Washington. The shameful acquiescence of Democrats to Bush's agenda came as little surprise to shrewd observers, owing to both the pull of bipartisanship and the continued moderating legacy of Clinton within the party born of corporate-defined "centrism." Indeed Clinton's own presidency was conservative on most issues, the outgrowth of a centrist electoral formula geared to winning political office at all costs. In world politics the compelling idea had been for Democrats to adopt a more aggressive military stance than Republicans, and that carried through the 2000 campaign. Clinton's response to the new militarism: "I approve of what is being done in Iraq now [2003] and the way it's being done, but it's not enough."[5]

At a crucial turning point in U.S. history, the Democrats were fully unable to forge any alternative responses or initiatives, perhaps fearful they would be branded as unpatriotic or soft on terrorism. The bankruptcy of Bush's justification for war, including his many false claims regarding the Iraqi threat, went scarcely contested within the political arena, as national chauvinism and ideological conformism ruled the day. House Majority Leader Dennis Hastert (R–Illinois) loudly proclaimed, "We must not let evil triumph," and the Democrats quickly took up the rhetoric. Representative Tom Lantos (D–California) spoke for the majority of Democrats when he said: "Just as leaders and diplomats who appeased Hitler at Munich in 1938 stand humiliated before history, so will we if we appease Saddam Hussein today."[6] The preposterous comparison of Hitler's Nazi war machine with Hussein's weak, beaten, surrounded, impoverished nation of twenty-three million was never made an issue in Congress. Senator Robert Byrd (D–West Virginia), a Bush critic mainly on constitutional grounds, did say: "I'm in my 50th year in Congress and I never thought I would find a Senate which lacks the backbone to stand up against this stampede, this rush to war. I think we are making one horrible mistake."[7]

The stifling narrowness of American politics, with its conformist discourses and absence of real debate, became even more obvious by the end of 2002 and early 2003 with the appearance of a broad antiwar movement, which for the United States was unprecedented in its scope and diversity. Despite the "unity" of mainstream politicians and the incessant push for war by elites and the mass media, the notion of an urgent regime change in Iraq was met with cynicism and disbelief by growing numbers of ordinary Americans. The gulf between elite discourse and popular feeling about war had widened dramatically by February 2003, when antiwar mobilizations reached their peak.

By early 2003 the lies Bush was feeding the public helped galvanize the resurgent peace movement, which brought tens of millions of people in the streets and squares of American cities. Few outside the Washington elite circles actually believed that Iraq was a major threat to U.S. security, or that the secular Baathist regime was somehow aligned with al Qaeda—or indeed that Bush was really concerned about bringing democracy to Iraq, insofar as the United States had a long history of supporting authoritarian regimes in the Middle East and elsewhere. Equally ridiculous were claims about WMD: Iraq's military capacity was reduced by 80 percent following the first Gulf War, and it (unlike other nations in the region) was the site of recurrent UN weapons inspections. By January 2003 the inspectors had found no evidence of WMD and no indications of chemical, biological, or nuclear armaments, but instead of welcoming this as good news Bush merely stepped up his denunciations of the Iraqis, calling for full disarmament at the very moment the United States and Britain were expanding their own arsenals and preparing to invade. Given the extremely dangerous level of military stockpiles in dozens of other countries, some (like Pakistan) with unstable regimes, this isolated discourse of WMD was patently fraudulent to any careful observer. As Robert Scheer wrote: "The entire world is astonished that the president is lying not about personal indiscretion but about the most sacred duty of the leader of the most powerful nation in human history not to recklessly endanger the lives of his own or the world's people."[8] But while Clinton's "personal indiscretion" in the Oval Office was met with the full wrath of Congress and the media, Bush's outrageous lies—with their life-and-death implications—were met with almost total silence. Neither Democrats nor Republicans offered any telling criticisms of Bush's rush to war, even as the Pentagon was shown to have contingency plans for the use of nuclear weapons (the most destructive of all WMD) in the Persian Gulf.

Evisceration of the public sphere became all the more obvious as the antiwar movement began to push the limits of official discourse, revealing just how detached politicians and the mainstream media had become from large sectors of the population. The opposition included not only a variety of leftist and peace groups but also a good many mainstream organizations like churches, unions, the National Organization for Women, the NAACP, Greenpeace, and local city councils, which passed hundreds of antiwar resolutions. Even before the outbreak of war, this movement was able to achieve more than what had been gained during more than a decade of anti-Vietnam war mobilizations. Local groups like Neighbors for Peace and Justice flourished across the country, with local vigils, marches, teach-ins, and demonstrations becoming virtually daily events. On February 15, 2003, the largest mass mobilization in American history took place, with turnouts of more than a hundred thousand in major cities a strikingly familiar sight. Even the traditionally conservative AFL-CIO Executive Council unanimously passed a resolution opposing war. Such grassroots opposition, however, never penetrated the inner sanctums of government or the major parties, nor did it have much impact on the mass media.

As the Bush administration geared up for war against Iraq, the groups mobilizing against military action and the elites operating within the institutional political arena could be seen as inhabiting entirely different worlds. Few Democratic Party leaders stepped forward to voice even minimal objections to the course of U.S. foreign and military policy. With the United States on the verge of a costly, imperialist war, the genteel U.S. Senate conducted business as usual, with Democrats and Republicans mired in a brawl over the appointment of a single federal judge and passing a resolution mourning the death of Mr. Rogers. Members of Congress seemed wholly disconnected from the turbulence swirling around them, delegating their constitutional power to declare war to President Bush. Congressional deference to the president had become nearly routine in modern U.S. history, at times reducing the legislators to the status of cheerleaders. Referring to the imminent war, Senator Byrd said in late February 2003, "We stand passively mute, paralyzed by our own uncertainty, seemingly stunned by the sheer turmoil of events. We are truly sleepwalking through history."[9] The leading Democratic presidential contenders such as Senator John Kerry (the ultimate candidate) lined up uncritically behind Bush, including those who had earlier voiced strong reservations. Congressman Dennis Kucinich (D-Ohio) was virtually alone in standing up against the Bush juggernaut, proclaiming himself a "candidate for peace" even as he was reduced to marginality within his own party. Leaving moral and political concerns aside, even the staggering economic costs of war and occupation (predicted to run into hundreds of billions of dollars) seemed hardly sufficient to upset the rigid uniformity of Congress and indeed the entire political establishment.

PATRIOTISM AS ELITE LEGITIMATION

The collapse of the Soviet Union removed the only serious counterweight to U.S. geopolitical domination. The circumstances of 9/11 and the war on terrorism enabled the Bush administration to move full speed ahead toward a more ambitious grand strategy, which the PNAC statement had earlier affirmed. U.S. global supremacy would now become post–cold war reality— a reality to be achieved and sustained by military force, where necessary. As the lone superpower, therefore, the United States would strive to prevent any rival centers of power or independence. The National Security Strategy that Bush presented to Congress in September 2002 was abundantly clear on this point. In seeking to amass such unchallengeable worldwide power, the United States was now committed to erecting and sustaining the most awesome military machine ever known.

In domestic politics, however, hegemony cannot be established by force alone, or even primarily by force: as Antonio Gramsci argued several decades ago, institutional power cannot last very long in the absence of supporting belief systems. In the case of U.S. military power, the war economy, and Empire, patriotic ideology furnishes the main legitimating values, myths, and attitudes to be instilled in the general population—or so the political and military leaders fervently hope.

The United States has been intensely nationalistic throughout its history, a country blessed with a special political mission reflected in such references as "Manifest Destiny," "the American Century," and, more recently, "The New American Century." From the time of the Revolutionary War,

American leaders have anointed themselves with a noble calling legitimated by the founding of constitutional order, ideals of liberty and democracy, the westward frontier push, and a sense of progress rooted in Enlightenment values of science, technology, and industrial growth. Beneath these seemingly benign virtues can be found an uneasy but often virulent mix of capitalism, racism, imperialism, and militarism—first visible on a global scale with the Spanish-American War and then, more powerfully, after the military victories of World War II. Although nationalism in the United States in some ways takes on the character of a secular religion, it has always been presented as more benevolent, superior to the cruder forms associated with rival powers, with Fascism, or with the third world. As Barbara Ehrenreich observes: "By convincing ourselves that our nationalism is unique among nationalisms, we do not have to acknowledge its primitive and bloody side."[10] Americans have enlisted God and history on their side to justify imperial expansion and military conquest, beginning with the Indian wars, defined at the time as a crusade for white/European civilization. Superpatriotism took hold during the Spanish-American War, which laid waste to the Philippines and inaugurated the rise of U.S. global power. Through all the patriotic symbols and sacred rituals, through a long series of military triumphs, Americans have increasingly come to define themselves as something of a chosen people—a beacon of freedom, democracy, and progress to be judged according to different standards than others. Within this ideological matrix patriotism would be recurrently fueled by war and the struggle to tame foreign demons. Patriotism would provide a sense of national catharsis, feelings of unity that might compensate for the harsh realities of daily life. The celebration of war and the defeat of terrible alien forces took on new meaning during the first Gulf War, witnessed by a rapt population as a flag-waving media spectacle.[11]

Patriotism shapes the entire American landscape: media, popular culture, sports, politics, foreign relations. With 9/11, the war on terrorism, and then the invasion and occupation of Iraq, the press eagerly adopted the language of war and patriotism, endorsing uncritically every move by Bush and joining the government in a common enterprise. CBS news anchor Dan Rather said he would follow any orders laid down by the president. ABC's Cokie Roberts said: "Look, I am, I will just confess to you, a total sucker for the guys who stand up with the ribbons on and stuff, and they say it's true and I'm ready to believe it."[12] Judging from the degree to which right-wing interests have permeated the corporate media, confessions of this sort probably turned out to be close to the norm. Further, as we have seen, dissent after 9/11 was commonly attacked as a sign of treason in much the same way critics were scorned during the cold war as un-American, Communists, or fellow travelers of the USSR. Efforts to understand recent terrorism in the historical context of U.S. military interventions and proxy wars—that is, in terms of blowback—are deemed not worthy of discussion. In November 2001 the American Council of Trustees and Alumni, founded by Lynne Cheney, launched its Defense of Civilization Fund to support the study of "American values" and isolate "blame America" academics, all with the support of corporate foundations. Bush administration spokespersons gave speeches celebrating the presumed superiority of American traditions and institutions and justifying their export to supposedly backward reaches of the world, beginning with the axis of evil. Demons had to be slayed. And if people from other nations and cultures felt hatred or resentment toward the United States, this was simply a matter of jealousy, as the elite intoned— envy over American freedom and prosperity. Not surprisingly, such attitudes were reflected across a wide spectrum of the population. One citizen randomly interviewed said what might have been fairly representative: "I guess it's my plain old American arrogance. We are the best. I think we've proved that over and over. We're vastly educated, we're vastly experienced, we're stable—plus we have resources."[13]

If the war on terrorism—however justified—serves elite power, a more robust patriotism becomes the cornerstone of its mass legitimating ideology. It might be argued, as Norman Mailer has, that 9/11 provoked a "mass identity crisis" in American society, introducing new levels of anxiety, fear, and paranoia into public life. Dismissing the notion that the attacks brought a heightened sense of national unity, Mailer finds instead an "odious self-serving patriotism" contaminating an American politics already diminished by the cult of violence, the fetishism of technology, election frauds, and corporate scandals.[14] Mailer is not the only commentator to find an ideological emptiness in American society tied to an erosion of effective governance, brought to the surface by 9/11—a predicament that also provided new opportunities for solving the legitimation crisis. One way out has been to extend U.S. global power in the face of new enemies, with hopes of refashioning a domestic consensus. Surely an energized patriotism wedded to a revitalized militarism constitutes one possible remedy for a nation that long ago had grown ideologically and culturally stale.

Corporate globalization, the war on terrorism, the doctrine of preemptive strikes, aggressive moves in the Middle East, an expanded military-industrial complex—all this is the work of an imperial agenda having precious little to do with the requirements of national security. Patriotic ideology, however, lends an aura of necessity to these trends, and the terrorist attacks provided the fuel. After 9/11, Mailer writes, "we were plunged into a fever of patriotism. If our long-term comfortable and complacent sense that America was just the greatest country ever had been brought into doubt, the instinctive reflex was to reaffirm ourselves. We had to overcome the identity crisis—hell, overpower it, wave a flag."[15] And these highly emotional attitudes were made palatable to a public bombarded with the incessant rantings of a jingoistic media. It is easy enough to see how warfare could become a safety valve for a variety of challenges, from economic stagnation to resource needs to the electoral worries of politicians. War and preparation for war can revive the national psyche, as shown during the first Gulf War, offering the illusion of empowerment mixed with the allure of high-tech entertainment. And terrorism, even more than Communism before it, represents the perfect target. It conjures images of unspeakably criminal villains carrying out evil designs against innocent civilians, whereas Communism, though godless and evil, was always a more distinctly *political* threat. The time-honored idea that patriotic citizens ought to stand up, fight back, and help vanquish the evildoers fits domestic even more than the global needs of the system. In Mailer's words: "Flag conservatives truly believe America is not only fit to run the world but that it must. Without a commitment to Empire the country will go down the drain."[16] If Mailer proves to be correct, the future implications of such desperate maneuvers might be too horrifying to contemplate.

Patriotism furnishes the most important source of ideological legitimation for militarism, war, and Empire; it is absolutely necessary if elite adventures abroad are to be justified. The seductive power of patriotism, moreover, naturally intensifies at a time of war or preparation for war. A global superpower clearly requires a strong consensual basis—a point that will be more fully explored in the final chapter. At the same time, however effective patriotism might be in helping secure legitimation domestically, its ideological availability for American power in *world politics* is destined to fall drastically short, as the sources of opposition to Empire flourish in a context of superpower ultrapatriotism and militarism. We know that history is filled with the wreckage of states seeking imperial power through military force.

THE MEDIA: CONDUIT OF MILITARISM

If an open, diverse, accessible mass media is the sine qua non of a functioning democracy, prevailing trends at work in American society are moving in the opposite direction: corporate megamedia structures have come to dominate the terrain, including TV, radio, film, cable TV, print journalism, and the Internet. Through giant multinational business empires like General Electric, Viacom, Disney/ABC, and News Corporation, elites have a greater capacity to influence the flow of ideas, information, and entertainment than at any time in the past, increasing the power to shape governmental decision making and popular consciousness. The mainstream media have become an extension of dominant corporate interests, not to mention government and military agendas—hardly a recipe for viable democratic

politics involving active citizen participation. As a structural adjunct to the
Pentagon system, the U.S. media have evolved into probably the most significant conduit of patriotism and militarism.

The vast majority of Americans receive the bulk of their news and its
interpretations from TV and talk radio, hypercommercialized venues that
depend on advertising for their revenue. These venues are not only overwhelmingly conservative but generally (except for times of war or crisis) de-
vote little coverage to foreign affairs. In global politics the emphasis tends
toward chaos, corruption, and violence in other nations, especially those
(like Russia and China) seen as potentially hostile. The broad consequence
of media culture, for both domestic and global issues, has been a profound
depoliticization—with the exception of those moments when warfare consumes public attention. As Robert McChesney writes:

> The commercial basis of U.S. media has negative implications for the ex-
> ercise of political democracy: it encourages a weak political culture that
> makes depoliticization, apathy, and selfishness rational choices for the cit-
> izenry, and it permits the business and commercial interests that actually
> rule U.S. society to have inordinate influence over the media content.[17]

At first blush this narrowing of the public sphere would seem to be contra-
dicted by all the national frenzy generated by around-the-clock coverage of
war; the result would seem to be a form of collective political *intensity*. Such
intensity, however, revolves around media-inspired spectacles, an essentially
manipulated process inducing an altogether different kind of passivity. This
ultrapatriotic transcendence of fragmentation and privatism, made possible
by the glorification of military prowess and national triumphs, is simultaneously ephemeral and false, instilling a provincial zeal hardly compatible with
a progressive, engaged citizenry. In effect the media war spectacle gives rise
to a caricature of politics.

The U.S. media presents the public with an entirely mythological view
of the world, one populated by foreign demons and evil monsters always
ready to bring great harm to a benevolent, innocent, peace-loving country.
While American society is upheld as the beacon of democracy, prosperity,
and progress, the global terrain, as presented through the lenses of Fox or
Disney, appears to be in a condition of Hobbesian chaos where corruption
and violence rule, where "they" violate human rights and norms of democratic governance. This is a world, predictably enough, requiring U.S. economic and political, and (where this fails) military intervention. Such views
are rather uniform across the mainstream media, a taken-for-granted representation allowing for no genuinely divergent opinions. TV, radio, and print
media are dominated by government officials and a large stable of "experts"
drawn from the corporate, state, and military sectors, resulting in a severely

limited range of opinions that only rarely deviate from the strong patriotic consensus. On *Nightline* and similar news shows, foreign policy discussion is framed by distinctly American interests and values, the rest vanishing into the Hobbesian global darkness where "other" cultures and experiences are routinely devalued.[18] The two sides to any military question are inevitably reduced to matters of tactics and phrasing, all the more so when the United States is engaged in warfare. Media coverage has all the character of a sports spectacle where, as in the Olympics, one-sided patriotic agendas prevail.

The sports metaphor, with its epic contests, winners and losers, heroes, and huge crowds reflects the extent to which media culture has come to be subservient to the imperatives of power, trading in double standards, myths, and various self-serving platitudes—for example, where "terrorism" is the label chosen to describe the actions of designated enemies. Gruesome episodes of combat are sanitized or aestheticized, or simply explained away as part of a process requiring endless repetition to be successful, as in Vietnam (where the process quickly broke down). All the production values of TV advertising and digital imaging are used to the fullest. As Norman Solomon and Reese Erlich write: "No product requires more adroit marketing than one that squanders vast quantities of resources while slaughtering large numbers of people."[19] Warfare carried out by a high-tech military machine turns out to be a sophisticated marketing phenomenon with an endless parade of packaged events, provocative viewing for audiences saturated with sports images, reality TV, and true crime; life and media converge. Leading TV commentators like Bill O'Reilly and Brit Hume on Fox TV can speak freely about bombing Afghanistan and Iraq to rubble, as if the carnage would be scarcely troublesome to audiences weened on video games and action movies. If Iraq is personified by a Hitler-like monster in Saddam Hussein, then all is rendered possible in a war made larger than life by the media embellishment of an epic crusade pitting good against evil. Referring to the media-charged buildup toward the second Gulf War, Scott Ritter, the former UN weapons inspector disgusted with the lies perpetrated by the media, comments: "We made it impossible for anybody to talk about Iraq in responsible, substantive, factually backed terms."[20]

Although the media has faithfully served patriotic ends and military interests since at least the Spanish-American War, marking the advent of William Randolph Hearst's "yellow journalism," it reached a pinnacle during the first Gulf War—essentially a TV war glorifying U.S. technowar exploits by means of endless, graphic, live depictions of modern warfare. Crowning every military victory as a great extravaganza, the media emerged as a powerful agency of the war hysteria that swept America, appearing to finally signal a break with the lingering Vietnam syndrome of defeat and humiliation. The result was nothing short of a deepening militarization of American culture, already well advanced during the cold war but having languished during the 1970s and 1980s, following the Indochina debacle.[21] Never before had media power been so flagrant, so comprehensive, so fully capable of molding popular consciousness. At the time of Desert Storm the media came to colonize popular life in a way theorized earlier by Marshall McLuhan but not yet completely realized within the social order. Following the Iraq invasion of Kuwait the results would be ominous, as Douglas Kellner points outs:

> And so, George Bush, the U.S. military, and the military-industrial complex were the immediate beneficiaries of the Gulf War. Bush was transformed from wimp to warrior and the U.S. military was able to overcome its humiliation in Vietnam and its past failures. The U.S. appeared to be the world's sole remaining superpower, a high-tech military colossus dominating Bush's New World Order.[22]

It would be a stunningly short-lived, and rather Pyrrhic, victory for both the senior Bush and the American people, as both foreign and domestic social problems momentarily obscuring the Pentagon extravaganza would soon reemerge; though of course militarism itself was hardly about to disappear.

Since the first Gulf War, and more emphatically since 9/11, the American press has seized hold of its patriotic role and taken it to new heights. In the case of U.S. foreign policy, the media has dropped any pretense of journalistic objectivity, adopting a Manichaeistic view dividing the world between "us" and "them," between a civilizing American global mission and a wide array of alien demonic forces. Fox TV has been especially shrill in its jingoism, but much the same pattern has held for CNN, NBC, ABC, and CBS, along with the bulk of mainstream newspapers and radio programs. Such frenzied partisanship guarantees a failure to explore the larger historical and social *context* of events in the news. Issues surrounding 9/11 and its aftermath offer a prime case in point: from the outset the media did little to situate and interpret the events, explore the history, scrutinize Bush's mistakes, report egregious intelligence lapses, or question the efficacy of an almost exclusively military response to terrorism. The very *possibility* of blowback was largely ignored. Instead, the media took off in the direction of patriotic celebration, focusing on those wondrous American freedoms that people around the world so angrily resented.[23] The terrorist attacks were simplistically framed as the work of diabolical Arabs bereft of any conceivable moral compass or political motive, a discourse that willfully overlooked the clear ideological significance of the targets. Events were depicted so as to justify an immediate military reaction—a pattern that would be duplicated later as the media culture provided crucial legitimation in the buildup toward war against Iraq.

The conservative patriotic media came into full swing as Bush's war drive picked up momentum after summer 2002. The campaign was based on a number of half-truths and lies that elites and pundits across the spectrum repeated ad nauseum, and never challenged: false statements about an imminent Iraqi military threat and possession of WMD, ridiculous claims about Hussein's collaboration with al Qaeda, phony evidence brought forth to support the notion that Iraq was rapidly accumulating nuclear materials, shameful coercive methods (often futile) used to win UN members' approval of war, disinformation about the projected costs and consequences of a new Gulf War, and so forth. Few corporate media outlets paid much attention to these issues, eschewing any watchdog or investigative role—long a staple of first-rate journalism—in favor of unabashed war-making propaganda. The supposedly liberal media took its cues almost exclusively from the government and Pentagon, closing off even the mildest dissent, which became particularly noisome once actual combat was underway. As in the case of Desert Storm, TV shifted to nearly around-the-clock coverage of U.S. military operations, dwelling most spectacularly on the Pentagon's initial "shock and awe" tactics, which unleashed as many as four hundred cruise missiles on Baghdad alone in the first days of the assault. The campaign was framed as "Plan Iraqi Freedom"; the military overthrow of Hussein was uncritically packaged as the liberation of the Iraqi people from despotism and their eventual move into an era of political democracy. The spectacle focused almost exclusively on the logistical and technical aspects of military invasion, with crucial ethical and political questions pushed aside. Guests on TV news programs, interview shows, and talk fests were drawn from a familiar stable of right-wing pundits: Fred Barnes, George Will, Charles Krauthammer, Ben Wattenberg, Pat Buchanan, Ann Coulter, William Kristol, Madeleine Albright. Prowar intellectuals like Kenneth Pollack and Robert Kagan became media stars at Fox and elsewhere. And of course the "defense experts," as in Desert Storm, were omnipresent. The antiwar side of the debate was almost entirely ignored until popular demonstrations and other actions in the United States and around the world became too large, with far too many repercussions, to be denied, at which time media outlets presented grotesquely caricatured and distorted pictures of what was happening. At the very moment the huge American war machine was preparing to attack Iraq, the vast material, human, environmental, even global consequences of this imperial gambit were overlooked or downplayed.

In 2002 and 2003 the *Washington Post* featured a series of op-ed pieces, editorials, and news reports that amounted to cheerleading for a second Gulf War. Despite its liberal reputation, the paper took on the character of essentially a mouthpiece for government and Pentagon agendas, championed by such writers as Jim Hoagland, Henry Kissinger, James Baker,

Robert Dole, Richard Holbrooke, and Robert Novak. An ensemble of prowar discourses was filled with outpourings of imperial arrogance, seeming indifference toward the costs of war, and rigid intolerance of those dissenting from the official government line. The few critical voices permitted on the opinion pages of the *Post* focused mainly on tactical concerns such as logistics, timing, and the need to mobilize broader support. A majority of contributors were present, or former government officials, typically referred to as "experts." Foreign viewpoints were largely absent.[24] In fact the *Post* approach turned out to be de rigueur for American journalism, both print and electronic, during the buildup toward war. The *Wall Street Journal* enthusiastically joined in the warmongering, as did *Time* and *Newsweek*, with special issues devoted to unveiling the evils of Hussein's Iraq, its possession of deadly weapons, and the glories of U.S. military technology.

Diversity of political opinion, long championed as part of the American democratic legacy, was increasingly difficult to locate within the established public sphere. Fundamental opposition to Bush's policies was nonexistent, unworthy of serious consideration in the press or political arena, with directly competing views (including virtually anything coming from the Arab world) dismissed outright as crude propaganda. Some media outlets chose to present coverage of official Iraqi statements, but these too were discredited as the diabolical work of Hussein or al Qaeda. In January 2003 CNN was set to cover a live press announcement from Baghdad in which Iraqi officials were to make rebuttals to Bush's statements and policies that were being carried twenty-four hours a day. Immediately after an Iraqi representative began making his case against war, the network cut away to breaking news from the White House: Bush would be giving a preview of his State of the Union address. There was never any return to the Iraqi official who had been interrupted in midstream. Although Bush predictably wound up saying little that was novel, the abrupt break gave CNN a plausible excuse for silencing a strong counterviewpoint. There was also Dan Rather's interview with Hussein in late February 2003—itself roundly condemned by politicians and pundits as an egregious willingness to give time and respect to the enemy. Giving his first extended foreign interview in several years, the Iraqi leader made a passionate appeal for peace, for stepped-up diplomacy, for friendly relations with the United States. A nearly full-page report on the interview in the *Los Angeles Times* (February 27, 2003) began with the bizarre observation that Hussein's statements were not newsworthy and then proceeded to ignore the actual text of the interview; the report strangely contained no quotes of responses to questions. In their place was a lengthy series of critical attacks on Hussein, five in all, by supporters of Bush's war policy, including White House spokesperson Ari Fleischer. Hussein's views, for better or worse, received attention only by virtue of their negation—a strange journalistic practice but one that became increasingly common during the rush to war.

Even the facade of media objectivity is readily abandoned once we enter the sacred "bipartisan" realm of U.S. foreign and military policy; something close to official propaganda takes over, transforming the news into a form of sports contest and political discourse into the language of patriotic conformism. Double standards inevitably prevail: rival and in some cases allied governments and their leaders are vilified for exactly the same international behavior the United States carries out with much great regularity, and with impunity. Media coverage dwells on a long list of horrors and abuses in Russia, China, and Iraq, while even more grotesque violations by the United States and its client states go unreported or, when reported, are downplayed. Thus possession of WMD by other nations is treated as an ominous threat to human civilization, while the taken-for-granted, infinitely larger (and more often used) WMD arsenal of the United States becomes part of the natural terrain, scarcely worthy of comment. When embarrassing realities simply cannot be ignored—as in the case of the Gulf War syndrome and the Abu Ghraib prison scandal—government counterresponse usually merits far more attention than any fact-finding investigations. The very *idea* that the United States might be held guilty of war crimes is, for the media, not worthy of reflection. The prewar situation in Iraq constitutes one of many recent examples: U.S. military action, routine bombings, and harsh economic sanctions carried out for well more than a decade brought enormous casualties (mostly civilian) to Iraq, but the little coverage this commanded in the media was largely confined to the back pages, minimized, or framed as if the carnage had been entirely the fault of Hussein and his circle.

With the growing concentration of the mainstream media, American political culture seems to have become rather inoculated against genuinely diverse viewpoints and open debates: terrorism, as we have seen, is looked on as nothing more than an evil scourge, the work of evil monsters addicted to hatred and violence, while the benevolence of U.S. global intentions remains just another matter of faith. As Ziauddin Sardar and Merryl Wyn Davies show, U.S. public opinion is shockingly provincial, marked by a profound lack of curiosity about how people in other countries live, think, and act.[25] Despite unprecedented affluence, mobility, and access to information, despite huge enrollments at colleges and universities, Americans at the start of the twenty-first century turn out to be remarkably insular and ethnocentric. Surveys continue to reveal a frightening ignorance of global issues. Thus it is easy to see how, with the end of the cold war, the label "terrorist" could be so routinely affixed to individuals, groups, and states deemed hostile to U.S. interests or policies just as the "Communist" stigma had been invoked before it. The recurrently asked question in the mass media, "Why do they hate us?" reveals a good deal about the political culture. While "they" now usually refers to Arabs and Muslims, the "us" part of the formulation naturally assumes a wounded innocence, a victim status that seems appropriate to a nation surrounded by threatening enemies. If the focus shifted to concrete policies and actions of an aggressive superpower, then the questions would have to be posed differently, focusing instead on how and why the United States so routinely intervenes—economically, politically, and militarily—in other countries around the world, why it is often so quick to deploy military force on behalf of narrow geopolitical objectives, why it has so often violated international treaties and laws.

In any balanced forum, such questions would naturally enter into the public debate; they would be seen as helping to enrich the political culture. One reasonably logical point of view would be that "hatred" might be the predictable response of people who have been victims of superpower intervention over which they had no control. That some of these victims might channel their deep resentment in the direction of violent actions should hardly come as a surprise to informed observers, but this very concept (part of blowback) is largely excluded from the corporate media or, where acknowledged, is simply mocked and trivialized. For those millions of people harmed directly by U.S. military ventures, "terrorism" will likely be viewed as a just reaction against what they experience as an even more terrible form of violence, *state* terrorism. History of course is replete with epic struggles against state oppression and violence: American and Irish independence movements against the British, the Algerian movement against the French, antiapartheid movements in South Africa, partisan battles against the Nazis in World War II, to name just a few. For most Americans it has become more comforting to view the predictable and recurrent violent actions of others as undistilled evil, bereft of any human rationality or motivation. Sardar and Davies argue that the well-worn media fixation on foreign devils ultimately serves as a cover for willful ignorance, xenophobia, and, in the end, military attacks on the designated malignancy.

In the weeks leading up to the second U.S. war against Iraq, the airwaves of major TV networks were dominated by prowar voices—many of them xenophobic and aggressive, according to a FAIR study of the American media. Of 397 total guest appearances during that period, fully 75 percent of the U.S. sources were present or former government officials, mostly national-security or military people, all strongly endorsing Bush's agenda of preemptive war. Just *four* voices from what had become a huge and diverse antiwar movement were given any kind of forum. A scattering of antiwar critics (twenty all told) was chosen from mainly *foreign* sources, many of them Iraqi government officials—the message being that such views were not to be taken seriously. The vast majority of TV broadcasts dwelled on the search for *military* solutions—"solutions" to a "crisis" that was, in the final analysis, clearly American made. Official news releases and press conferences, many coming directly from the Pentagon and State Department, were routinely taken at face value, as were Bush's endlessly repeated false pretexts for war.[26] Such media bias came at a time when opinion polls in other major industrial countries showed that 80 percent of their combined populations opposed military action, while even in the United States more than half those surveyed were hostile to Bush's unilateralism and rush to war. Given the overall trajectory of media culture, the American public now receives news and information almost exclusively from mainstream sources with direct ties to the White House, Pentagon, State Department, and a variety of conservative think tanks, along with a small but influential circle of academics ready to support hawkish military actions. One problem is that any news organization hoping to get access to the structures of power, always vital during combat situations, must go along with the hegemonic parameters maintained by those same centers of power. Above all, the Pentagon influence on corporate media outlets has grown immensely, especially since 9/11, reflected in the increased glorification of military power at Fox, CNN, ABC, *Time* magazine, and most talk-radio stations (the majority owned by Disney/ABC and Clear Channel)—not to mention the more frequent release of Hollywood combat films dramatizing "good war" themes since the late 1990s. The popular media, inseparable from the war economy and structures of corporate power, has become essential to the legitimation of U.S. imperial and military agendas.

MILITARISM AND THE INTELLECTUALS

In modern society a growing stratum of intellectuals (scholars, teachers, literati, professionals, and cultural workers) carries out tasks crucial to ideological domination, which of course extend to the global arena. One way such tasks can be effectively performed is for the military itself to go largely unmentioned in the various discourses; the Pentagon system, behemoth that it is, conveniently escapes mention and scrutiny. Another is for the goals of U.S. imperialism to be explicitly acknowledged and then embraced, even celebrated—a tendency more visible since the end of the cold war. Yet another way intellectuals perform such tasks is by explicitly recognizing the worldwide American presence while denying it has anything to do with geopolitical interests or militarism. To the degree ideological domination is solidified, the power of an emergent critical intelligentsia is correspondingly devalued.

Viewed historically, the American system of higher education has since the 1950s become increasingly interwoven with corporate, state, and military power, partly in response to the expanded legitimating role performed by the knowledge industry, partly because of the role played by education in the development of science, technology, and industry. The growth of colleges and universities, in numbers and in scope of influence, has meant the simultaneous expansion of intellectual venues and activities. Since the 1950s planners in higher education have linked their agendas to a variety of systemic objectives: corporate marketing and advertising, military research and development, techniques for streamlining administrative control and efficiency, general technological development, foreign intelligence, and so forth. The bulk of research sponsored within academia is funded by government and corporations (including foundations), meaning that elite interests have come to shape a wide range of scholarly pursuits. Academic funding rarely flows in the direction of scholarly projects that in some way critically scrutinize the status quo, all the more so when such projects concern foreign policy and world politics. Within the major universities strong economic and bureaucratic interests, working in tandem with highly specialized research agendas, help bolster established institutional values and practices. Such logic has deepened with the massive growth of transnational corporate power, the high-tech global economy, sophisticated telecommunications systems, and the military-industrial complex. Here American intellectuals, always with notable exceptions, play a central legitimating role in sustaining U.S. global power. Since 9/11 this role has become more visible, more extensive, perhaps more emotionally charged than ever.

With the end of World War II and the onset of the cold war, American intellectual life became enmeshed in a confluence of developments: anti-Communism, the war economy, expanded higher education, increasingly grandiose U.S. foreign-policy ambitions. Massive flows of resources were directed toward Pentagon-style Keynesianism. Cold war ideology evolved into a mixture of patriotism, militarism, imperial arrogance, and standard anti-Communism all revolving around the containment of Soviet power and Third World insurgencies—integral to the outlook of American intellectuals, liberals and conservatives alike. From the late 1940s through the collapse of the Soviet Union critics of U.S. imperial power were marginalized, kept beyond the pale of "serious" discourse; with few exceptions, political campaigns did not incorporate debates around questions of American foreign and military policy. On the whole intellectual work was subordinated to the imperatives of class and state power, to the dictates of Pentagon agendas. As throughout U.S. history, "pragmatism" was the supreme virtue of intellectual life, and departure from it was labeled "ideological" or "extremist." With intellectuals becoming a privileged stratum within the professional-managerial class, their outlook—within and outside of academia—was more than anything technocratic, rarely straying very far from the matrix of power. As the intellectual culture merged with the hegemonic discourses, the costs and consequences of U.S. global power were either ignored or justified on grounds of American exceptionalism—that U.S. behavior in the world, however far-reaching and violent, was uniquely a function of democratic, peace-loving values. Very few cold war intellectuals and scholars chose to investigate or criticize the dark side of Empire. As Noam Chomsky observes: "To this day, the fact that the United States attacked South Vietnam has not penetrated American scholarship, intellectual life, or indeed most of the left."[27] While the American media clamors for Japanese apologies regarding World War II atrocities, U.S. leaders have never acknowledged their crimes in Korea and Vietnam, in Hiroshima and Nagasaki, much less in Central America or the North American continent itself, where millions of native inhabitants were exterminated. A large stratum of American intellectuals derives its income, status, and sense of empowerment by means of its ties to the universities, the media, corporations, government, and, in many cases, the military. Academics especially adhere to a fairly rigid set of professional norms, ostensibly scientific and value free, that barely cloak often strong underlying ideological biases. A close relationship to the power structure ensures rewards and status vital to successful work: grants, promotions, travel, the ability to get published in the right circles, and so forth. In some academic disciplines (for example political science, international relations, economics, history) intellectuals can enter the rarefied sphere of upper-echelon politics—the State Department, Pentagon, CIA, even the White House. More of them, however, wind up performing technocratic roles within higher education, the corporations, and the government. Elite scholars like Arthur Schlesinger Jr., Walt Rostow, George Kennan, Henry Kissinger, Zbigniew Brzezinski, Jeanne Kirkpatrick, and Robert Reich have occupied high-level offices close to the president. Working in the service of such professional interests, large numbers of academics have willingly joined the propaganda system, endorsing the various rationales for expanded Pentagon spending and power, for armed interventions abroad, and perhaps even for U.S. global supremacy (until recently rarely defined as Empire or imperialism). The notion of a benevolent, peaceful, democratic, even humanitarian U.S. foreign policy is usually taken as an article of faith, as is the tendency to invoke double standards in situations where violence is used for political ends. Where criticism does come into play, it usually follows the discourse of "mistakes," the personal misjudgments of leaders, and the success or failure of tactical decisions. The intellectual role in reproducing ideological hegemony extends to liberals and conservatives, Democrats and conservatives alike, joined sometimes by progressives anxious to show their anti-Communist and patriotic (or, since 9/11, antiterrorist) credentials. Many have been inclined to go along with different variants of "humanitarian" intervention, looking to the supposedly democratic and liberating potential of U.S. military action. The cold war started during the Truman years and achieved its peak expression during the John F. Kennedy administration, which recruited liberal academics from Ivy League schools to help forge an aggressive anti-Communist foreign policy. The Council on Foreign Relations (CFR), always integral to the national-security establishment, has been bipartisan, as have such venues of academic influence as the George-town Center for Strategic Studies, the Hoover Institute, and the Brookings Institute. Some, like the Center for Strategic and International Studies (CSIS) and the American Enterprise Institute, have become more stridently right wing over time. The Reagan presidency witnessed the rise of a new generation of neoconservative, hawkish intellectuals with an aggressive mil-itary outlook: Richard Perle, Paul Wolfowitz, Richard Cheney, Kenneth Pollack, Robert Kagan, and Elliott Abrams, among others. This group was affiliated with such groups as CFR, AEI, and CSIS and such journals as *Foreign Affairs*, *Commentary*, and the *Weekly Standard*. As we have seen, in 1997 many core members of this neoconservative circle founded the Project for a New American Century (PNAC), dedicated to the goal of U.S. world domination. Through the cold war and into the 1990s, these intellectuals—working with Democrats but more often Republicans—forged a consensus behind the idea that the United States has the right, indeed the *obligation*, to carry out its grand strategy for remaking the world. It was around this con-sensus that such doctrines as preemptive strike were born.

While institutions like CFR, the Hoover Institute, and CSIS work be-hind the facade of academic rigor and scholarly objectivity, their agendas are hardly secret: enhanced Pentagon spending, wider U.S. military presence around the world, militant defense of Israel, a readiness to intervene on be-half of geopolitical interests, and of course Empire. These agendas have become more focused and uncompromising since the Bush presidency and 9/11, but they are not radically new. Extreme partisanship is rather easy to uncover beneath the surface of professionalism and scholarly neutrality. The CFR, for example, has always been dominated by large corporate interests, the major source of its funding. The largest think tank in the area of inter-national relations, it is fully immersed in the business community; twenty-three of the biggest American banks and corporations have four or more di-rectors who are CFR members.[28] In this arena intellectuals carry out research and writing that is often inseparable from priorities of the corpora-tions, the government, and the Pentagon. By means of its long-term presence and publication of its journal *Foreign Affairs*, the CFR has established strong ties to disciplines like political science, history, and international relations. The Hoover Institute too has benefited from the financial largesse and polit-ical support of big-moneyed interests since its founding in 1919, when it emerged even then as the hub of anti-Communist studies in the United States. Hoover expanded in size and prestige after 1960, growing from six to eighty-five fellows by 1990, with an endowment of $125 million, and get-ting a boost from wealthy donors like Joseph Coors and Rupert Murdoch.[29] While Stanford University imparted to Hoover an aura of scholarly respectability, in effect Hoover became a major forum within which the Reagan-Bush foreign-policy motifs would be developed and refined.

The Council on Foreign Affairs has been a dynamic force behind the formulation of postwar U.S. global doctrines and to the growth of the national-security state. In its financing, leadership, and membership (over four thousand in 2003) the CFR is enmeshed in the world of transnational corporations, oil companies, large banks and insurance firms, and military-related businesses. As Laurence Shoup writes: "The importance of the Council stems from its role as the central link that binds the capitalist upper class and its most important financial and multinational corporations, think tanks, and foundations to academic experts in leading (mainly eastern) universities, and government policy formation and execution."[30] A key objective of CFR is to keep public debate regarding U.S. foreign policy within bounds acceptable to the power structure. Leading business contributors have included AOL Time-Warner, ABC, AT&T, Nike, Prudential, Lockheed-Martin, Shell Oil, and Verizon. A proliferation of study groups, roundtables, forums, workshops, and conferences are continuously being organized through CFR's New York offices; at these gatherings members focus on key issue and geographical areas, often arriving at recommendations that find their way into journals like *Foreign Affairs* and *World Politics*. The terrorist attacks of 9/11 stimulated an outpouring of CFR activity that would help streamline the goal of an American-dominated New World Order. In the eighteen months following 9/11 council scholars wrote a total of ten books, twenty major journal articles, and more than one hundred op-ed pieces in widely read newspapers. They also made over one thousand TV and radio guest appearances, testified before Congress, and gave briefings to a multitude of government officials.

A major thread running through all this activity was the idea of a preemptive attack on Iraq, the sooner the better—most forcefully articulated by Pollack in his spring 2002 *Foreign Affairs* article "Next Stop Baghdad." An Iraq strategy was simply one step in the larger goal of establishing U.S. economic, political, and military control over the Middle East, with its prized natural resources and its key geographical location. While neocons have always been a driving force behind this agenda, its *bipartisan* character needs to be emphasized: the CFR venue is shared equally by Democrats and Republicans, indeed more so today than in the past. Leading Democrats like Richard Gephardt, John Kerry, Christopher Dodd, Bill Clinton, Joseph Lieberman, and Albert Gore are CFR members, as are leading members of Bush's foreign-policy team—Colin Powell, Condoleezza Rice, Cheney, Wolfowitz, and the new ambassador to Iraq, John Negroponte. All endorsed Bush's decision to invade and occupy Iraq—that is, preemptive war for "regime change"—a scheme with origins in the first Gulf War. Beyond this, the CFR has long pushed for a global Pax Americana in which the United States would have no significant challengers, a view clearly reflected in the 2000 PNAC statement and the September 2002 Bush military strategy outlined in the document "National Security and Strategy of the United States." Here lie many of the foundations of a new militarism: unilateralism, the spurning of international treaties, distrust of the UN, a keen readiness to intervene militarily to secure national interests, a renewed focus on the weaponization of space, global supremacy.

This is one flagrant instance where a sizable intellectual stratum, manifestly conservative, technocratic, and patriotic, has been able to exercise strong ideological influence within the upper reaches of government. Academics critical of U.S. foreign and military policy can be found in large numbers at American universities, but their leverage seems to pale in comparison with that of the neocons and others closer to the corridors of power. The myth of scholarly objectivity remains, but its professional veneer has become increasingly transparent. The facade wears thin precisely because the major universities depend so heavily on the largesse of corporations, wealthy donors, foundations, and the federal government (largely for military research and development). These institutions are governed by trustees or regents drawn for the most part from corporate ranks. This is one reason why critical scholarly work on the war economy, U.S. militarism, and Empire has been so limited in its scope and influence. In economics and foreign relations especially, the intellectual culture has evolved into a bastion of established discourses. A smaller substratum of critical intellectuals has exerted influence within the larger culture, mainly through a variety of discourses on the fringes of intellectual and political life: critical theory, neo-Marxism, feminism, ecology, postmodernism, cultural studies. Such discourses have revitalized scholarly work, but their scope has been mostly hyperspecialized, compartmentalized, and in most cases depoliticized, consistent with the norms of professionalized academic culture—quite in contrast with the neocon pattern of highly politicized work. The postmodern tendency, with its emphasis on ambiguity, indeterminacy, and the collapse of master narratives, has contributed to this impasse of critical scholarship.

The reality is that few intellectuals are truly independent, able to work outside the relatively narrow institutional and political boundaries of academic and media culture. Most are forced to adapt to the inducements of prestige, rewards, and leverage. Even the most critical vocabulary, even when it is sustained over time, usually loses its power and relevance once it is overcome by the seductive ideological pull of mainstream venues, methods, rewards, and frames of reference. Ironically, whatever their political commitments, most critical intellectuals wind up more detached from the public sphere than their mainstream counterparts, ever prepared to collaborate with the centers of power. Scholars at elite universities particularly refrain from strong criticism of U.S. foreign policy, understandable given their quest for tenure, promotions, grants, and publications—all requiring rather strict adherence to rules of the academic game. Many critical intellectuals (for example, Marxists, postmodernists, and feminists) commonly refuse to extend their otherwise probing, subversive discourses into the realm of world politics; dissonance ends at the water's edge, it would appear. The examples of Domhoff and Hardt and Negri, discussed earlier, fit this pattern exactly: analyses of the power structure and globalization rarely make contact with the actualities of war economy, militarism, and imperial domination.

One can carry this line of thinking even further: the truism that critical thinking stops when it comes to assessing U.S. foreign and military policy becomes even more valid during wartime, or preparation for war. It would seem that the aftermath of 9/11, signaling a perpetual war on terrorism, has produced just such a milieu, in which superpatriotism, fear of attack, and obsession with national security combine to either close off or marginalize even the most tepid dissent, especially in the year following the attacks. Writing in such journals as the *New Republic, Dissent*, the *Nation*, and the *New York Review of Books*, or contributing op-ed pieces to major newspapers, a surprising number of left-wing intellectuals wrote passionately in defense of patriotism and U.S. military power, supporting (often uncritically) Bush's operations in the war on terrorism while chiding critics for their "naive pacifism" and tendency to "blame America first," traditional refrains of the right. References to the *historical context* of terrorism, to the obvious realities of blowback, were dismissed for making light of the 9/11 victims or for being soft on terrorism. Well-known progressives like Todd Gitlin, Michael Walzer, Christopher Hitchens, and David Corn denounced both the critics and the growing antiwar movement for failure to recognize the virtue of "just wars" on behalf of U.S. global interests. A strange form of anti-intellectualism overtook the culture, with severe consequences: the avoidance of contextualizing political issues, jettisoning of critical viewpoints at a time when they were urgently needed, and refusal to address long-term *future* ramifications of U.S. military interventions.

Other reputedly progressive intellectuals, writing in the aftermath of 9/11, abandoned any sense of nuance or complexity, their response hardly differing from that of the neocons: the terrorist attacks were interpreted as nothing but an evil assault on the American bastion of democracy and modernity. Along these lines Alan Wolfe wrote of a new citizen solidarity that flourished after 9/11, inspired by the defense of political freedoms, democracy, and religious tolerance, all of which terrorists placed under attack. The United States, in Wolfe's view, represents a social order that is opposed to hatred, discrimination, and violence, a "culture of nonjudgmentalism."[31] Wolfe saw a revival of trust in government, along with a broadening public sphere and, more incredibly, a reinvigorated push toward social equality. Thus: "It is difficult to imagine government operating blatantly in the interests of only one class when people from all walks of life were killed in the attacks." Bush was depicted as a president "who acts on behalf of all the people," just as the current political leadership "acts and speaks from the heart."[32] Moral conditions in the nation have improved dramatically, marked by a rebirth of "civic engagement" along with a heightened interest in world affairs. Wolfe believes the United States is widely despised not because its global presence might have brought harm to tens of millions of people but simply owing to its undeniable benevolence, remarking that "some fanatics hate us so much for doing so many things well."[33] These kinds of platitudes—none of which are taken very seriously by even the ruling elites—were in fact a staple of post-9/11 responses in the media and political system, repeated endlessly. Writing in the *New Republic*, Martin Peretz echoed the insularity of mainstream intellectual opinion when he argued that "the frisson of death, of killing others and dying oneself in the process, is so alien to our culture. In the West, large numbers of people no longer experience an emotional thrill or shiver of excitement at the shedding of blood—even the blood of our enemies."[34] Soon enough, of course, the American public would be getting ready for a second bout of Gulf War carnage, yet another media/combat extravaganza that would boost TV ratings to all-time records.

Many long-time critics of U.S. foreign policy—examples include Todd Gitlin, Michael Walzer, and Christopher Hitchens—shifted rightward in the 1990s, emphatically after 9/11 defending Bush's initiatives from what increasingly appeared to be a neocon outlook. Perhaps the best case in point is Hitchens' book *A Long Short War* (2003), a loosely assembled series of brief essays (initially written for the online magazine *Slate*) amounting to little more than an occasionally witty but strong brief for an aggressive U.S. imperial strategy. The author of such provocative works as *The Trial of Henry Kissinger*, Hitchens seems to have been politically reborn, prepared to accept virtually any Pentagon or White House claim in favor of military intervention in the Middle East. In *A Long Short War* he stridently favors Bush's war against Iraq, presumably so that the demonic Hussein, a mixture of Darth Vader and Joe Stalin, can be removed from the political scene, allowing for the democratization of Iraqi society. Hitchens was convinced that Iraq had become a "patron" of al Qaeda, that Hussein was a "bad guy's bad guy" with no business controlling 9 percent of the world's oil reserves, a leading member of the "madman-plus-WMD club."[35] The U.S. goal, Hitchens says, is to bring pluralism, tolerance, and peace to the Middle East, to create new geopolitical conditions in the region, to establish institutions in which downtrodden populations can finally govern themselves.

This goal would be accomplished under the auspices of the Pentagon, helped along by a few detachments from Britain and other coalition partners. The costs and consequences of such intervention do not seem to bother Hitchens, for the main issue is the moral and political correctness of the policy at hand: "There's nothing like the feeling of being in the right and proclaiming firmness of purpose."[36] As for prospects of additional blow-back, of heightened rather than reduced global terrorism, we are informed that "warfare is an enterprise where, very noticeably, nice guys finish last." Military action is surely worth the price, since the United States is obliged (as in the Balkans and Afghanistan) to defend "civil society" against the horrors of "theocratic nihilism"—never mind the near inevitability that U.S. invasion and occupation would only undermine the constituent elements of a thriving "civil society." As for Bush, he is praised as a moderate, rational, wise leader who was unduly patient before deciding to invade, extending deadline after deadline. (Of course Bush's "patience" was a function not of his moderation or wisdom but of the UN refusal to go along with the invasion plans.) One cannot find a single Hitchens' criticism directed at Bush, probably the most reactionary and dangerous president in historical memory. As for the great warrior Wolfowitz, he gets strong praise for being "right" about regime change in Iraq before anyone else, as early as 1978 (even before Hussein consolidated his power).

Hitchens' seeming penchant for U.S. military action resonates throughout *A Long Short War*. Moving through Iraq in the company of U.S. and British troops during the invasion, he writes triumphantly of rapid military victories and the strong welcome "liberated" Iraqis gave to advancing soldiers, with cries of "Boosh, Boosh!" coming even from young children—hardly, as it turns out, a prelude to the coming nightmare of occupation. Hitchens refers to the warmhearted presence of "big, happy, friendly, gullible Western officers,"[37] taking another page from Hollywood's World War II propaganda movies. It turns out the officers had every reason to be happy: they were on the road to a heartening achievement, getting rid of all the thieves, rapists, murderers, and other monsters lurking about Iraq on their way to uncovering vast hidden caches of WMD. The sprawling allied military convoys were to link up with the brave Kurds engaged in "fighting a battle for all of us"[38] —a battle, predictably, that U.S. forces were reluctant to support on the ground. Hitchens observes that the invasion not only liberated Iraq but saved the oil from Hussein's clutches "with scarcely a drop [of blood] spilled."[39]

Next to Hussein as a modern incarnation of Stalin, Hitchens saves his most venomous prose for the antiwar movement that, to his great dismay, grew during 2002 and early 2003 to mobilize millions of people worldwide. Hitchens was not particularly impressed: he says (without evidence) that the movement was organized by people who do not think Hussein is such a bad guy and supported by "blithering ex-flower children" and "ranting neo-Stalinists in the streets."[40] If the "potluck peaceniks" had their way, the world would be overrun by monsters like Milosevic and Hussein, because the misguided activists are sadly obsessed with fighting *American* power instead of those monsters. Hitchens writes of phony antiwar protests based on hysterical predictions and puerile beliefs about the inflated role of corporations in American political life.

Like the neocon hawks, Hitchens envisions a "new imperialism" where armed force is to be celebrated, where U.S. military intervention lays the groundwork for democracy and human rights, emboldened by a combination of lethal weapons and the ideas of Thomas Paine and Frederick Douglas, who (unlike the protesters) believed that liberty was well worth fighting for. We do not know whether the Bush-Rumsfeld-Wolfowitz crowd ever paid much attention to Paine and Douglas as architects of the New World Order, in contrast to, say, the pressing resource needs of an all-consuming industrial-military machine that utilizes 25 percent of global resources. Of course the old-fashioned imperialism always dressed itself in the ideological garb of freedom and democracy, but Hitchens knows *this* imperialism is entirely different—benevolent, generous, out to slay all tyrants, true to its official proclamations. Today, moreover, there is yet another familiar rationale behind preemptive warfare—the war on terrorism. Hitchens' willingness to go along with the most crude propaganda emanating from the Pentagon and White House is difficult to fathom. Moreover, he seems totally oblivious to the fact that continuous U.S. military intervention (however righteous its claims) itself leads to blowback, that is, even more terrorism. Like the neocons, Hitchens is convinced that state-organized violence is a separate phenomenon, since, while undeniably more systematic and lethal, it is more "rational" than the "asymmetrical" violence practiced by terrorist groups like al Qaeda. What makes substate terrorism distinctly fearsome and immoral, he notes, is its shadowy, random, irrational character. Hitchens does not try to deny that the violent pursuit of political aims is and has been more or less universal. But he never explains how terrorist networks are uniquely irrational, nor why their actions should be any more reprehensible than the supposedly "rationalized" military actions carried out on behalf of U.S. global domination, the destructive impact of which is many times greater. After all, even the Nazis employed organized military power to achieve "rational" (i.e., state-defined, geopolitical) agendas, but it is unlikely Hitchens would defend Nazi methods against the more sporadic, localized, "shadowy" terrorism of the partisan groups fighting Nazism.

Little historical investigation is required to show that U.S. military operations around the world have served primarily corporate and geopolitical interests—above all where the resource-laden Middle East and Central Asia is concerned. As the elites themselves know quite well, democracy scarcely figures in these plans. Oddly, as imperial ambitions have become more naked and ruthless the myths and deceits shrouding them seem more attractive to former leftists like Hitchens, the neocons, and other assorted intellectual defenders of Empire. The tendency has been to ignore the costs of such imperial ambitions: wide areas of death and destruction, economic and political collapse, ecological disaster, global blowback, growing international hatred of the United States, lopsided domestic priorities, a growing culture of violence. The barbarism of groups like al Qaeda is more than equaled by an arrogant and technologically awesome U.S. military, though none of this can be expected to deter intellectual apologists from eagerly looking forward to the next "regime change" and next monster slaying as a new chapter in the history of world democracy.

SECURITY STATE AND AUTHORITARIAN POLITICS

The postwar solidification and growth of the permanent war economy has contributed to an increasingly authoritarian political culture and institutions, especially visible since 9/11. Warfare and preparation for war by their very nature require subordination to norms of patriotism, loyalty, discipline, and violence within the governing system. For the United States, however, with its firmly established military-industrial complex, the ideological effects have been deeper, more long-term; they reflect a transformation of popular consciousness cutting across regional, class, racial, gender, and age divisions within American society. The military impulse, reaching far beyond the confines of the Pentagon, is fueled by the national drive for vital resources, the cult of technology, patriotism, and a sense of imperial supremacy. It might be argued that escalating levels of military production, deployment, and intervention serve as a relegitimation agency at a time when globalization and domestic economic problems aggravate dysfunctions within the corporate-state system. Left to expand the way that it has in the United States, militarism could well lead to a quasi-fascist ideology characterized by superpatriotism, imperial chauvinism, racism, and the glorification of violence—all well-known responses by elites and other groups within a society undergoing rapid change and great stress. Where power is more centralized, it penetrates new areas of economic, social, and personal life as the governing apparatus becomes more integrated within the political culture. A convergence of economic, political, and military rule, anticipated by C. Wright Mills but going far beyond what he observed during his time, constitutes the basis of the U.S. national-security state.

The war economy thrives on foreign threats, real or contrived, to American national interests that are essentially marketed to the public as a menace to the very security and survival of ordinary citizens. Since World War II a series of "threats" to U.S. security have justified not only massive deployment of military force but its expansion across many different areas of the world. In this context a heightened readiness for armed intervention—and the recurrent *actuality* of intervention—favor an elite impulse toward military ventures, bureaucratic routine, technological efficiency, and patriotic mobilization. Superiority in military strength readily equates in the elite mind with moral supremacy, further adding to xenophobic and chauvinistic sentiments—a linkage starkly visible at the time of the two Gulf Wars. Within this matrix state power easily develops into an object of (elite) deification, the very embodiment of ethical national goals, following a trajectory outside the scope of democratic processes. During both Gulf Wars, war making by and through the security state provided an aura of monolithic unity where doubts, ambiguities, and reservations were concealed or suppressed, if only temporarily. In the euphoria of war the public can find strength in the exercise of brutal military force, transferring loyalties and aspirations onto the terrain of state power and thereby helping to sustain the Leviathan.

The security state relies on a highly rationalized system of bureaucratic and coercive functions: military, law enforcement, surveillance, an enormous security apparatus. Historically the rationale for this system was furnished by Communism and the Soviet Union, but with the end of the cold war the focus shifted toward global terrorism and rogue states. Public support for authoritarian measures has always been relatively easy to galvanize in the face of menacing enemies, and this was no less true for Bush in the wake of 9/11, when both patriotism and fear of external threats reached their highest levels since World War II. In his 2002 State of the Union address Bush proposed a military budget of nearly $400 billion, including requests for new high-tech weaponry, mobile antiterrorist units, and space militarization—not to mention bulked-up spending for intelligence and homeland security—all of which passed with little debate. If terrorist operations were intended to destabilize the system, as dictated by the "strategy of tension," their impact on the American power structure turned out to be just the opposite: the political system actually gained new legitimacy in the face of mounting domestic and global crises, while the security apparatus gained new license to expand. In part this was the result of "wartime" mobilization which fed into a series of planned responses that won quick approval: strong initiatives to bolster military, surveillance, intelligence, and law enforcement capabilities. It was also facilitated by the rapid growth of new technologies, such as space-based surveillance and tracking, championed by the Pentagon, the space establishment, and the National Security Agency.

If the American economy suffered an initial staggering blow from 9/11, the main authoritarian levers of state power—the military, intelligence, and law enforcement—gained an unprecedented boost, the long-term consequences of which will take many years, perhaps decades, to fully grasp. A Homeland Security Office was set up in November 2001 to coordinate more than forty government agencies. Given what was expected to become a perpetual national state of alert, such agencies as the CIA, FBI, Immigration and Naturalization Service (INS), Internal Revenue Service (IRS), ATF, and NSA are sure to command far more resources and institutional reach, and thus greater control over people's lives.

The USA Patriot Act antiterror bill was passed by Congress in October 2001 by a vote of 337 to 79 in the House and 96 to 1 in the Senate, moved to resolution virtually without public input or congressional deliberation. Representative Barney Frank (D-Massachusetts) remarked that passage of this landmark legislation involved "the least democratic process for debating questions fundamental to democracy that I have ever seen." The 342-page act gave the federal government sweeping new powers to investigate and monitor electronic communications, personal and financial records, computer hard drives, and other individual documents. Wiretap authority was greatly broadened. Due process was suspended in many areas of the criminal justice system—for example, the right to a speedy trial, freedom from arbitrary police searches, prohibition against indefinite incarceration and incognito detentions. The act lays out an elastic definition of terrorism making it possible for law enforcement to crush ordinary acts of dissent and protest, threatening a range of basic constitutional rights of free speech and assembly at a time when the parameters of public discourse were already severely narrowed. At the outset this legislation had the effect of intimidating protesters in the bourgeoning antiglobalization movements that, owing to their anticorporate politics, could be linked in the dominant ethos to the jihadic destroyers of the World Trade Center. The war against terrorism took the United States into a new period of governmental controls and surveillance that readily feeds off an atmosphere of paranoia, fear, and insecurity, with enemies presumed to be lurking around every corner, not to mention those sixty-plus nations identified by Bush as havens of al Qaeda and other terrorist groups.

While long-term trends toward popular distrust in government might have been momentarily arrested in the aftermath of 9/11, by early 2002 the focus on citizenship and solidarity gave way to a mood of insecurity and despair, owing in part to the economic downturn, in part to the very mixed results of operations conducted against terrorism. Meanwhile, the elites' anticipated move to "revitalize" political institutions revolved mainly around the bureaucratic and *coercive* side of power—the Pentagon and security state. Authoritarian methods of rule were deemed necessary to secure domestic and global order, since, as Bush has intoned on several occasions, terrorist networks must be recognized as "heirs to fascism," and, as in World War II, the only way to fight such enemies must be through all-out military combat. As he puts it: "We're fighting against men without conscience but full of ambition to remake the world in their own brutal images. . . . They have the same will to power [as fascists], the same disdain for the individual, the same mad, global ambitions. . . . Like the fascists, the terrorists cannot be appeased; they must be defeated."[41] In his glib references to "remaking the world," Bush could more appropriately describing his own agenda, above all the drive to control and shape the New World Order by any means necessary—an agenda carved out by the neocons several years before 9/11.

The USA Patriot Act, building on Clinton's antiterrorist legislation of 1996, has much in common with earlier repressive measures: the Alien and Sedition Act, the post–World War I Palmer Raids, the Smith Act, the House Un-American Activities Committee, McCarthyism, and COINTELPRO of the Vietnam era. In the wake of 9/11, however, such authoritarian moves against social protest, unpopular views, and aliens were more easily cloaked behind appeals to patriotism, and they were more eagerly accepted. As Nancy Chang writes: "The Act stands as radical in the degree to which it sacrifices our political freedoms in the name of national security and consolidates new powers in the executive branch."[42] Everything in the act, above all its loose definition of terrorism, is so elastic as to be easily abused by an administration obsessed with law and order; abuse is made all the more likely, moreover, by the lack of judicial or congressional oversights. Citizens' rights to privacy are essentially gutted: section 213 of the act allows federal agents to conduct "sneak and peek searches"—covert investigations of a person's home or office—with no advance notices, while section 215 extends the Foreign Intelligence Surveillance Act of 1978, allowing easy seizure of people's books, tapes, and computer disks in connection with investigations of "international terrorism." Restraints on governmental surveillance were almost totally stripped away. According to section 216, federal agents can track all phases of Internet transactions, with few guidelines to keep them in check. All this amounts to nothing less than an outright abrogation of Fourth Amendment rights within an expanded security state permitting fewer mechanisms of appeal.

After 9/11 it became possible for the federal government to detain persons accused of a crime indefinitely, showing only probable cause; as of spring 2004 a few scores of such detainees remained incarcerated. Due process for noncitizens was jettisoned altogether. The FBI, INS, and local police unleashed a wave of investigations, aggravating the public mood of fear, paranoia, and intolerance, and encouraged citizens to report on the activities and beliefs of their neighbors and coworkers (a scheme that quickly failed). The patriotic mettle of individuals was challenged in the media, popular culture, political campaigns, and academia, with possible sanctions awaiting transgressors judged to be too soft on terrorism or too uncritical of al Qaeda or Saddam Hussein's Iraq. The list of "terrorist" organizations grew rapidly in the immediate aftermath of 9/11. The act, working through the Homeland Security Office, established a new labyrinthine system of databases to detect potential threats. Guilt by suspicion or association could be established for persons involved with, or donating to, any number of protest organizations that flourished during the antiwar mobilizations of 2002–2003. Many such organizations were infiltrated by police agents. The mere speculation that violence might be used in protest actions could be grounds for federal investigation. As Chang observes: "With the advent of electronic record-keeping, the FBI is likely to maintain far more dossiers on law-abiding individuals and to disseminate the dossiers far more widely than during the COINTELPRO era."[43] The consequences for reputations, jobs, and careers, not to mention personal freedom, would conceivably begin to match those of the McCarthy period. The events of 9/11 were seized on by the Bush administration as a pretext for expanding coercive governmental powers and restricting the ability of the press, the public, and legislatures to make the executive accountable for its heavy-handed actions.

By early 2002 the Bush administration had listed 153 groups as terrorist organizations to be monitored and investigated, greatly expanding Clinton's smaller list assembled in 1995 and 1996. People affiliated with such organizations, even remotely, can under the new laws be interrogated, arrested, deported, and have their assets frozen. Using the combined resources of the Departments of State, Treasury, Justice, and Defense, the federal government is now empowered to use its vast administrative power to fight terrorism, with groups and individuals targeted according to vague, arbitrary criteria, and protest movements rendered vulnerable to attack owing to their "violent" or "disruptive" character. Robert Dreyfuss comments: "Taken together, the lists have emerged as a handy tool to suppress dissent, dissuade Americans from backing insurgent movements overseas, and deport immigrants tied to the groups."[44] In early 2003 Attorney General John Ashcroft hired John Poindexter, convicted felon in the Iran-Contra scandal, to set up an Orwellian Total Information Awareness System, making it easier for government agencies to track suspects. Poindexter was charged with setting up databases for the Pentagon to create an intimate electronic portrait of every person in the United States. While the initial outcry against this scheme (and Poindexter's involvement) forced its abandonment, its planned functions are still likely to be dispersed among other scattered agencies and institutions, including above all the Pentagon.

Local criminal-justice agencies too have assumed a more powerful role in the security state, cooperating with the FBI, CIA, and INS, creating their own intelligence units and antiterrorist squads, and building community dossier systems that strongly reinforce the Patriot Act. Joint Terrorism Task Forces were set up and run by the FBI, operating out of war room–like antiterrorism centers. The task forces were permitted to scrutinize a vast range of personal documents and were even allowed to seize records of bookstores and libraries to find out what people were reading. In the aftermath of 9/11 large-scale antiterrorist mobilization seemed natural and rational enough, but its deeper impact could be to augment an already gargantuan national-security state—all the more so as the war on terrorism continues over a period of many years or decades.

One of the most alarming trends since the 1990s is the deepening involvement of the military in the criminal-justice system, again pushed further along by 9/11. Most significant is the Pentagon's role in high-tech surveillance, as well as its increasing contribution to drug and immigration enforcement along the United States–Mexico border. Indeed the long-standing war on drugs figures centrally in these trends, stemming from that moment in the early 1980s when President Reagan identified crime and drugs as twin evils and portrayed their elimination as a major cornerstone in the defense of national security. Like terrorism, Communism, and other designated evils, drugs (though always mainly a domestic issue) were seen as a *foreign* scourge; interdiction became essentially a military priority. The result was that the armed forces and the criminal-justice system began to work in tandem as agencies not only of law enforcement but of ideological and social control—an underlying thrust of the war on drugs from the outset. Local police paramilitary units (PPUs), modeled after the Navy SEALS, carried out thousands of drug raids yearly and then gradually broadened their range to include the war against terrorism. By 2002 all major American cities had PPUs that conducted extensive surveillance, made thousands of arrests, and engaged in regular shootouts with criminal suspects. While the Pentagon welcomed this development as an opportunity to expand its power and promote its military ideology, local law enforcement came to accept (if reluctantly) the federal intrusion onto its terrain as a step toward greater efficiency. Among other things, this development signaled a precipitous erosion of the famous Posse Comitatus Act of 1878 outlawing collusion of the military and domestic police operations.

The new circumstances likewise favored reinvigoration of the intelligence apparatus, its reputation grossly weakened throughout the 1990s and its competence severely questioned after the terrorist attacks. Whatever their previous failings, the FBI, CIA, INS, ATF, NSA, and other surveillance organizations now became more deeply embedded in domestic life, largely under the guise of protecting homeland security. In fact the Homeland Security Office was established to coordinate the work of intelligence and law-enforcement groups, but clearly not all of them. Not only were the Pentagon and criminal justice agencies more integrated, so too were the international and domestic realms of intelligence. Whatever its institutional and operational inadequacies, the power of surveillance at the disposal of U.S. intelligence and law enforcement cannot be overstated. The NSA alone, with its nearly two hundred million computers, processes tens of millions of communications items literally every hour—by far the largest processor of information in the world. Billions of dollars are spent to encircle the world with thousands of miles of fiber-optic cable, rendering those frightening Orwellian scenes from *Enemy of the State* already obsolete. The NSA possesses sixty-eight separate e-mail systems and is constantly rationalizing its massive supercomputer facility geared to the most sophisticated eavesdropping. With its more than seventy-five acres of floorspace, the agency is poised to share information with any military or law enforcement agency, stationed anywhere in the world, as part of its National Security Operations Center (NSOC), set up after 9/11.

The unprecedented growth of intelligence technology, of course, does not guarantee high levels of efficiency or desired results. Politicized to the maximum, agencies like the FBI, CIA, and NSA have often turned out to be domains more of institutional control, with their own ideological agendas, than of measures to secure public safety. In the first place, elaborate technology does not in itself furnish a deep understanding, or useful contextualization, of the massive amounts of information received daily; more likely it ushers forth an endless glut of data that in the end obscures more than it reveals. Within the highly computerized intelligence empire it has actually become humanly impossible to keep pace with the remarkable flood of information—at least in a way that permits human beings to carry out the kind of in-depth analysis needed for coherent, rapid political response. Secondly, political elites operate according to ideological biases that routinely subvert clear paths to decision making: data is often ignored, denied, suppressed, or simply ridiculed when it conflicts with specific agendas and priorities, or it can be exaggerated when it fits those agendas and priorities. One flagrant instance of such high-tech informational limits was the NSA's woeful performance in the war on terrorism. Despite the agency's unlimited access to electronic intercepts, its managers turned out to be surprisingly clueless about long-term plans by al Qaeda for major terrorist operations against the United States—a failure that extended to the CIA, FBI, and other agencies leading up to 9/11. As James Bamford observes: "In the days leading up to the September 11 attacks, a great deal of planning took place right under NSA's giant ear, in the agency's bedroom community of Laurel."[45] If the war against terrorism gave the NSA a new mission and increased resources, it would not necessarily endow surveillance and intelligence functions with greater capabilities. Bamford adds: "But despite the valiant human effort and the billions of dollars spent on high-flying hardware and super-complex software, for at least two years before the attacks, the NSA had no idea where Osama bin Laden and his key associates were—or even if they were still in Afghanistan."[46] As for the second problem with U.S. intelligence, a recent telling case in point was the Bush administration's stubborn decision to ignore or distort CIA information that conflicted with its drive toward war on Iraq, a stratagem set in motion already in the days following 9/11. It has become clear that CIA reports debunked the idea of Iraqi connections with al Qaeda, while agency director George Tenet (in late 2002) wrote a letter to members of Congress stating that Iraq posed no threat to U.S. security interests. (Two years later, none of these claims by Bush have been proven.) Dismayed by such reports, the war makers bombarded the CIA with harsh criticisms, insisting on some form of incriminating evidence to justify their obsessive push for invasion of Iraq. One senior Bush official was quoted as saying that CIA briefers "are constantly sent back by the senior people at Defense and other places to get more, get more, get more to make their case."[47] Such willful manipulation of data, though consistent with familiar patterns, adds still another disturbing element to power machinations within the security-state apparatus.

The extension of homeland security institutions and measures across the United States signals a blurring of lines dividing military and law enforcement functions, with the military now operating more aggressively on the home front under cover of the war on terrorism. The Posse Comitatus Act of 1878 had long prohibited the military from getting involved with domestic law enforcement, but that was informally overturned after 9/11, with precedents having bet set already in the 1990s. Many local police forces have been militarized, with sophisticated command centers set up along with tightening links between the Pentagon and intelligence agencies. As surveillance powers were broadened under the USA Patriot Act, the CIA, NSA, and other bodies historically concerned with international operations wound up more deeply involved in domestic security, given the historical (and likely future) presence of terrorist groups on U.S. territory. Collaboration among multiple levels of law enforcement, the intelligence agencies, and the Pentagon was heightened. Such developments were already visible with the war on drugs and were given a boost by President Clinton in his 1996 antiterrorist legislation, but were taken to new levels in the post-9/11 emergency situation.

This militarization of law enforcement coincides with strenuous efforts by the Bush presidency to extend its scope of power beyond conventional limits set by law and custom, beyond the reach of Congress and the courts. Arguing that the terrorist threat places the United States in conditions akin to a state of war, Bush moved to apply the rules of armed combat to people apprehended as suspects in the war on terrorism, meaning that anyone could be detained without charges, incarcerated indefinitely without due process, and could otherwise be denied rights that would normally apply within the criminal justice system. Suspects could be brought before specially constituted military tribunals where, again, ordinary legal rights would be suspended. The laws of warfare remain vague enough to be given the harshest interpretations—for example, allowing a suspect to be abducted from a foreign country or a detainee to be summarily killed. Consistent with his leadership style, Bush has pushed for unfettered presidential power, as commander in chief, to cope with a state of emergency, that would if realized essentially obliterate the long American tradition of checks and balances. According to Steven Shapiro, national legal director for the American Civil Liberties Union, "this president has taken an aggressive and extreme view of his power to act unilaterally without congressional or judicial review. They [Bush's supporters] have imposed maximum secrecy whenever possible, and they have asserted their actions are unreviewable by the courts."[48] However, two federal court challenges in late 2003 ruled against Bush, stating he had overstepped his authority. At the same time a federal judge admonished Attorney General John Ashcroft for misconduct in the government's courtroom handling of terrorist cases. By spring 2004 the stage was set for a clash between the Bush administration and the Supreme Court on the scope of presidential power, with at least five cases scheduled for deliberation. The outcomes of these cases will go far in determining the extent to which the security state will be able to further consolidate its already unassailable powers.

The shrinking political realm, potentially devastating to the future of American democracy, is a product of several convergent trends: economic globalization, the growth of domestic corporate power, the increased sophistication of high-tech surveillance and control, the war on terrorism, the expanding Pentagon system. By the start of the new century the political culture was hardly consonant with democratic practices and values, with citizenship degraded and popular involvement in decision making diminished—nowhere more so than in the crucial sphere of foreign and military policy. The decline of the public sphere is starkly visible in the mass media, political system, popular culture, and workplace. After 9/11, and especially with the invasion and occupation of Iraq (itself decided by a small authoritarian clique), the gulf between the centers of power in Washington and New York and the general population has widened perhaps further than ever. In this milieu it was possible for a small nucleus of neocons with vastly disproportionate influence in the media and politics, harboring jingoistic, wildly imperial delusions not long ago regarded as outlandish, to shape global policy with little concern for domestic or international repercussions. Even more frightening, we have reached a point where the most dangerous military-industrial complex in history has to confront surprisingly few restraints on its hell-bent quest for world domination.

4

THE CULTURE OF MILITARISM

The phenomenon of war and war making in the United States reflects a developmental pattern grounded in a deepening culture of militarism, increasingly visible since the early 1980s. It may not be too far-fetched to suggest that, beneath the "civilized" or "enlightened" norms of democratic society and modernity, one can detect a legacy of both domestic and global violence associated, at times, with outright militarism and barbarism. This was certainly the powerful message of Michael Moore's Oscar-winning 2002 documentary *Bowling for Columbine,* which established an intimate linkage between regularized outbreaks of violence in everyday American life and continuous U.S. armed interventions around the world since World War II. A long history of aggressive militarism—typically carried out in the name of grandiose ideals—has been made possible not only through the workings of the political system and economy but through the legitimating mechanisms of culture understood in its broadest sense. This encompasses a syndrome of beliefs, attitudes, and myths running through the mass media, popular culture, educational structures, the workplace, family life, and community life, a syndrome gaining more currency (as of 2004) while the United States accelerates its drive toward world domination. Militarism is integral to a Manichaeistic view of reality in which the forces of light and goodness are destined to confront evildoers wherever they lurk, with the United States (by definition) representing the forces of light and goodness on a global scale.

The evolution of a permanent war system reveals just how deeply-ingrained and multifaceted the military realm has become, involving the systems of production, consumption, work, communications, politics—and inevitably culture. The Pentagon labyrinth has established firm roots in historical and cultural patterns going back to the first Indian wars of conquest. If the United States does not yet qualify as a "warrior society" at the level of Sparta, ancient Rome, Nazi Germany, or even contemporary Israel, its militarism is surely just as pervasive, likely even more so, owing to the unique international scope of American power. While few Americans strongly identify with their country's outright pursuit of armed conquest, invasion of foreign countries, and Empire, the vast majority do remain intensely patriotic, easily seduced by ideological justifications for continued U.S. military adventures abroad. Indeed for many decades the United States has been a kind of fortress order sustaining popular beliefs around expansionary goals: patriotism, national chauvinism, rights of intervention and control of resources, the use of massive armed violence in the service of political ends. Never in history has a culture and ideology of militarism been so far-reaching, so sophisticated and yet so illusory, dependent on appealing myths.

The second Gulf War demonstrated, like Desert Storm before it, the extent to which a rabid patriotic mobilization has a deep presence in the American mass psychology—in popular fears, needs, aspirations, and prejudices. The ordinary person encounters a seemingly monolithic wall of militaristic myths, lies, distortions, and celebrations that would be tempting to attribute to the propaganda apparatus alone, but which goes far beyond the discrete functions of the media and political system in manufacturing consent, vital as that is. Spectacular celebrations of war, violence, conquest, and triumph have a profoundly cathartic, empowering dimension rooted in discourses of patriotism, American exceptionalism, and racism in the midst of a society priding itself on its special enlightenment, its wondrous educational and technological achievements, its sophisticated civic culture. While systematically ignored throughout the intellectual and academic culture, militarism has in reality become fully integrated into the vast framework of ideological hegemony, crucial to the reproduction of corporate and imperial domination.

PATRIOTISM AS SECULAR RELIGION

The military web of institutions and belief systems in American society demands a simple, yet highly romanticized, image of the national interest and mission, a patriotic ideology strong enough to call forth heroism, conquest, and armed missions in faraway places. Seen in this light, probably no country in the world is more intensely patriotic than the United States, where the mass media, the educational system, culture, and politics converge to generate pervasive hegemonic ideals. As Mary Wertsch writes: "In the theatrical world of the warrior society, where costumed actors rehearse their movements and their lines, patriotism is in the atmosphere of every set."[1] Doctrines of Manifest Destiny and the American Century were organically tied to such notions, justifying the early colonial push westward and then (beginning around 1900) outward toward Asia and Latin America. Patriotism reached its zenith during the "good war" against Nazi Germany and Japan, and sunk to its low point during and after the Vietnam War. This low point was followed by a resurgence during the two Gulf Wars, when national military pride became a media spectacle. By 2003 patriotic mobilization, though naturally uneven across the population, seemed commensurate with a nation bent on uncontested global supremacy.

In upholding war making as a noble, heroic calling, patriotism serves to rationalize the horrors and costs of military action: death, destruction, the uprooting of local populations, environmental chaos, the very threat of planetary extinction. The ideology of warfare justifies, even celebrates, moral atrocities such as the saturation bombing of civilian areas or the use of terrible weapons that might ordinarily be met with scornful outrage. The pursuit of national interest is invoked to legitimate the atomic leveling of Hiroshima and Nagasaki, harsh economic sanctions and blockades directed at civilian populations, the torture of prisoners, scorched-earth policies, and occupation of distant nations. Patriotism furnishes a convenient framework defining common objectives, shared fears and dangers, agreed-on enemies. Barbara Ehrenreich refers to the "sacralization of war," where patriotism takes on the character of a "civil religion" endowing large populations with a sense of loyalty, solidarity, commitment, and empowerment.[2] As both the ends and means of war become sacred, enemies are readily demonized while mass killing is all too often turned into a heroic obligation.

The national identity of Americans has been shaped by a long history of militarism sustained by a complex variety of experiences, attitudes, beliefs, and myths. From the outset patriotism converged with militarism, both having deep foundations in the early revolutionary and settler periods and continuing through the twentieth century. As Ward Churchill observes: "Racially oriented invasion, conquest, genocide and subsequent denial are all integral, constantly recurring and thus defining features of the Euroamerican makeup from the instant the first boat load of self-ordained colonists set foot in the 'New World.'"[3] The legacy of colonization tied to military conquest has been reproduced endlessly in literature, art, music, film, TV, and ultimately within the daily lives of ordinary citizens; this is no strictly elite phenomenon, but resides within the larger collective national psyche. Chris Hedges writes that this pattern of war making amounts to a powerful drug peddled not only by business leaders and politicians but by writers, journalists, filmmakers, and others within the popular culture: "It dominates culture, distorts memory, corrupts language, and infects everything around it."[4] Tied to patriotism and militarism, the idea of war has given Americans a large ensemble of psychological impulses: sense of purpose, adventure, heroism, nobility, superiority. War making permits, indeed encourages, the depiction of other nations and cultures as alien, primitive, uncivilized, barbaric—eligible to be attacked, conquered, even exterminated—framed by a self-conception that is noble and benevolent.

Patriotism is usually taken as a higher value, a source of obvious political truths, yet as a mass belief system it typically embellishes the worst of human impulses, legitimating ethnocentrism, racism, and violence while sanctioning any variety of atrocities and war crimes. It offers a simplistic, anti-intellectual, parochial view of a world reduced largely to "us" and "them," friend and enemy, allies and demons, liberators and terrorists. It lifts popular spirits, especially during wartime, by furnishing a sense of collective empowerment that, however, is neither genuinely *empowering* nor very durable. It inspires and glorifies warfare as a virtuous human activity, rationalizing conduct that, as Hedges writes, "breaks down long-established prohibitions against violence, destruction, and murder."[5] In the United States this syndrome has become more pronounced over time, as deeply ingrained patriotism serves to mobilize popular support for the Pentagon system, military priorities, and pursuit of global economic, political, and armed power. Here the Gulf wars represent something of a turning point, helping rekindle American patriotism linked to armed adventures, the glorification of weapons technology, and the celebration of war as media spectacle. War, and especially *triumphant* war, amounts to the ultimate national catharsis, a form of ideological hegemony appropriate to U.S. global military domination.

The impact of the military on American political culture thus turns out to be just the opposite of its benign representation in the high-school textbooks. Military action that stimulates mass xenophobia not only legitimates the war economy itself but protects elite domination by deflecting attention away from urgent domestic issues. This works most effectively where military campaigns are waged against a well-defined diabolical enemy (Noriega, Milosevic, Hussein), are dramatically and quickly successful, and result in minimum (U.S.) casualties—as in the first Gulf war and the Balkans. We know that warfare by its nature requires popular subordination to norms of patriotism, loyalty, and obedience, but for the United States, with its entrenched war system, the ideological consequences are more profound and long-term than elsewhere, having transformed crucial elements of popular consciousness and culture. Hence the widespread jingoism (stirred up by the media), the ease with which a majority of Americans can be mobilized behind military intervention, the willingness of so many (up to 45 percent during Desert Storm) to consider the use of nuclear weapons against a designated enemy, the often callous indifference toward foreign casualties, the public celebrations of armed violence. While such attitudes can be attributed to the power of media and governmental manipulation, in reality they have a strong resonance with the popular culture and national psyche. Both Gulf wars, for example, reveal a virulent nativism embedded in a mass psychology that demonizes Arabs and Muslims. The conclusion of the first Gulf War brought Bush senior a resounding 91 percent approval rating, not quite reached by Bush junior in 2003, when military triumph produced a 73 percent approval rating. It seems that the mass public was prepared to believe any lie or myth spun by politicians and the media, allowing war makers greater flexibility.

American nationalism has always been informed by a messianic belief in national destiny merged with notions of historical progress—a sense that people can have mastery over the course of events, a certitude about national supremacy and its entitlements, a unique civilizing mission. Here we have an ideology, simultaneously elite and mass, embracing American exceptionalism, religious fervor, and elements of racism mixed, inevitably, with the idea of attaining virtue through military action. No U.S. president epitomized these values more than Theodore Roosevelt, with his fervent belief in Manifest Destiny and its colonizing agenda. Bush II fits perfectly within this trajectory, upholding the concept of a uniquely American crusade to establish global hegemony ostensibly to rid the world of evil. For Bush and his small circle of neocon ideologues, military power and imperial expansion become the lever of renewed fundamentalist, messianic goals, a recycling of the "white man's burden" where religious and humanitarian ideals help crystallize and legitimate the struggle for domination. In January 2003 Bush said: "We'll do everything we can to remind people that we've never been a nation of conquerors; we're a nation of liberators." It follows that such "liberation," as previously experienced by the Indian nations, the Vietnamese, Panamanians, or Iraqis, would have to be carried out by American noblesse oblige, through the barrel of a gun.

From all we can glean from Bush's personal background and outlook, what emerges is a fierce patriotism long associated with Christian evangelical notions of "good" triumphing over "evil," U.S. global ambitions being endowed with the blessings of a higher power. Empire, though scarcely acknowledged as such, is the manifestation of God's will, justified as religious imperative. Where monstrous evils must be extirpated by any means, where biblically inspired apocalyptic visions of the future are embellished with great fervor, reliance on military force cannot be far from sight. For the second Bush presidency, therefore, the United States possesses not only the right but the *obligation* to remake the world in its own image—a sentiment reflected in the president's bizarre contention (in early 2003) that it would be immoral for the United States *not* to attack Iraq. Herein lies a unique convergence of ideological tenets guiding U.S. foreign and military policy at the start of the twenty-first century: religious fundamentalism, sense of national exceptionalism, patriotism, militarism. While it has been argued that a small nucleus of neoconservative "defense intellectuals" were able to "hijack" American politics after Bush II's ascension to power, in fact the values they represent and the policies they advocate have strong resonance across U.S. history, shown by the strong bipartisan support for the invasion of Iraq. The agenda is roughly the same—the main difference being how aggressively it is pursued. Here Bush has not really deviated from well-established imperial priorities, as can be seen from a reading of Bob Woodward's *Bush at War*.

The two Gulf Wars galvanized patriotic feelings on a scale rarely seen in previous U.S. history, owing in part to the jingoistic influence of mass media, in part to efforts to purge the Vietnam syndrome, in part to the wonders of technowar and its glorification. Seemingly new departures in foreign policy made war fashionable again, indulging the popular attraction to spectacles, games, heroic victories, and technological gimmickry. Outpourings of patriotism come with quick military conquests of weak, yet easily demonized, targets. For a populace conditioned by media culture, war is easily reduced to *images* of combat violence that saturate people's living rooms, where they remain at a safe, passive, sanitized distance from the immediate horrors of warfare. Political and ethical concerns are jettisoned from view, leaving people in a state of catharsis linked to the spectacle of military triumph, the destruction of a dreaded enemy. As Hedges writes: "We dismantle our moral universe to serve the cause of war."[6] Media *representations* of armed intervention help aestheticize acts of human violence to an extent rarely known throughout human history. The aftermath of war brings not horror, shame, and forgiveness but rather the *celebration* of war itself, now commodified and glamorized. Thus following the second Gulf War vast merchandizing operations came to the fore to take advantage of the (momentary) triumphal euphoria: on eBay alone it was possible to buy three thousand war-related items, including Iraqi coins and bills, Hussein condoms and puppets, wristwatches, terrorist body bags, wacky T-shirts, talking military dolls, Iraqi most-wanted playing cards, and special flavors of Iraqi ice cream.

For the United States as unchallenged world hegemon, patriotism and militarism help ideologically underwrite global strategic ambitions. The narrative of military adventure and conquest—usually denied or obscured in the official discourse—winds up fixated on a particular target (terrorists, Arabs, Muslims) that can be defined as irrationally hostile to the West, modernity, and democracy. It follows that American patriotism is tightly interwoven with the presumed civilizing process itself, a bulwark against brigands, criminals, outlaws, gangsters, and terrorists, indeed against the whole legacy of irrationality and barbarism. And the logic of this connection seems absolutely overpowering: the stronger the armed power of the state, the stronger must be the patriotism, which legitimates virtually any U.S. military intervention regardless of its distance from American shores. American patriotism at the start of the twenty-first century, internalized by the vast majority of the population, is the belief system of a chosen nation—a nation that is to carry out its peculiar historical destiny by means of economic, political, cultural, and military power.

GUN CULTURE AND CIVIC VIOLENCE

Owing in great measure to its long history of imperialism and militarism, to its endless fascination with guns and combat, the United States had by the 1980s easily become the major hub of global violence: repeated armed interventions abroad found their domestic parallel in the world's largest prison system, an epidemic of civic violence, an out-of-control gun culture, homebred terrorism, gang warfare, militias spread around the country, domestic violence, spontaneous outbursts of youth violence like the one at Columbine High School in Colorado, a mass media saturated with images of violence and bloodshed. While such a culture of violence was not new, its expanding scope and its increasingly transparent connection with the military-industrial complex were. The close linkage between military and civilian forms of violence is the outgrowth of the role the Pentagon has come to play in so many areas of politics, the economy, culture, media, and everyday life. If governmental and military elites appear as regular purveyors of death and destruction worldwide, then an ethos of violence can be expected to develop locally, within civil society, as ordinary people follow the lessons taught by the power structure. As a government-supported mode of violence, militarism brings with it a definite form of *legitimation*, one of the consequences of which is that added impetus is given to individual and small-group violence. Such violence results not only from a deeply militarized foreign policy but from a social order steeped in gross social inequality, anomie, fragmentation, and powerlessness, and in which politics has lost its capacity to inspire or mobilize people, to get them involved as civic participants.

At the turn of the new century the United States was clearly the most violent of nations, even as its political leaders customarily stressed high-sounding themes: peace, human rights, civic culture, law and order. This shameful condition grew out of a strong convergence of trends—global and domestic, military and civilian, national and local. And a culture nurtured on violence, on the resort to weapons and guns in solving conflicts, seems to require increasingly heavier doses of the medicine, as the 2003 war on Iraq once again confirmed. It could be that this culture has in some fashion become addicted to war, as the title of one book on U.S. militarism suggests.[7]

As Richard Rhodes argues, civic violence is typically rooted in human experiences that desensitize people to suffering, pain, and death—harsh economic realities, media images, personal encounters, prolonged exposure to war and/or civil insurrection. Foremost among personal encounters is military training and service, designed to induce transformative individual changes that make killing more psychologically and ethically permissible, while even romanticizing and glorifying it. Combat experience in particular tends to strip away social and moral constraints historically related to violence and killing.[8] Acts producing death and destruction need not always be a function of direct combat, of course, especially in the age of technowar, when the military is more likely to produce its deadly effects from a safe distance, its process more detached, impersonal, clinical. The point is that military training instills in recruits a preparedness to kill with few questions asked. This logic of psychological conversion, according to Rhodes, has shaped the lives of tens of millions of Americans whose return to the civilian world carries with it the fruits of that conversion. Those who served in Vietnam, Korea, and the two Gulf Wars were no doubt uniquely and permanently transformed by such brutalizing experiences. One result is that the distance between combat violence and everyday criminality in the United States has been narrowed considerably, as the military ethos spills over into civic life in myriad ways.[9]

Rhodes speaks of "unmitigated violent phantom communities" that, to varying degrees, support all manner of brutal activities or at least desensitize people to such activities. Indifference toward suffering and pain is a product of military socialization and is reinforced by harshly violent messages contained in the mass media and popular culture. Combat experiences, moreover, usually engender feelings of anger, revenge, frustration, and cruelty that reproduce codes of violent conflict elsewhere, including militias, cults, gangs, murders, domestic assaults, and terrorism. Many veterans of the military returned to civilian life intoxicated by images of armed combat, as shown dramatically in the case of Oklahoma City bomber Timothy McVeigh. More generally, it seems that the more violence characterizes individual or group experiences, the more that individual or group is prepared to engage in further violent acts—a phenomenon that applies equally to those whose lives appear quite normal, replete with comfortable jobs and homes, families, and strong religious ties.[10] Beneath the surface of a militarized society can be found a wide range of dark impulses capable of producing the most terrible deeds, which, though visible in any culture, have uniquely pervaded the American landscape.

A major phenomenon associated with civic violence is what might be called "reactionary populism," first noticeable on a large scale in the mid-1980s in the form of a bizarre variety of cults, sects, militias, and enclave groups. Attractive to the familiar "angry white male," reactionary populism is a diffuse ideology embracing diverse impulses: gun culture, xenophobia, conspiracy thinking, nativism, Christian fundamentalism, racism. It is fueled by many of the same conditions that gave rise to historical Fascism such as joblessness, fear of change, hostility to social movements, and alienation from politics. With the decline of the two-party system and the stranglehold the corporations have on the government, many local groups came to view politicians and officials as corrupt, untrustworthy, incompetent, remote from immediate social problems, and indifferent to the ordinary person's needs. Inevitably, violent confrontations erupted between local groups and the state—the FBI assault at Ruby Ridge, the Waco standoff and massacre at the Branch Davidian compound, the Oklahoma City bombing, the lengthy holdout of the Montana Freemen, the Amtrak train derailment in Arizona, and hundreds of lesser episodes involving angry public encounters, shootouts, and bombings. Federal agents were frequent victims of threats, acts of intimidation, and verbal attacks. Reactionary populism of this sort went into decline by the late 1990s, hastened along by the impact of 9/11, but given its deep roots in U.S. history and the persistence of conditions that foster such local mobilization, the eclipse could well be temporary.

The paramilitary groups carry forward a long-standing American tradition of disenfranchised people fighting for identity, recognition, and local control against distant, impersonal, elite interests. Most see themselves as bearers of renewed citizenship to be won with great difficulty in a harsh, threatening world. Their obsession with conspiracies, with mysterious schemes and plots, and their glorification of gun culture often draws them into a zone of domestic terrorism. The militias' hostility to state power, officialdom, and international agencies is visceral, going beyond the targeting of specific officeholders and politicians, beyond any simple hostility toward bureaucracy. Their grassroots impulses are compromised, however, by a sometimes virulent racism, a staunch social conservatism, an intensely parochial defense of turf not too different from that of gang culture, and a superpatriotism. They rarely energize people toward any positive, transformative ideals, dwelling instead on fear of disruption, material insecurity, and the scapegoating of minorities, immigrants, gays, and others defined as outsiders, often leading to a kind of Rambo syndrome—a macho revolt against elites in the vein of the outlaw hero and the frontier ethos of rugged individualism.

The importance for the militias of a weapons subculture, of preparation for armed combat, based on the idea of everyday people locked in a struggle against mortal enemies, can hardly be stressed enough: they are simply taking to extremes the worship of guns and violence already embedded in postwar American social life. In the year 2000 there were an estimated 240 million guns in civilian hands across the country, including several million combat-grade weapons owned by people roaming freely across the rural and urban terrain. The hard-fought and well-financed lobbying campaigns and propaganda efforts of the National Rifle Association have done much to legitimate and solidify this gun culture. Add the influence of a mass media and popular culture saturated with images of violence, along with a turbulent civil society that feeds a multiplicity of angry, paranoid responses, and the resonance of messages predicting apocalyptic warfare involving ordinary citizens (as in Larry Pratt's *Armed People Victorious*) becomes fathomable.

As William Gibson observes in *Warrior Dreams,* guns and violence have been a distinctly male obsession in the United States at least since the Vietnam War.[11] The weapons fetish has spread rapidly across regional, class, and ethnic lines; more than five million assault rifles alone were purchased between 1980 and 2000. Various expressions of male violence have been on the upswing since the 1960s, from street crime to domestic violence to serial murders and terrorism. Hollywood films devoting macabre attention to mass killings—and just regular everyday mayhem—like *Silence of the Lambs, Reservoir Dogs, Pulp Fiction, Natural Born Killers, Very Bad Things, XXX*, and the *Terminator* episodes have become objects of cult fascination. The immense popularity of TV coverage of the two Gulf Wars is well known. Reflecting on the origins of this trend, Gibson points to the emergence of a "new warrior hero" in American society that mirrors a shifting masculine ethos, focused not only on soldiers and cops but on an everyday warrior life, where the disenfranchised take up arms, join quasi-military groups, and "prepare for heroic battle against the enemies of society."[12] So the modern male warrior, whether in the guise of the Montana Freemen, patriot organizations, gangs, skinheads, or even a hermetic figure like the Unabomber, becomes the archetype of the renegade hero who in earlier times tamed the frontier, robbed trains and banks, or simply took the law into his own hands to fight various alien intruders.

This search for a male warrior identity goes back to the Minutemen, frontier settlers, and foreign adventurers like Teddy Roosevelt's Roughriders; these groups attracted men looking to conquer the world, or at least hoping to defend their own turf, through the medium of armed combat. The male warrior identity runs through the myths and rituals of the mafia and organized crime, as well as urban street gangs. During the 1980s and 1990s it appealed more to young white men than to any other social category—to men feeling threatened by a heartless and encroaching urban world and often driven by feelings of racial superiority, sexism, male bonding, and ultrapatriotism. As Gibson notes: "American men—lacking confidence in the government and the economy, troubled by changing relations between the sexes, uncertain of their identity or their future—began to dream, to fantasize about the powers and features of another kind of man who could retake and reorder the world."[13] Here we witness a convergence of trends at both the elite and mass levels of American society.

Paramilitary culture was shaped in part by a national mood of defeat and pessimism stemming from the failed Vietnam War—a mood seemingly ameliorated by the euphoria of the first Gulf War. The Indochina debacle

was a great blow to the collective American psyche, the end to a long tradition of U.S. military victories; it eclipsed, at least momentarily, the national
sense of Manifest Destiny, of "progress" achieved by means of armed intervention abroad. U.S. military power was dramatically challenged and defeated, in one geographical locale and for one historical moment, creating
broad psychological disruptions leading to a "crisis of self-image" in the
general culture most disorienting for those in and around the military subculture. During a period of rapid, far-reaching change, including the impact
of feminism and erosion of traditional gender roles, a large percentage of
men felt driven to recapture the patriarchal ethos of an earlier time. Many
sought out images of violent power, which they found validated in diverse
arenas of popular culture: film, MTV, video games, comics, and so forth. But
for such drives to make sense, to have real credibility, they would have to
confront purported enemies: Communists, foreign terrorists, drug dealers,
illegal aliens, nebulous conspirators, even the federal government itself. In
this paranoid milieu the national predicament intersected with a variety of
identity crises and material hardships that seemed to cry out for direct
action.

As with cult organizations like the Branch Davidians, a conspiratorial
siege mentality came to typify right-wing extremists, who formed the backbone of rural groups such as militias, survivalists, the Aryan Nations, Christian Identity, the Order, and the Order-2, often based in Western areas like
Idaho, Utah, Montana, and eastern Washington. Richard Butler, long a fixture in the white supremacist Aryan Nations, set up an enclave of twenty
acres behind barbed-wire fences in northern Idaho where members could
meet, practice target shooting, and generally vent their rage at disparate
aliens, enemies, and conspirators. Butler's goal: a "10 percent solution" that
would save one-tenth of the United States as a "white homeland" while let-
ting the rest of the country rot in its corruption and decay. Funded partly
by Silicon Valley high-tech money, Butler and his followers rejected the
Klan and John Birch Society for being "too liberal"; by 2000 they had established close contacts with various neo-Nazi groups worldwide. Referring to the Bible as a "book of separation," displaying photos of Hitler, and
fascinated with both punk rock and German marching music, the Aryans
envisioned a protracted "war of freedom" involving armed combat and insurgency. The Aryans and kindred groups derive much of their inspiration
from survivalism, looking to refuge in the wilderness through tightly knit,
isolated communities wanting to preserve conventional lifestyles. The term
"survivalist" was first coined by Kurt Saxon in the early 1960s—referring
to people bonded together in remote areas, prepared to outlive cataclysmic
events such as nuclear war. By the 1990s survivalist ranks grew to tens of
thousands—mostly marginalized, poorly educated white males—and the
groups took on increased organizational and ideological coherence. Their

élan was boosted by the influence of neo-Nazi texts like William Pierce's *The Turner Diaries*.[14]

Already in the 1980s survivalists had merged with some militias and other right-wing populist forces, building on a milieu that included tax resisters, posse groups setting up their own political domains, religious fundamentalists, gun enthusiasts, and the ever-present cults. Within this violent subculture many adopted the veneer of military structures replete with uniforms, chains of command, ribbons and medals, large arms caches, shooting ranges, and the lingo of an armed outfit. Looking at their abundant literature and videotapes, some militia groups believed that "urban warfare" and "race war" were imminent, that American citizens were obligated to mobilize for the coming Armageddon—an outlook shared by more than a few gangs and cults. At the same time, militia partisans liked to carve out an image of simple folks just out for fun and games in the woods or desert. While many groups had disbanded by the late 1990s, hundreds remain, often adopting a lower profile at a time when the war on terrorism limits their room to maneuver.

The culture of violence extends to acts of domestic terrorism, which in the 1990s found fertile soil on the terrain of reactionary populism. Proto-fascist episodes of violence directed at public targets were frequent, the work of seemingly ordinary people taking some very ordinary American ideas (freedom, rugged individualism, patriotism, the right to bear arms) to fanatical extremes. Such actions have been, at least indirectly, encouraged by the gun lobby, media images, gang subcultures, generally high rates of violent crimes, the revitalized war economy, and plentiful examples of U.S. military intervention abroad. Local incidents of terrorism proliferated throughout the 1990s: according to the ATF, in the peak year 1993 there were almost 2,400 bombings across the nation, leading to 70 deaths and 1,375 injuries. Reportedly hundreds of other actions were intercepted by the FBI and police agencies. The heightened interest in bombs and guns, including sophisticated assault weapons, was fueled by mail-order companies that cater to paramilitary enthusiasts, not to mention what is available through the Internet, shortwave radio, fax systems, and talk-radio programs hosted by militia sympathizers. Aided by the Internet and alarmed by domestic and global threats, hate groups have multiplied since just the late 1990s. In 1998 observers from Klanwatch and the Militia Task Force documented an all-time high of 474 hate groups in the United States, an increase of 20 percent from 1996. The targeting of many groups of Arabs, Muslims, and immigrants was sharpened in the aftermath of 9/11, and the number of crimes directed against those minorities also multiplied. This orbit includes biblical doomsayers often inspired by violent rock lyrics; collectors of high-powered weapons; builders of chemical devices and bombs; architects of Internet websites that coordinate literally hundreds of reactionary groups.

Right-wing terrorism was of course responsible for the bombing of the Oklahoma City Federal Building in April 1994, but this bold attack was simply the tip of the iceberg; politically motivated violence became a durable element of the culture, though it virtually disappeared on the Left after the 1970s. Recurrent assaults on women's health clinics took place, along with increasing numbers of attacks directed against minorities, gays, Arabs, and Muslims. The violent mood has been nourished by a mounting sense of powerlessness in American society resulting from several factors: economic globalization, the growth of bureaucratic and corporate power, influence of media culture, and popular cynicism over the rather boring, meaningless character of normal politics. The violent mood is exacerbated by the spread of paranoid, conspiratorial beliefs that often come with fears of nebulous intruders or some kind of imminent apocalypse.[15] Paranoid obsession with black helicopters, alien creatures, drug cartels, and secret military missions—all seen as possible elements of a tyrannical new order—can be understood in this milieu. Such beliefs can produce a violent demonology, which, when combined with genuine fears of terrorist attacks, furnish a convenient substitute for familiar cold war images of the Communist devil.

Domestic terrorism is hardly synonymous with reactionary populism, but the ideological milieu established by the latter helped nourish the former. As noted above, thousands of politically motivated acts of violence were carried out in the United States during the 1990s, with no doubt thousands more intercepted before they could be launched. These figures dwarf anything attributed to al Qaeda, but this homegrown variety of terrorism received little media attention. At the time of the Oklahoma City bombing by Timothy McVeigh and his accomplices, militia groups were at their peak, with membership estimated to be as high as four million (including over four hundred thousand paramilitary activists). Just before the bombing former CIA director William Colby said:

> I watched as the anti-war movement rendered it impossible for this country to conduct or win the Vietnam war. . . . This militia and patriot movement is far more significant and far more dangerous for Americans than the anti-war movement ever was. . . . It is not because these people are armed that America need be concerned. They are dangerous because there are so many of them.[16]

According to standard reports, McVeigh was just a regular kid from a blue-collar family in upstate New York. He developed an intense love of guns at an early age, obtaining a .22-caliber rifle at age thirteen and a shotgun when he turned sixteen, at which time he began stockpiling food and large barrels of water in his basement. In 1986, upon graduating from high school, McVeigh and a friend bought several acres of property where they could camp out, wear army fatigues, build bombs, and carry out regular target practice. As Joel Dyer writes, during this period "McVeigh continued his survivalist behavior. He would camp out on the property at night and practice his shooting from sunup to sundown."[17] McVeigh joined the army in 1988, was quickly promoted to corporal and then sergeant, compiled an excellent overall record, and served in the first Gulf War, where he received battlefield commendations. He became an avid reader of survivalist and gun-related magazines and was fanatical about the right to bear arms, at one point complaining that the NRA had not taken a strong enough stand against gun control. He read the Christian Identity newsletter, *Patriot Report*, filled with antigovernment conspiracy theories, and then got hold of Pierce's *The Turner Diaries*, which, by several accounts, transformed his life. The Waco events in 1993, however, were the most traumatic: he saw the federal assault as a government-sponsored massacre, directed against the Second Amendment. He visited the Waco site on numerous occasions. Here McVeigh apparently turned to Pierce's novel, in which Earl Turner decides to fight back after the government passes antigun legislation. Turner blows up a federal building that houses the FBI with a fertilizer and fuel-oil bomb concealed in a truck—a scenario almost identical to that of the Oklahoma City bombing.[18]

In his correspondence with Gore Vidal, spanning three years, McVeigh justifies his actions as a necessary moral and political response to an authoritarian, oppressive, and militarized government that was waging war at home and abroad. He writes:

> For all intents and purposes, federal agents had become "soldiers" (using military training, tactics, techniques, equipment, language, dress, organization, and mindset) and they were escalating their behavior. Therefore, this bombing was also meant as a preemptive (or pro-active) strike against those forces and their command and control centers within the federal building. When an aggressor force continually launches attacks from a particular base of operations, it is sound military strategy to take the fight to the enemy.

He adds:

> Bombing the Murrah Federal Building was morally and strategically equivalent to the U.S. hitting a government building in Serbia, Iraq, or other nations. Based on observations of the policies of my own government, I viewed this action as an acceptable option. From this perspective what occurred in Oklahoma City was no different than what Americans rain on the heads of others all the time.[19]

Elsewhere in his correspondence McVeigh writes: "Our government is the potent, the omnipresent teacher. For good or ill it teaches the whole people by its example."[20] From this standpoint McVeigh's brand of terrorism can be seen as *doubly* the product of a militarized culture—a result of the gun craze and a government and military that encourages violence through its own actions.

Violence within the paramilitary milieu has parallels in sectors of youth culture, including gangs, skinheads, and other groups that rove across the urban, suburban, and rural landscapes. Often reactionary in ideology, the skinheads— in contrast to the militias and cults—have been more closely linked to the urban (and suburban) gang subcultures. Their origins go back to the Teddy Boys, a youth subculture that spawned the rival Mods and Rockers in England during the early 1960s. Skinheads came together around dispersed gangs of young males alienated from social convention, feeling hopeless about the future, and looking for scapegoats to attack as the presumed sources of their economic misery and social powerlessness. Their targets were mainly immigrants and racial minorities, symbols for them of a corrupt, oppressive, and threatening world. Skinheads first established a presence in the United States during the late 1970s, when they were associated with punk rock, "screwdriver music," episodic acts of violence, and gestures toward white supremacy. While not overtly ideological, they often adopted the rhetoric of a racist, sexist, xenophobic subculture bent on reproducing the division between initiates and outsiders, between (usually homogeneous) youth groups and stereotyped "others."[21] They frequently took on the symbolic paraphernalia of historical Fascism, adorning themselves with swastikas, German Eagle medals, and tattoos, listening to German marching music, celebrating Hitler's birthday, and so forth. Like many cults and militias, skinheads attracted youth from poor, marginalized, semieducated sectors, above all young males without strong roots in family or work— although their influence eventually spilled over into the suburban middle class. In a context where few good jobs and careers seemed available to young people, where family life had deteriorated as a source of cohesion and identity, and with politics viewed as a waste of time, skinheads epitomized the anomie and nihilism of youth in general. Much like cults and militias, violent youth-based groups furnish solidarity where it might otherwise be absent. By the end of the 1990s the skinheads (loosely defined) numbered probably no more than three thousand across some thirty-one states, mainly in the West, but their social impact was no doubt greater than such numbers suggest.

On April 20, 1999, possibly in commemoration of Hitler's birthday, two students at Columbine High School in Littleton, Colorado, went on a shooting rampage, killing twelve fellow students and a teacher before committing suicide. Michael Moore's documentary *Bowling for Columbine* depicts the suburban, middle-class environment where the students—Eric Harris and Dylan Klebold—lived and presumably were socialized into their violent youth subculture, such as it was. Both became attached to neo-Nazi ideas and symbols, listening to heavy-metal music, playing video games that celebrate violence and guns, and watching movies like Oliver Stone's *Natural Born Killers*. Both were former Boy Scouts but then in high school formed the "Trenchcoat Mafia," which focused its hatred on blacks, Latinos, Jews, and other minorities, and on the in-group of school elites. At a bowling class just before the killing spree, Klebold wore a T-shirt that read "Serial Killer," advertising a symbol that would soon achieve its bloody realization. In the film Moore visits the nearby Lockheed-Martin plant, which manufactures and sells a huge arsenal of high-powered missiles and other weapons of mass destruction, setting up a strong parallel between the two cultures of violence. It turns out that many students at Columbine High had parents working for Lockheed-Martin, carrying out their routine business in the midst of a seemingly peaceful suburban community.

If, as Rhodes argues, violence directed against human beings is in great measure rooted in people's exposure to certain brutalizing experiences and images, then we should hardly be surprised to find the United States—with the world's largest military machine and prison system, the most violence-saturated media, a fanatical gun cult, and a civil society permeated with criminal activity—to be the global leader in mass murders and serial killings, among other violent crimes. The episodes seem endless, many perpetrated by individuals who have military training and/or combat experience, or have done extensive jail time. Clearly, war and preparation for war thrives on an ethos that extends to the civilian population; the quick readiness of elites to use military action, or threaten such action, inevitably leaves its psychological imprint on the general population. It is no coincidence that a dramatic upswing in violent crimes occurred in the 1970s, coming on the heels of protracted U.S. warfare in Indochina, which destroyed three countries and killed at least three million people, including fifty-eight thousand American troops. Hundreds of thousands of veterans returned after exposure to the horrors of brutal war, with predictable consequences for everyday life in families, workplaces, and communities. We have already noted how both the Oklahoma City bombing and the Columbine shooting spree bear some relationship, directly or indirectly, to the deepening culture of militarism. As for serial killings, they increased tenfold in the 1970s alone and have shown no signs of abating since.

As Darrell Hamamoto has shown, the huge increase in mass murders and serial killings in the United States originates largely in a military apparatus that pervades virtually every sphere of American life.[22] We know that Night Stalker Richard Ramirez, who brutally killed at least thirteen people in the Los Angeles area during 1985, was "coached" into violence by an older cousin who had served in Vietnam and boasted of freely slaughtering large numbers of "Vietcong." A decorated war hero, the cousin took credit for twenty-nine confirmed kills in Vietnam. He inspired in Ramirez a hatred of Asians while teaching him secrets of guerrilla warfare that Ramirez used for his nighttime attacks.[23] One of the most notorious serial murderers, Dr. Michael Swango, who relished poisoning dozens of patients under his care at several hospitals, had been a diehard marine with a fancy for combat and guns. His father, Colonel John Virgil Swango, had been stationed in Vietnam and passed on his glorification of military life to his son. The younger Swango enjoyed being at the scene of gruesome disasters as a paramedic, was obsessed with firearms and kept a small arsenal at home, and dwelled on news reports of mass murder, such as the July 1984 shooting spree at a McDonald's restaurant in San Ysidro, California. In his book on the Swango case, James B. Stewart writes: "Serial killers typically betray a fascination with the military and law enforcement, careers in which people are armed, and they often fantasize about violence and disasters in which they emerge as heroes."[24] Swango fit this profile almost perfectly. Stewart adds: "Swango spoke often of his absent father, glorifying Virgil's career in Vietnam [while] . . . his fascination with disasters, with killing, and with weapons echoed similar interests he perceived in his father, as when he learned that Virgil also kept scrapbooks of disasters."[25]

Yet another serial killer, Arthur Shawcross, rationalized his murder of eleven women between 1972 and 1989 by claiming it was a result of post-traumatic stress disorder following his duty in Vietnam. In Vietnam, he claimed, he murdered two girls, raping one and roasting and eating the severed leg of the other; this set him off on a pathological killing mission.[26] The man who came to be known as the Genessee River Killer admitted to having killed at least twenty-six Vietnamese in cold blood. The famous Zodiac Killer, who went on a murder rampage in the San Francisco Bay area during the 1980s, was believed to have been on active military duty at the time. More recently, John Allen Williams (Muhammed), the 2002 sniper killer in the Washington, DC, area, was a Gulf War combat veteran. Just as U.S. military intervention around the globe has no historical precedents, just as government and military elites have been able to commit war crimes with impunity, so too can it be said that the hundreds of documented serial murder cases in the United States since the 1970s have no parallel elsewhere.

The militarization of culture permeates other areas of daily life in American society. In 1991 Operation Desert Storm set in motion a new craze for large, powerful, aggressive vehicles—sports utility vehicles (SUVs), manufactured by every automobile company, and the even more awesome Hummers, originally created for military use. American Motors General began making

Hummers in 1992, the first one going to the king of male action films, Arnold Schwarzenegger. A major idea behind SUVs and Hummers was to give drivers a stronger command of the road, but the result was an increase in violent behavior behind the wheel including manifestations of road rage. As Sheldon Rampton and John Stauber observe, SUVs and Hummers "exploit fear while actually doing nothing to make people safer. They make their owners feel safe not by protecting them, but by feeding their aggressive impulses."[27] Not only do the huge luxury vehicles (costing up to $50,000) get far worse gas mileage than cars, they have a 6 percent higher death rate—so the feelings of command and intimidation turn out to be illusory. Throughout the 1990s SUV sales skyrocketed in the United States, tied in part to fear-based marketing and a subliminal appeal to violent impulses that have no parallel in any other society. After 9/11 SUV and Hummer sales further exploded, but then by 2004 Hummer purchases began to drop as gas prices increased.

If the deepening ethos and practice of human violence against other humans (and indeed against nature) in the midst of a militarized culture is part of a transformed world, it all takes place *within* the framework of modernity, not *against* it. There is much to suggest that barbarism is in many ways facilitated by the tools and modalities of advanced industrial society, in contrast to what is generally assumed. The main instruments of violence—high-tech military, WMD, bureaucratic structures, media culture, elements of instrumental rationality—have now become more refined and concentrated, more capable of bringing massive death and destruction across the globe. Horrendous acts of violence become more routine, depending on modern forms of planning, calculation, and technique that easily widen the distance between the perpetrators and the objects or victims of violence. The idea of a civilizing, pacifying Enlightenment ethos has turned out to be a cruel myth. As Zygmunt Bauman writes: "Contemporary mass murder is distinguished by a virtual absence of all spontaneity on the one hand and the prominence of rational, carefully calculated design on the other. It is marked by an almost complete elimination of contingency and chance, and independence from group emotions and personal motives."[28] Hence the militarized culture, reflected in its great reliance on aerial terrorism, the setting up of brutal regimes and death squads, the domestic gun craze and serial killings, and celebrated media images of vast destruction occurring in real combat situations (the Gulf Wars) or in simulated warfare (*Star Wars, Black Hawk Down, Behind Enemy Lines*), is bolstered and legitimated by the very workings of modernity.

The refined practice of technowar, pushed to its routinized maximum in the United States, could just as easily be carried out by computerized robots and pilotless drones like those replicated in sci-fi and action films, video games, and TV spectacles of the two Gulf Wars—all glorifying violence in a setting that separates actors from their victims, rendering the *object* of military action impersonal, detached, clinical, even invisible. Impediments to terrible acts of violence are stripped away as barbarism winds up integrated into the structures and norms of modernity itself. In Bauman's words: "Reduced like all other objects of bureaucratic management to pure, quality-free measurements, human objects lose their distinctiveness. They are already dehumanized."[29] Here the institutionalization of violence within modern society readily places the human targets and victims outside of any ethical or social consideration. The triumph of U.S. military power over weak, defenseless "enemies" is approached with the same kind of moral detachment as a Super Bowl contest. Rather than providing greater restraints and safeguards against the horrors of militarism, the technocratic ethos embedded in modernity erodes such restraints and safeguards, whether ethical, political, scientific, legal, or religious.

For the U.S. war machine, its scope unmatched in history, the notion it would have to adhere to universal legal, political, and ethical precepts enshrined in the UN Charter and international law is considered preposterous, beyond discussion. Violence becomes a purely technical or strategic question, immune from normal countervailing pressures, just the way it is presented in the corporate media. Where the instruments of modernity are turned toward barbarism, the culture of militarism elicits less commentary and criticism, less outrage within the political system and mass media. Mechanisms and relations of power are all that seem to matter to elites who manage the war economy. In this context protofascistic tendencies within American society—militarism, authoritarianism, xenophobia, racism, the weapons cult—can be assimilated into a rationalized state capitalism, which already possesses a vast concentration of economic, political, and military power. This kind of power structure hardly requires the familiar accoutrements of historical Fascism, like swastikas, medals, concentration camps, organized military processions, and führers. Geared toward corporate domination and imperial expansion—and legitimated in part by the culture of militarism—this system already embodies many powerful features of historical Fascist states, all behind a liberal-democratic facade. The long association of modernity with progress and civilization represents a superficial veneer rationalizing the U.S. drive toward global supremacy through expanded economic and military power.

PATRIARCHY AND WARRIOR CULTURE

With few exceptions the military has been a domain of patriarchal, masculinist traditions—social hierarchy, violence, conquest, sexism, homophobia, gun worship—and the U.S. military has never been one of the exceptions. The warrior culture (from training to combat) has always been a repository of patriarchal values, from the early Minutemen to the frontier settlers, cavalry, and cowboys to the later uniformed participants in global wars and the more recent gangs, cults, militias, terrorists, and weapons fetishists. It is within and around these historical activities and legacies that the predominantly male mythology of warfare has evolved, built on the motif of fighting off demons and evildoers with maximum force, on imposing order by violent means in a chaotic Hobbesian world. This is a milieu of masculine action heroes looking to make history, hoping to achieve redemption through conquest and domination. Warfare has routinely provided an opportunity for men, as warrior protagonists, to rebuild psyches beset with some combination of anxiety, crisis, defeat, and impotence.

The Rambo phenomenon, dramatized in a series of 1980s Hollywood films starring Sylvester Stallone, is just one recent example where male warrior heroes have been endowed with iconic status in American popular culture, Arnold Schwarzenegger in his *Terminator* series being another. A superpatriot and gun cultist, Rambo embodied the ideal of heroic individualism won through military action. Aligning strong masculinity with the power of the gun, the films constructed a larger-than-life mythic personality who relishes violence as a means to rid the world of evil—a narrative falling within the tradition of Superman, the various *Star Wars* heroes, *Indiana Jones*, *Top Gun*, and literally hundreds of other combat and Western films or TV shows. Wars giving visceral expression to patriotic valor, technological virtues, and masculine conquest fit this pattern. Within such a narrative the Vietnam War wound up frustratingly messy and confusing, while the two Gulf Wars easily fit into the historical desired pattern, reinvigorating the national psyche (deflated by the Vietnam syndrome) in a triumphal war over a demonized opponent. The Gulf Wars furnished some of the most dramatic, compelling images of technowar replete with sophisticated gadgetry, flashy spectacles, graphic explosions, victory celebrations, and male expertise used to decode (and justify) the events witnessed by mass audiences. If Vietnam disintegrated into a terrible morass, then the Gulf Wars could be understood as clean, neat, resolute, and technically efficient, with obvious winners and losers, all packaged in the masculine philosophy equating victorious military power standing for moral rectitude. Unfortunately for U.S. war planners, however, this fantasy began to unravel quickly once the second invasion of Iraq degenerated into a Vietnam-like nightmare.

In her path-breaking exploration of military life, Mary Wertsch analyzes a socialization process that is distinctly patriarchal, rooted in norms of discipline, order, and obedience in the service of a (masculinized) national ideal. She refers to a "fortress morality" known for its uncompromising rigidity, where easy acceptance of violence is combined with a "purity of vision" regarding duties and obligations.[30] An indelibly male vision saturates the military world, with women deemed valuable in nothing more than supportive, adorning roles. Thus: "Women are tolerated inside the fortress on one all-encompassing condition: in appearance, dress, speech, and behavior a woman must at all times reflect her complete acceptance of the ultimate patriarchy and its implications for women. By that rule any woman inside the fortress is automatically an accomplice in her own devaluation."[31] Within such patriarchal culture—depicted with some exaggerations in the *The Great Santini*—women are expected to live out male expectations and fantasies. Wertsch's generalizations are based on dozens of interviews with members of military families conducted in the early 1990s. While more recent socialization patterns have been altered by the increased entry of women into the armed forces, the change seems not to have fundamentally transformed gender relations.

Wertsch observes that within military culture it is male authority figures who consistently prevail in both professional work and everyday life, where virtues of duty, conformism, and hierarchy operate to keep women and children in line. The sense of powerlessness experienced by women, above all wives, can be rather extreme in the military setting.[32] Moreover, all this is exacerbated by other dysfunctions permeating military family life: rigid controls, alcoholism, frequent travel and separation, fear of intimacy resulting from constant loss of friendships, and so forth. It goes without saying that the traumas of war itself, with its emotional horrors, uncertainties, and constant exposure to violence, create added tensions and conflicts that inevitably further marginalize the status of women and children, with family relations commonly harmed by feelings of guilt, rage, and violence. The armed-services milieu gives rise to extremely high rates of domestic violence and child abuse insofar as the familiar dysfunctions of "normal" family life and gender relations are simply aggravated. As Wertsch states: "One of the things characterizing life inside the fortress is the exaggerated difference between masculine behavior and feminine behavior, masculine values and feminine values. Macho maleness is at one end of the spectrum; passive receptive femininity at the other."[33] Conflict often turns out to be particularly harsh and violent. The problems that arise within military families—domestic violence, child abuse, alcoholism and drug abuse, relationship breakdowns—are rarely if ever adequately handled by the military brass which itself remains trapped within the same "fortress." The capacity of women to confront marital problems is undermined by their already devalued status within military culture. In the end, the ongoing travails and miseries of military family life are concealed (not always effectively) by an elaborate social facade of order, harmony, duty, patriotism, and outward status. All this takes on greater significance as the military comes to occupy an increasingly central place in American foreign policy and social life.

In the conjuncture of an expanding war economy, Empire, and recurrent U.S. armed interventions, one can detect a merger of corporate, bureaucratic,

military, and patriarchal forms of domination, each overlapping and reinforcing the others. The stubborn fact is that military institutions continue to be
ruled by men and pervaded by masculine norms; at the start of the twenty-
first century men comprise more than 90 percent of U.S. armed-services personnel and fully 100 percent of those entering direct combat. The historical
impact of the feminist revolution on Pentagon culture has been limited. As
Claire Snyder observes, militarism in American society reinforces a wide
range of conventional social and sexual values, a tendency strengthened by an-
tifeminist backlash linked to official fears that a large-scale influx of women
into the military inevitably compromises training standards, weakens morale,
creates sexual tensions, and disrupts combat situations.[34] The dominant Pentagon thinking is that a kinder, gentler armed forces cannot hope to win wars:
it is best to rely on the skills of men, with their supposedly innate drive toward aggression, violence, and martial exploits. Given tough leadership, military organizations can harness those masculine traits into forms of bonding,
heroism, and brute physical strength required for war—although the shift
from conventional ground warfare to new modes of technowar would seem
to render such assumptions obsolete. In any event, the deeply entrenched patriarchal values defining military life can easily shade into misogyny, as reflected in the canons of basic training, where drill instructors often use
woman-hating ridicule to shame recruits seen as lacking "manhood" or sexual potency. As depicted in films like *Full Metal Jacket*, femininity is repeatedly
deprecated while the weapons of combat are identified with male genitalia;
sexism becomes a tool to secure male bonding. The U.S. military thrives on
authoritarianism, conformism, cult of violence, and misogyny that, in civilian
life, are generally regarded as signposts of fascist ideology.

As the military extends its presence in governing institutions and civil
society, it further reproduces gender inequality and social hierarchy consonant with increased violence against women; militarism and patriarchy together generate an even more explosive culture of violence. The forms of
sexist outlawry in wartime are well known: women become widespread victims of combat, atrocities are visited on civilian populations, homes and
neighborhoods are destroyed, people are dislocated, prostitution spreads
along with sex trafficking, rape, torture, and domestic violence.[35] Established
social and moral restraints against extreme patriarchal violence usually disappear in warfare, giving women fewer protections and safe havens as they
often wind up the targets of ideologically and sexually charged acts of violence. It might be argued that women have actually suffered more grievously with the advent of technowar, characterized by aerial bombardments,
long-distance attacks, and the destruction of civilian infrastructures. Domestic violence seems an enduring feature of military family life, even in the
absence of wartime experience. The hypermasculinity and misogynism that
flourish in and around battlefield situations often enter directly and tragi-

cally into the household. Wertsch's interviews reveal dozens of such violent episodes. A more recent case in point is five highly publicized domestic killings at Fort Bragg, North Carolina, in summer 2002, three of which involved elite Special Ops troops. The murders grew out of extreme levels of marital conflict resulting, in part, from aggressive behavior that military men so routinely bring home from work, from their entire hypercharged milieu. In many instances common taboos against violence simply disappear as the warrior mentality allows men to believe as if they are above the law. Problems like marital infidelity can be met with such extraordinary anger that they can, as at Fort Bragg, lead to brutal attacks and murder. Those killings were no doubt the tip of the iceberg, rendered visible because there was a cluster of actions spanning a relatively short time span.[36] Marital conflict in the armed services is aggravated by regular (and sometimes lengthy) periods of separation and by the fact that men—themselves victims of suffocating hierarchy and discipline—have very little control over their lives, a power deficit they can easily overcome with a vengeance in the household. In the tragic Fort Bragg episodes, marital conflict quickly got out of control, helped along by the army's own code of silence as well as a traditional devaluing of therapeutic solutions. Military culture serves to inhibit families from getting badly needed help. The Pentagon brass, moreover, usually turn a deaf ear to reports of distress that might harm the image of the U.S. armed forces.

The predicament of women in the military academies reflects this pattern to a surprising degree. At the Air Force Academy in Colorado Springs, for example, several years of reports by women claiming rape, stalking, and general harassment were ignored or downplayed by administrators and students steeped in patriarchal military values and the code of silence surrounding them. This history of charges came to light when a female student in the 2002 class, Andrea Prasse, filed charges against a male classmate who was accused of stalking and harassing her for more than a year. In the end, however, her desperate complaints were turned against her by the academy: she was charged with dishonesty and expelled. Subsequent investigations discovered an educational milieu largely devoid of respect for women—a milieu actively fostered and defended by the male officers in positions of authority. Officials received fifty-six reports of rape and sexual assault that were not acted on, while perhaps hundreds more incidents were never reported to what had become an unresponsive bureaucracy. As Prasse's mother stated: "These boys just don't get it. They are being raised to have no respect for women, and the attitude is fostered by the male officers in charge. My daughter asked for help, and they ignored her all the way up the chain of command."[37] As in the case of Prasse, who had spent four (wasted) years studying to become a pilot, charges brought forward by the other women were frequently turned against them, as victims. After dozens of reports, in

fact, not a single air force cadet was court-martialed. The situation was reportedly no better at West Point or Annapolis, where an entrenched code
of silence was maintained by patriarchal gatekeepers to avoid "scandals"
detrimental to the upper echelon of the armed services.

Many features of patriarchal militarism thus remain firmly embedded
in American society, despite historic gains of feminism and increased entry
of women into the different services. It is staunchly defended by such intellectual figures as Christina Hoff Sommers, Robert Bork, Lionel Tiger, and
Stephanie Gutmann, not to mention the vast majority of male politicians
across the ideological spectrum. It continues to draw cultural strength from
the male warrior mythology that even after the year 2000 serves the Pentagon's elitism so well. If women are valuable to the U.S. military, it is mainly
in largely peripheral, subordinate, devalued roles consistent with the traditional sexual division of labor, exactly the pattern of gender relations that
has been challenged (and to some extent overturned) within the larger
society.

HOLLYWOOD AND THE PENTAGON

War and the preparation for war resonate through virtually every region of
artistic expression, though perhaps nowhere so extensively as in the Hollywood filmmaking enterprise. More often than not American cinema has celebrated the virtues of patriotism and militarism, from the earliest Western
movies to the later combat, action, sci-fi, and blockbuster genres. At the
hands of dozens of directors, military action has been romanticized, beauti-
fied, and in most cases relativized, insofar as violence is represented as a positive thing for the American military but always negative for the demonized
enemy. While much of this cinematic output has been excellent, practically
all of it has served propaganda functions for the government and Pentagon—
vital functions indeed owing to the immense global power wielded by the
Hollywood film industry. And today, perhaps more than at any time except
World War II, motion pictures constitute a significant ideological and cultural weapon in the service of U.S. foreign and military policy.[38]

In the months and years leading to the second Gulf War—and the war
on terrorism launched after 9/11—Hollywood helped lay the cultural
groundwork for public endorsement of military action with its plethora of
combat and action movies glorifying U.S. supremacy in a world riddled
with chaos and evil. These films are saturated with images of Americans
waging a virtuous fight in which (typically white male) heroism knows no
limits and terrible violence is meted out to those villains who would stand
in the way of the United States, a country dedicated to modern progress,
democracy, human rights, peace, and just plain decency. Where villains were

once Indians, Communists, and Asian hordes, today they are more likely to be Arabs, Muslims, Serbs, terrorists, and drug traffickers. The spate of films (and books, TV programs, and video games) about war and terrorism during the 1990s and beyond all share a certain imperial hubris that coincides with the U.S. drive toward unfettered world domination. The evidence is hard to miss: the great success of the fifth *Star Wars* episode; the blockbuster popularity of films like *Saving Private Ryan*, *Pearl Harbor*, and *Black Hawk Down*; the Rambo-like xenophobic celebrity of Vin Diesel in *XXX* and new California governor Arnold Schwarzenegger in *Terminator 3*; growing collaboration between Hollywood and the Pentagon; even five-minute film shorts prepared by the Navy and Marines and shown in theaters around the country to advertise the war on terrorism. Probably more than any other artistic medium, movies fuel the illusions of an eternal, benevolent U.S. global domination.

Nowhere are the horrors of war portrayed with more dazzling imagery than in cinema—one need look no further than *Apocalypse Now*, *Platoon*, and *Saving Private Ryan*, strong technical achievements directed by three of the very best filmmakers in the United States. At the hands of Hollywood auteurs combat is experienced by audiences as a wondrous spectacle where the realities of violence, death, and suffering are aestheticized, kept at a rather safe distance. Tragedy and art become organically linked just as war and beauty are connected, encouraging a form of voyeurism attuned to death and destruction. Such cinematic "realism" can only help reinforce, indeed legitimate, U.S. military power and its interventions around the world.

The connection between filmmaking and patriotism/militarism has a long tradition in Hollywood, starting with the earliest renditions of the westward push and Indian wars. At least two thousand Westerns were produced over several decades (mostly between 1910 and 1969), depicting the heroic exploits of the U.S. cavalry and white settlers against a bestial, diabolical, primitive enemy standing in the way of progress and civilization. Even the very best films made in this tradition, by such directors as Michael Curtiz, Howard Hawks, Raoul Walsh, and John Ford (*Stagecoach*, *She Wore a Yellow Ribbon*, *Fort Apache*, etc.), established this theme, putting civilized East against primitive West while presenting fully distorted narratives of such massacres as Sand Creek and Wounded Knee. As Ward Churchill points out, the brutal colonization of American Indians was most graphically depicted in movies, which, however, wound up romanticizing and sanitizing the true history. In literally millions of cinematic frames Native Americans are presented as bereft of any humanity and individuality—objectified and degraded as savage warriors to the degree that their annihilation could be seen as justified, even desirable.[39] Vital to the Hollywood construction of the Western was demonization of the racial other, a motif carried forward into other genres. In Churchill's words: "Having attained such utter decontextualization, filmmakers were free to indulge themselves—and their audiences—almost exclusively in fantasies of Indians as warriors. Not just any warriors, mind you, but those of a most hideously bestial variety."[40]

The Western formula, repeated ad nauseum by all studios well into the 1960s, portrayed Indians (always young male warriors) as a fearsome menace to innocent, hard-working, peace-loving white settlers forced to defend themselves as they traveled to their destiny, as in *Stagecoach*. The only good Indians were either dead or working with settlers or the cavalry toward the aim of Manifest Destiny; bad Indians were those, like Geronimo and Cochise, who fought to hold their ancestral land. Surely in no other artistic form was the mythology of western conquest, of the triumph of good over evil, conveyed to the American public more extensively and more directly than through the medium of Hollywood movies, and this naturally set the pattern for later combat and action pictures that embraced the same Manichaeistic, patriotic, demonizing narratives, with Asians, Serbs, Arabs, and generic Communists or terrorists supplanting the Indian enemy that in any event had been largely decimated by genocidal colonialism.

Films about World War II embraced this model of the idealized combat genre often to the point where they degenerated into little more than prowar propaganda releases. The war, after all, was fought by the Great Generation as a noble cause to defeat Fascism and save democracy—yet another recycling of the civilizing mission. The movies, the majority produced during the war as part of a supreme patriotic effort, involved plots featuring groups of courageous men embarking stoically on dangerous missions to destroy sinister, semihuman antagonists, made all the more demonic if they were Japanese. Noteworthy pictures embracing the mythic concept of the good war include *Wake Island* (1942), *Air Force* (1943), *Destination Tokyo* (1943), *Guadalcanal Diary* (1943), *Thirty Seconds over Tokyo* (1944), and *They Were Expendable* (1945), along with a series of film shorts entitled *Why We Fight*, assembled by several great directors of the period. In the postwar years such films as *Flying Leathernecks* (1951), *From Here to Eternity* (1953), *The Bridge at Remagen* (1969), *A Bridge Too Far* (1977), and of course *Saving Private Ryan* (1998) kept alive the good-war patriotic tradition. These movies generally shared certain motifs in common: male bonding, patriotic ardor, triumph of American technology and ingenuity, group heroes, coolness in the face of danger, the obligatory mass of sinister, evil-looking villains.[41]

The cold war period too featured an enormous output of movies depicting epic battles between forces of good and evil, civilization and its enemies—now focused on the Communist (or Russian) threat, typically in noncombat situations. A deep strain within Hollywood cinema was the mood of fear and paranoia that, by the late 1940s, was already sweeping American society and feeding into McCarthyism and other forces of ideological provincialism and intolerance, in the context of U.S.–Soviet super-power conflict and the emerging nuclear balance of terror. There were still plenty of demons lurking about, only now they had managed to infiltrate American social and political life at its very core, crazed in their desire to attack Western civilization. Don Siegel's *Invasion of the Body Snatchers* (1956) dramatized the role of unified community action in defeating a group of aliens (i.e., Communists) working clandestinely and ruthlessly to destroy the U.S. government and enslave its citizens. This cinematic motif was repeated endlessly throughout the 1950s and 1960s, extending even to comedic representations like Norman Jewison's *The Russians Are Coming! The Russians Are Coming!* (1966).

Throughout the cold war era into the 1990s, Hollywood cinema reproduced time and again its combat formulas developed and perfected in Westerns and World War II dramas, with their masculine, patriotic, gun-toting heroes prevailing over a variety of evil, and scheming but ultimately hopeless, opponents of Western civilization. Tony Scott's *Top Gun* (1986) provides one of the best examples of this methodology, its hero a navy fighter pilot (Tom Cruise) who relishes the anti-Communist crusade as both good and winnable. Douglas Kellner claims the *Top Gun* figure, along with Rambo and kindred military heroes of the 1980s, is a "Reaganite wet dream," glorifying combat while celebrating a host of conservative values.[42] Indeed the 1980s witnessed a constant torrent of books, TV programs, and films revolving around the U.S. obsessions with getting rid of the Vietnam syndrome, which connoted military failure, and renewing the cold war against the newly labeled "Evil Empire." Tom Clancy's best-selling tech-nothrillers *The Hunt for Red October* (1984) and *Red Storm Rising* (1986) helped popularize this trend, which rapidly became a cultural rallying point for neoconservatives and Pentagon hawks clamoring for increases in military spending.[43] Clancy's novels indulged a mass psychology of American global supremacy, glorifying the exploits of combat and the wonders of technowar. (Turned into a film by John McTiernan in 1990, *The Hunt for Red October* was somewhat toned down to reflect a mellowing in U.S.–Soviet relations by then, even as warfare remained a purifying event.)

Indispensable to this revival of cinematic militarism in the waning years of the cold war were the famous *Rambo* episodes, beginning with *First Blood* (1982), directed by Ted Kotcheff and starring Sylvester Stallone as John Rambo, a Green Beret Vietnam veteran abandoned by the very system he fought to defend. Having to face off against the treacherous system, bureaucrats, weak and indecisive elites, and of course hardened Commies, Rambo emerges as the ultimate macho, superpatriotic combat hero, a larger-than-life John Wayne, able to triumph over every obstacle thrown in his path. According to his commanding officer, Rambo's task in Vietnam "was to dispose of enemy personnel. To kill, period. Win by attrition. Well,

Rambo was the best." Rambo became an icon within the popular culture and national psyche. This series inspired numerous later combat and action films, for example *Missing in Action* (1984), in which Chuck Norris rescues soldiers held prisoner in Vietnam by means of an incredibly daring commando raid, and the *Terminator* series with Arnold Schwarzenegger. From this standpoint, Rambo can be understood as the resurrected warrior, a self-disciplined macho hero with awesome mental and physical powers—not to mention the capacity to kill vast numbers of enemy soldiers.

During the Reagan-Bush years Rambo came to serve as a symbol of patriotic, dedicated, betrayed manhood, ready to overcome any roadblocks. Indeed Reagan's own advisers made expert use of the Rambo icon in the pursuit of hard-line anti-Communist foreign policy and a rekindling of the cold war. Susan Jeffords argues that Stallone's portrayal of a military superhero, coupled with Schwartzenegger's violent macho roles in such movies as *The Terminator*, became an integral part of Reagan's presidential imagery. She writes that "these hard bodies came to stand not only for a type of national character—heroic, aggressive, and determined—but for the nation itself."[44] In July 1985 Reagan said: "Boy, I saw *Rambo* last night," after thirty-five hostages held captive in Lebanon had been released. "Now I know what to do the next time this happens."[45] As Michael Rogin observes, "Reagan's demonology was not marginal, a sign of personal disturbance. It was the norm."[46]

The 1990s witnessed a dramatic resurgence of conventional military films, usually made with Pentagon collaboration, that celebrated a rebirth of heroic, noble war making and generally meshed with U.S. imperial agendas. To recover a sense of the good war in the absence of fearsome enemies, Hollywood filmmaking turned to the great achievements of World War II. The movie industry was free to build on the *Rambo* series, cold war spy dramas, action genres, and blockbusters like *Star Wars*, including the work of directors Steven Spielberg, George Lucas, Francis Ford Coppola, Paul Schrader, and John Milius, all previously involved with the New Hollywood renaissance of the 1970s. What emerged within the new cinematic militarism was a narrative schema according to which U.S. military intervention became necessary to protect American values and Western civilization from hordes of demons and monsters lurking about in the post–cold war Hobbesian turbulence—the same state of nature confronted by frontier settlers, cowboys, sheriffs, and cavalry units in Western films. The theme, familiar not only from Westerns but from films in the combat and action genres, involved good guys imposing law and order in a disorderly, threatening world.

Terrence Malick's *The Thin Red Line* (1998) depicts the harrowing and bloody Battle of Guadalcanal, a key 1943 U.S. engagement against the Japanese in the Pacific Theater. As with Andrew Marton's 1964 picture of the same title, also based on the James Jones novel, two messages appear simultaneously: war is hell, but it is nonetheless exhilarating, necessary to advance (unquestionably noble) American national interests. The main characters in the movie, grunts from every background, are seen as terribly battle weary, but they (and the audience) clearly recognize the moral imperative of the fight before them. Spielberg's *Saving Private Ryan* (1998) also recaptures the safe, comforting terrain of the good war, bringing to the screen the resounding achievements of the Allied invasion of Normandy in June 1944. Having spent time in Vietnam, Spielberg focused much of his creative energies on World War II as a watershed historical moment that deeply influenced him during his childhood years. His father served as a radio operator on B-25 bombers. The good war provided a setting for no fewer than *eight* of Spielberg's movies, including *1941* (1979), three *Indiana Jones* films (1981–1990), *Empire of the Sun* (1987), and *Schindler's List* (1993), as well as *Private Ryan*. In 2002 he completed yet another wartime epic for HBO, a spin-off of *Private Ryan* titled *Band of Brothers*. In the case of *Private Ryan,* starring Tom Hanks, Ed Burns, Tom Sizemore, and Matt Damon, Spielberg dramatizes the travails of a private who urges his would-be rescuers to do something heroic for the war effort; the rescuers quickly agree to help Ryan destroy a German armored convoy in France, enlisting all their battlefield skills to defeat the Nazis, who are shown as demonic enemies fighting for an evil, doomed cause. The Allies are seen as courageous, skilled, and fighting for a just objective. Perhaps more than any combat film of its time, *Private Ryan* follows the formulaic pattern of the 1940s and 1950s Hollywood war movies.

One of the most absorbing celebrations of U.S. victory in World War II—surely intended as a morality tale for the new century—is Jonathan Mostrow's submarine-warfare thriller *U-571* (2000), which in effect rewrites history by rendering the heroic exploits of British sailors as the deeds of an *American* submarine crew. The director subverts historical authenticity by recasting British success in detecting the Enigma German secret code as a U.S. breakthrough, presumably with the idea of (falsely) reassuring viewers of America's leading role in fighting the Nazis. Mostrow himself stated: "If it's possible to call a war a 'good war,' that label would have to apply to World War II. Never before in our history was there such a clear-cut case of good versus evil. There is no ambiguity about our [U.S.] involvement in that war."[47] In this fashion *U-571* pays cinematic homage to past U.S. military glory, and by extension the nation's contemporary hegemonic role in global politics, by deliberately falsifying actual events.

Michael Bay's epic *Pearl Harbor* (2001) goes beyond the films of both Spielberg and Mostrow in its dramatic romanticization of World War II. Much like the earlier blockbuster *Titanic*, *Pearl Harbor* revolves around a standard, all-consuming love affair (Ben Affleck and Kate Beckinsale), with the fascinating and often controversial historical events relegated to backdrop.

And, like *U-571*, it departs from historical accuracy for the sake of questionable dramatic objectives. As one example the film presents the heroic efforts of two fliers (Affleck and Josh Hartnett) to take on the Japanese aerial invasion, but in reality the surprise attack decimated the U.S. Air Force and left it unable to mount any serious aerial counterattack. Virtually all of the heroics—and there were many—occurred along Battleship Row. What we have with *Pearl Harbor*, despite its many gripping scenes of the bombardment and destruction of the U.S. Navy, is a marriage of love story and patriotic spectacle leaving viewers with a comic-book characterization of events, far inferior to what was earlier depicted in *Tora! Tora! Tora!* Moreover, Bay glosses over the failure of U.S. political and military leaders to anticipate the Japanese attack, ignoring conflicts in the upper echelons of the Roosevelt administration and viable reports that Roosevelt's senior military advisers had advance warning of Japanese plans.[48] What does emerge from the picture is a benevolent giant trapped into joining the quintessential good war at the very moment it loses its historical innocence—both highly questionable premises.

Film discourse in the 1980s and beyond has also been infused with the motif of terrorism, with its attention riveted mainly on the Middle East and the threat posed by Muslims and Arabs. If the political climate of the Reagan-Bush years helped nourish a cinematic war on terrorism, the Clinton period in fact brought little change, so that the cultural fallout from 9/11 and the new Bush presidency can be seen as *extensions* of what went before. For some time U.S. militarism and global terrorism have been joined in a dialectic cycle, as we have seen. The war against terrorism, in both its cultural and military dimensions, has long been a key part of the stratagem for projecting American power abroad. The film industry has fallen into line, producing dozens of movies celebrating U.S. military power and its struggle against dark, sinister (mostly Arab) enemies. With the eclipse of Communism, terrorism became the central focus of these pictures, including *Delta Force* (1986), *Iron Eagle* (1988), *Trident Force* (1988), *Iron Eagle II* (1988), and *Navy Seals* (1990). Films of this genre offer a number of predictable images: an ethnocentric view of other nations and cultures, especially in the Middle East; a presentation of Arabs as an undifferentiated mass; a global struggle between civilization and savagery, good and evil; the glory of American patriotism, notably as personified by its masculine heroes; a celebration of high-tech weaponry as a sign of U.S./Western moral supremacy.

The new militarism films of the 1990s, and even before, conjure up a world remade on the basis of a broad mélange of conservative ideals: rugged individualism, the sanctity of the patriarchal family, religion, jingoism, armed might. On reflection this amounts to a simple recycling of themes from the Western genre, with its simplistic East-versus-West dichotomy and colonizing ethos. Of course the issue of terrorism injected these motifs into a new historical framework, even before 9/11. Pictures of the 1990s portray terrorism as a threat to all of the era's conservative ideals; the threat emanates from an assortment of barbarians, as in the *Die Hard* series, *True Lies* (1994), *The Crying Game* (1992), *Sudden Death* (1995), *The Siege* (1998), and *Rules of Engagement* (1998). All these contain harsh stereotypes of Arabs—dark, aggressive, unwashed, crude, violent—that today could never be duplicated for any other ethnic group.[49] Hollywood employed a variety of action/adventure narratives to depict the good war against terrible, primitive demons, James Cameron's *True Lies* providing an excellent instance of this methodology. As Mehdi Semati writes: "*True Lies* in its attempt to combat international terrorism within the confines of the discourse of the family becomes sitcom, a variation of domestic comedy. This film is the 1990s answer to patriotism in the cycle of films made in the 1980s." The film, he adds, "takes the mix of terrorism, sex, and violence to a new political imagery."[50] The Arabs in *True Lies* are shown offering prayers before detonating atomic devices, beating up women, kidnapping children, and generally acting like subhumans.

In *The Siege*, a group of terrorists sets off a series of explosions terrorizing an entire city; a busload of people is shown being blown to pieces. With the FBI and CIA unable to crack the case, the army enters the picture and martial law is imposed. Arabs become the immediate target of investigation and revenge. As a flight into fantasy, terrorists are shown being trained in Iraq. Edward Zwick's film oddly indulges certain liberal sensibilities, at one point presenting the terrorists as themselves somehow getting caught up in a wider matrix of conflict, but in the end the predictable Manichaeistic theme reappears, with evil Arabs getting totally vanquished by the all-powerful U.S. military. Awesome high-tech weaponry once again saves the day. As in Cameron's film, successful male warriors are depicted simultaneously as good family men, thereby mixing family values with patriotism and the warrior ethic. Despite the movie's multicultural veneer, the stark images of scheming Arab villains come across with great power. Of course the notion of Islamic terrorists wreaking great damage in the heart of a major U.S. city turns out to be prophetic indeed. Yet, as in the actual war on terrorism, *The Siege* offers no historical context within which events take place, recycling diffuse images of Arab enemies who carry out their evil deeds largely outside any fixed time and space.[51]

The events of September 11, 2001, seem to have further consolidated trends of cinematic militarism that were already in place. We know that combat pictures serve to congeal patriotic, and to some extent xenophobic and violent, sentiments, especially among youth. Of twentieth-century U.S. military experiences, however, only World War II has been consistently portrayed as a good war in which the lines between good and evil, friend and enemy come across as obvious to all viewers. One dimension of the Hollywood war machine has been the effort to force other wars (Korea, Vietnam,

Iraq) into the good-war mold, usually achieving only mixed results. With 9/11 the prospects for rekindling cinematic good wars resurfaced as the U.S. embarked on its perpetual war against global demons. If that "war" turns out to be diffused, scattered, without many clear-cut victories, then it might be possible to link more direct forms of military intervention (Afghanistan, Iraq) with the memories of patriotism, heroism, and victory associated with World War II. Such a linkage would validate anew the sense of national (or global) mission. No doubt this is why many symbols of that good war—fear of "appeasement," references to "genocide" and concentration camps, the bitter fight against Hitler and the Nazis, accusations of war crimes—have been resurrected by politicians and the media in the context of such arenas as the Balkans and the Persian Gulf.

In the aftermath of 9/11 the Bush administration, with presidential adviser Karl Rove in the lead, sought to enlist Hollywood creative talents in the war on terrorism—the first such efforts since World War II. Conservative politicians hoped to see a convergence of U.S. foreign-policy agendas and film content; Bush himself argued for a "seamless web of unity" around the war effort. Of course the Pentagon has for many years insisted on the right to monitor film scripts dealing with military action before allowing its facilities and resources to be used in movie making, and more recently the CIA and NSA have followed this pattern. During Rove's visit to Hollywood after the election, however, many film industry people (for example, Robert Redford and Oliver Stone) expressed a strong reluctance to go along with the idea of Pentagon or White House control over film projects. While such resistance probably captures the general mood of the industry, the main thrust of combat pictures, deeply influenced by directors like Spielberg, Cameron, Bay, and Mostrow, can be expected to follow the lines established by a revitalized Hollywood war machine, building on patriotic and vengeful feelings unleashed by 9/11 and consolidated by the U.S. interventions in Afghanistan and Iraq. The jingoistic TV spectacle before and during the second Iraq war, along with the proliferation of combat-oriented video games modeled on Desert Storm I and II, could well anticipate Hollywood's own long-term response to terrorism and the continuing growth of U.S. militarism.

As early as October 2001 two brutally violent films depicting acts of terrorism, *Training Day* and *Don't Say a Word,* were released and immediately generated high box-office revenues. At the same time production was resumed on other pictures with terrorist motifs, *Behind Enemy Lines* and *Black Hawk Down,* both of which had been nearly completed by 9/11. *Behind Enemy Lines* depicts the harrowing adventures of a U.S. pilot (Owen Wilson) shot down over Bosnia during the U.S. intervention in Yugoslavia. A senior U.S. army officer bucks his superiors and orders a secret mission to rescue the flier from the grasp of the Serbs, portrayed here in all their ugly, Slavic bestiality. Ridley Scott's *Black Hawk Down* presents a botched 1993 military action in Somalia, where a Black Hawk helicopter was downed by hostile fire and eighteen soldiers were killed, a film described by producer Joe Ross as a "mature version of *Top Gun*." Here too the enemy is portrayed as sub-human, brutal, primitive. Other movies with powerful military themes were released within several months of 9/11, including *Collateral Damage*, *Big Trouble*, and *Windtalkers*. The great success of the movie *XXX* in 2002 no doubt owed much to the superpatriotic mood prevailing after 9/11. Star-ring Vin Diesel as a muscled, tattooed, bald combat hero, the film portrays a Herculean American struggle against terrorists ready to use weapons of mass destruction, an evil that lurks everywhere. Recalling elements of Rambo, the hero indulges in the cult of physical fitness, plays video games, is techno-savvy, and is xenophobic to the core—a character designed to fit the national zeitgeist exactly.

Perhaps the most virulent representation of militarized culture in Hol-lywood was Mostrow's film *Terminator 3* (2003), yet another vehicle for Schwartzenegger's jingoism, patriarchal swagger, and passion for technowar. Replete with its own official magazine, the movie spectacle glorifies the most sophisticated forms of weaponry—indeed an entirely new universe of machines—that can triumph over the most evil forces around. The maga-zine describes Schwartzenegger as "fresh off the assembly line and back in the role that made him a movie legend," namely, an "unstoppable cyborg." The hero, of course, is equipped with the most awesome attack weapons imaginable, including a variety of "T3" products made especially for the movie. There is also the "most advanced humanoid robot" ever, manufac-tured by Honda. But the key to *Terminator 3* is sophisticated futuristic tech-nowar, including new modes of "remote warfare" that fundamentally alter the character of military combat. Such warfare, already visible in the U.S. deployment of unmanned Predator drones in Afghanistan, can be expected to rely on various molecular and cellular devices made possible by nan-otechnology. According to one of the magazine's contributors:

> One of the most important things to note with remote warfare is that it distances soldiers from death. It is widely documented that soldiers don't have an easy time killing people and that, despite what we see in the movies, very few soldiers are of the bloodthirsty type. . . . With remote warfare, however, soldiers are removed from their actions and find it eas-ier to kill. A generation of children raised on violent video games could therefore be excellent future soldiers.[52]

The militarization of popular culture is reflected in the diminishing boundaries separating entertainment and war. Manufacturers have produced increasingly realistic combat video and computer games for children of all ages, with the full blessing and participation of the Pentagon, which launched its gaming operations in 1997. In 2001, even before the terrorist attacks, the U.S. military crafted a video game titled Tom Clancy's *Rainbow Six: Rogue Spear*, designed to mix fun and training for conducting small-unit operations in urban settings. In 2002, the army created *America's Army*, a training combat video game developed at the Naval Postgraduate School with the assistance of the THX Division at Lucasfilms, Ltd. The new videos are designed to recreate a virtual environment for warfare, allowing for more realistic combat scenarios and a more intimate sense of involvement. In 2004 the Pentagon began to unveil a new generation of combat video genres for Microsoft, beginning with *Full Spectrum Warrior*, which includes scenarios for fighting terrorists in such regions as Central Asia. The Full Spectrum games are a product of the Institute for Creative Technologies at the University of Southern California, a $45 million venture linking academics, technicians, and the Pentagon.

The success of these high-tech military programs, along with films like *XXX* and the pervasive national impact of the *Rambo* and *Terminator* series, reveals a growing convergence of Hollywood moviemaking, new trends in American popular culture, and the frightening contours of U.S. foreign and military policy at the beginning of the twenty-first century. Pictures like *Tears of the Sun* (2003), a Bruce Willis action vehicle, continue to replicate powerful elements of the traditional combat genre, weaving heroic, mythical narratives in a world of consummate evil, narratives that justify worldwide U.S. domination. In this fashion the culture of militarism operates fully in the service of Empire.

5

THE CRIMES OF EMPIRE

Consistent with the general political mythologies that shroud American foreign and military policies, namely that the U.S. has historically been a force behind human rights, democracy, and lawful behavior in global affairs, any serious public discourse around U.S. culpability for terrible abuses of democratic practice and international law has always been taboo, outside legitimate debate. This is also true, only more so, regarding U.S. culpability for war crimes or crimes against humanity. As far as the established media, political system, and academic world are concerned, the nation's international presence has been a taken-for-granted benevolent one, motivated by good intentions and dedicated to human progress despite occasional flaws or mistakes in carrying out its policies. War crimes are demonic, barbaric actions carried out by others—Nazis, Serbs, Iraqis, Rwandans, Chinese, and of course terrorists. Even where the United States and its allies or surrogates have been clearly shown to commit atrocities of one sort or another, these are justified within the larger humanitarian design of Western values and interests, or they simply wind up obscured to the point of vanishing from public view. This phenomenon has been deeply reinforced in the post-9/11 atmosphere, in which Hobbesian chaos produced by the terrorist menace requires ever harsher police, intelligence, and military responses in defense of an embattled society. Yet, if the war on terrorism has exacerbated already strong trends toward expansion of the security state and war machine, it has also pointed toward a different set of concerns: the need for universal laws and principles to restrain out-of-control military forces in their violent pursuit of political ends.

The historical reality is that the U.S. drive for economic, political, and military supremacy has led to massive and horrific war crimes, to repeated and flagrant violations of international law—a legacy easily documented but one that has been obscured or simply ignored within the national ethos of denial. The U.S. record of war crimes has been, from the nineteenth century to the present, a largely invisible one, with no government, no political leaders, no military officials, no lower-level operatives (with just a few scattered exceptions) held accountable for criminal actions. A culture of militarism has endowed *all* U.S. interventions abroad with a patina of patriotic goodness and democratic sensibilities beyond questioning or debate. Since 9/11 this situation has worsened: a nominally liberal-democratic system has moved ever more ominously along the road of corporatism, authoritarianism, and narrowing public discourses. American society today exhibits every sign of ideological closure, one-dimensionality, and erosion of civic culture, accompanied by the rise of national chauvinism and hostility toward foreign nations and cultures. Recent ideological trends involve a steadfast refusal to confront the larger context of U.S. foreign policy or to reflect on the terrible consequences of U.S. Empire, as if the terrorist attacks occurred in a historical void. The terrorist attacks have heightened the mood of national denial. Chalmers Johnson, as we have seen, observes in *Blowback* a fundamental refusal on the part of Americans to even consider the possibility that the U.S. role in the world amounts to an Empire.[1] Nowhere is this proposition more evident than in the sphere of war crimes discourse.

In their exhaustive volume *Crimes of War*, Roy Gutman and David Rieff follow this ethnocentric pattern, detailing a vast assemblage of military atrocities from every corner of the globe—the blame always squarely placed on *others*: Russians, Serbs, Iraqis, Rwandans, South Africans. References to war crimes attributed to U.S. allies or client states are careful to avoid any mention of American complicity, whether in furnishing arms, training, material and logistical supports, or political backing. Where reference to U.S. involvement could simply not be avoided, as in the Indochina War and the use of nuclear weapons against Japan, ethical and political issues are treated in a rather ambiguous fashion. The authors of this comprehensive text merely *assume*, contrary to all historical evidence, that U.S. foreign and military policies have been guided by noble ambitions: democracy, human rights, the rule of law. As for the canons of international law, here again the United States and its allies are presented as standing at the forefront in the struggle for universal principles of rights and obligations, valiantly striving to extend liberal ideals to a generally messy, violent, and recalcitrant world—as in the case of Iraq. Thus: "In the well-off Western countries, the canons of international law took hold."[2] The historic shift toward codification of worldwide humanitarian law, say the authors, was triggered by the awful events in the Balkans during the 1990s, when the Serbs under Slobodan Milosevic embarked on their program of "ethnic cleansing."[3] In his brief introduction to the volume, Lawrence Wechsler exults that we are presently in the midst of an important historical development—most clearly reflected in the Hague Tribunal for the former Yugoslavia—toward the expansion and codification of international law applied to crimes of war. We have reached a conjuncture where new global procedures, norms, laws, and conventions can be firmly established, thanks to the bold initiatives of Western powers.[4] That the seventy-nine days of NATO bombing of Yugoslavia, with its massive destruction of the public infrastructure and terrible civilian toll, was itself a gross violation of the UN Charter (article 2-4), which obliges member states to "refrain in their international relations from the threat or use of force against the territorial integrity or political independence of any state" is never mentioned. Nor is the fact that the Hague Tribunal, dedicated to prosecuting mainly Serbs, has not indicted any NATO leaders for war crimes, despite abundant evidence of such crimes.

As I argue in this chapter, the rules of engagement for U.S. economic, political, and military intervention are shaped far less by any ethical or humanitarian concerns than by sheer geopolitical *power* interests that, in the New World Order, seem to recognize no limits, as we have abundantly seen in Iraq. Indeed American national interests, even in an age of globalization, have been increasingly asserted over the canons of international law—most starkly visible in Bush junior's formulation of a military strategy based on the doctrine of preemptive strike. The rules of U.S. military action today have little to do with customs or morality or laws that might infringe on national interests or the transnational corporate power the country supports. It is probably fair to say that, for the United States, "ethics" has little if any meaning once we reach the water's edge; international law serves to protect the most powerful. What Sven Lindqvist writes seems especially relevant to the American modus operandi: "The laws of war protect [those] of the same race, class, and culture. The laws of war leave the foreign and the alien [and one might add weak] without protection."[5]

Today perhaps more than ever, U.S. foreign policy revolves around a harsh ("realistic") principle—that the U.S. military can intervene virtually anywhere in the world (or, indeed, in space) outside the jurisdiction of international justice and be beholden to no higher authority, while suffering minimal negative consequences for itself. Moreover, given the advent of high-tech weaponry, aerial and space-based surveillance, new sophisticated aircraft, and enhanced battlefield flexibility, the Empire has presumably entered a comfortable zone of "safe wars," enhanced by its global supremacy. U.S. military action has led, directly and indirectly, to terrible loss of human life since World War II, much of it the result of deliberate, planned, callous strategies.[6] Aerial bombardment in particular has been devastating, but artillery, infantry, armored divisions, death squads, and economic sanctions have taken an unspeakable toll. American crimes of war have been overt and brutally direct, as in the cases of Indochina, Panama, Iraq, and Yugoslavia, or mediated through proxy wars carried out in Central America, Indonesia, Turkey, Israel, and Colombia, although the agents of such crimes have usually managed to escape culpability.

NATO'S HAGUE TRIBUNAL

By the 1990s, after a full century of treaties, conventions, and tribunals designed to establish legal criteria for governing the military behavior of nations, no truly universal structure for this purpose had been established. Principles embodied in the various Hague and Geneva protocols, along with the Nuremberg and Tokyo courts set up after World War II—many of which found their way into the UN Charter of 1948—had never become internationally binding in legal or political terms. The great promise of Nuremberg to hold political and military leaders responsible for war crimes and crimes against humanity did not come to fruition. Finally, in 1998, the majority of nations (139 in all) met in Rome to ratify a treaty creating an International Criminal Court that would allow for binding global jurisdiction. The court would be a professional, impartial body charged with bringing leaders and others to justice for assorted war crimes, genocide, and crimes against humanity. In July 2002 the court became a reality, confirming long-held hopes of human-rights partisans around the world. Unfortunately, however, the United States took a fiercely hostile stance toward the court from the outset, first refusing to sign the treaty and then trying to sabotage the body's operations. The U.S. government, first under Clinton and then under Bush, insisted on guarantees that no American officials or military personnel could be brought before the tribunal; the nation with the only truly global military presence wanted immunity.

The United States was threatening to paralyze UN peacekeeping operations in Bosnia and elsewhere if it did not receive assurances that Americans would receive immunity from criminal court prosecution—a condition that backers of the court found politically and legally untenable. Having refused to endorse the tribunal, the United States then demanded special exemption from possible charges, arguing that it might be the target of "politically motivated" legal actions. Despite broad support for the court, Bush was able to affirm (in early July 2002) that the United States would refuse to sign on to the criminal court. Within a week of this statement, the United States muscled through the Security Council a resolution granting U.S. troops and officials a renewable one-year exemption from investigation or prosecution by the international court. But the U.S. exemption turned out to be outrageously illegal, not to mention politically corrupt. As one longtime observer at the UN remarked: "We do not think it is the business of the Security Council to interpret treaties that are negotiated somewhere else."[7] The resolution not only was in flagrant opposition to the world consensus, it also effectively validated the idea that the United States is free to stand outside the canons of international law. Such exceptionalism renders the court and its procedures a mockery, since laws and procedures require universality to be legitimate and effective. At precisely the time all this was taking place, Secretary of Defense Rumsfeld outlined a series of sweeping proposals that would drastically weaken congressional oversight of the Pentagon—the idea being to provide the military with more freedom than ever to conduct its domestic and global business, a move justified by the war against terrorism. Further, U.S. efforts to subvert the criminal court while expanding the scope of Pentagon power coincided with Bush's aggressive new strategy of preemptive strike, directed, for the moment, against Iraq.

Yet even as the U.S. government refuses the jurisdiction of international law for itself, its leaders remain ever vigilant in seeking to bring *others* to justice—notably those (like the Serbs and Iraqis) with the audacity to stand in the way of American geopolitical interests. The International Criminal Tribunal for the Former Yugoslavia (ICTY), set up by NATO powers in May 1993, has been convened in The Hague to try Milosevic and other Serb leaders for monstrous crimes supposedly carried out during nearly a decade of bloody civil wars in the Balkans. Milosevic was indicted in May 1999, at the very height of the NATO attack on Yugoslavia, on sixty-one counts that included genocide, crimes against humanity, and war crimes associated with Serb policies of ethnic cleansing in Bosnia, Croatia, and Kosovo. Milosevic was arrested in March 2001 and delivered to the Hague Tribunal in June 2001, after the United States simultaneously threatened the new Serb government and bribed it with millions in cash. The Western powers, with the United States taking the lead, portrayed Milosevic and the Serbs as modern-day Nazis responsible for an unspeakable holocaust filled with acts of mass murder, mass rape, torture, and ethnic cleansing that left much of the region devastated. These atrocities were so horrific as to demand immediate "humanitarian" intervention by NATO military forces. Once the bombing was finished, the NATO-supported and -financed Hague Tribunal would finally bring Serb leaders and their accomplices to justice.

In the United States, the media and politicians eagerly championed the new war-crimes trials, celebrating the ICTY as an inspiring "triumph of the civilized world."[8] By holding Serb leaders accountable for such terrible crimes the tribunal opened up a new era of international law. Former secretary of state Madeleine Albright referred to the Hague as the "mother of all tribunals," where it would now be possible to try, in the manner of Nuremberg, some of the greatest monsters in European history.[9] Caricatured as a Hitler-like dictatorial figure obsessed with building an ethnically pure Greater Serbian state, Milosevic was deemed the kind of war criminal the world desperately needed to bring to trial in order to avoid a condition of "international anarchy." Serbs were regularly demonized in the mass media, referred to by columnist Anthony Lewis and others as "beasts" and "monsters." The mainstream text *Indictment at The Hague* (2002) is subtitled *The Milosevic Regime and Crimes of the Balkans Wars*. In it, authors Norman

Cigar and Paul Williams set out to present a case for war crimes against the
Serbs, replete with documents from the Hague Tribunal and U.S. State Department; there is no mention of other parties to the Balkans civil wars, nor
to the role of NATO and the United States (in the context of war crimes).
"No matter how he personally meets his end," write the authors, "Milosevic shall remain one of the most villainous figures in the history of the
South Slavs." They add: "The atrocities committed by Serbian forces were
part of a planned, systematic, and organized campaign to secure territory for
an ethnically 'pure' Serb state by clearing it of all non-Serb populations."
The tribunal represents a historical breakthrough, they remind us, since by
"attacking liability for war crimes [it] will serve as a reminder to other
prospective war criminals that their actions will not be granted *de facto* immunity by the world community."[10]

Despite such overblown rhetoric denouncing genocidal Serb Nazis on
the march, it takes little effort to reveal the ICTY as an outrageous fraud.
From the very outset this tribunal was totally biased and one-sided, hardly
the product of universal jurisprudence—an inevitable state given that the
tribunal was set up and financed by the NATO powers (above all the
United States) and received the bulk of its investigative and informational
resources from these same powers, the very powers that had carried out
seven weeks of intensive military aggression against the Serbs. The fraudu-
lence is quickly shown by the flagrant one-sidedness of the indictments:
after many years of violent civil wars involving not only Serbs but Croatians, Bosnian Muslims, Kosavar Albanians, and myriad paramilitary groups
of varying ideological and ethnic makeup, not to mention the period of
covert and armed intervention by NATO powers, we are told to believe that
only the Serbs were guilty of atrocities, that all the others were simply victims of a singular evil force, that others were victims *only* while Serbs themselves were *never* victimized. This scenario, constructed mainly by Western
public relations firms and mass media, defies all logic. Indeed the Serbs could
be said to have suffered the *most*, especially when the U.S./NATO bombings are taken into account. Without doubt Serbs were responsible for
atrocities, but historical evidence from the field, unfiltered by propaganda,
shows convincingly that atrocities were committed on all sides, and that
Serbs were just as often on the receiving as on the culpable end of war
crimes. The Hague Tribunal completely ignored this complex history, dismissing those instances where Serbs experienced the violence of civil war—
for example, several thousand killed and at least 500,000 displaced in Croatia alone, and yet another 330,000 displaced in Kosovo in the wake of
United States–backed Kosovo Liberation Army (KLA) terrorism and
NATO aerial attacks. In August 1995 the United States and Germany supported a bloody Croatian military offensive in the Kraijina region, killing
thousands of Serbs and forcing another 200,000 from their homes.[11] Yet

when looking at such atrocities, the moral outrage over ethnic cleansing that so consumed NATO elites as they targeted Serbs suddenly vanishes. The failure of ICTY to address this terrible anomaly, to investigate and prosecute war crimes across the board, to pursue *all* combatants involved in the civil wars, demonstrates ipso facto its moral and political bankruptcy.

In reality the Hague proceedings do little more than conceal the long sordid involvement of the United States and its NATO allies in the Balkans; by now the self-righteous ruminations concerning genocide and ethnic cleansing should ring hollow. Nowhere has it been shown that Milosevic's supposed drive toward a Greater Serbia was motivated explicitly by goals of ethnic purity. Was ethnicity more a factor for Serbians than for Croatians or Bosnians, or for Kosovar Albanians? Belgrade itself was and remains an extremely diverse, cosmopolitan city, with Muslims, Albanians, and others by the hundreds of thousands living peacefully in close proximity. In no military operation of the civil wars was anything resembling a genocidal policy actually designed or carried out. The propaganda campaign dwelling on Serb atrocities was in fact not too far removed from the narrative contained in the film *Wag the Dog*. Such one-sided discourse totally ignores the role of Western powers in the post–cold war disintegration of Yugoslavia, the U.S. role in supporting the fascist Tudjman regime in Croatia, the horrors of the right-wing Islamic fundamentalist Izetbegovic regime in Bosnia, and the rampant terrorism of groups, such as the KLA, that were organized and funded by the United States. Also ignored is the increased NATO *military* presence in regions of Yugoslavia after 1995, not to mention long-standing U.S. geopolitical interests in the Balkans.[12] To believe that *only* the Serbs could have committed war crimes within such a historical matrix is so preposterous on its face that, for this reason alone, the credibility of ICTY should be seriously questioned.

In fact the most egregious crimes of war in the Balkans can be laid at the doorstep of the U.S./NATO military forces, guilty of carrying out seventy-nine days of high-tech aerial terrorism, with its extensive destruction of civilian targets and population, including large parts of the Serb infrastructure. Belgrade alone suffered upwards of ten thousand casualties, with thousands more scattered around the country. The attacks destroyed power plants, factories, apartment complexes, bridges, water plants, roads, hospitals, schools, and communications networks. NATO targets in Yugoslavia were 60 percent civilian, including 33 hospitals, 344 schools, and 144 industrial plants. The "humanitarian" air squadrons, relying on the comfort and safety of technowar, dropped cluster bombs and delivered missiles tipped with depleted uranium, spewing thousands of tons of toxic chemicals and radiation into the air, water, and crops, guaranteed to produce long-term health problems and ecological disasters. Beneath the rhetoric of human-rights intervention, a small, poor, weak, relatively defenseless nation of eleven million people was pulverized by the largest military machine in history. NATO Commander General Wesley Clark boasted that the aim of the air war was to "demolish, destroy, devastate, degrade, and ultimately eliminate the essential infrastructure of Yugoslavia."[13] This of course was no war but rather an aerial massacre of defenseless human beings, most of them civilians. Not only did the assault violate the UN Charter prohibiting offensive war against a sovereign nation, it willfully abrogated the whole tradition of Hague and Geneva protocols declaring illegal the wanton destruction of civilian populations. Whatever the crimes of Milosevic, they would pale in comparison with the U.S./NATO program of aerial terrorism in Yugoslavia. NATO leaders were indeed charged with monstrous war crimes in 1999, in a suit that named President Clinton, Defense Secretary William Cohen, Secretary of State Albright, and General Clark along with British leader Tony Blair. With massive evidence at their disposal, including calculated policies of mass murder, the plaintiffs took their case to the Hague Tribunal, hoping for an audience before Chief Prosecutor Carla Del Ponte—but the case was summarily thrown out after U.S. leaders protested vehemently, convinced of the mystical (but iron) principle of American immunity. As for Milosevic, Hague prosecutors were admitting (in September 2002) that the case against him—once trumpeted with arrogant confidence—was more flawed than earlier believed owing to difficulty in proving the Serb leader's actual connection with the atrocities in question.

As in the Persian Gulf War of 1991, there was never a bona fide war between NATO and Serb forces in the Balkans—simply a protracted, one-sided campaign of aerial annihilation carried out in direct violation of international law. As Michael Parenti writes: "In sum, NATO's aerial aggression accomplished nothing, except to deliver a magnitude of death and destruction across Yugoslavia far greater than any it claimed to arrest."[14] It has become clear that the United States targeted the Milosevic government not because of crimes against humanity—the ideologically charged nature of such claims made them bogus from the outset—but rather because it was seen as an impediment to U.S. domination of the Balkans, strategically close to the rest of Europe, Russia, the Middle East, and the Caspian Sea, a region rich in oil, natural gas, and other valuable resources.[15] U.S. plans were clearly laid out in a forty-six-page Pentagon document,[16] stating that the United States is prepared to militarily challenge any nation that stands in the way of U.S. policies and interests.[17]

As proceedings at the Hague Tribunal continued through 2003 and 2004, the political bias of the setup became increasingly transparent; U.S. and NATO interests were to be preserved at all costs. The mostly Serbian defendants' right to an open, public trial, for example, was consistently violated by the ICTY, especially in the case of Milosevic—justified often on the vague grounds of U.S. national-security interests. Thus the testimony of

General Wesley Clark before the tribunal, in December 2003, was held out-side the reach of public or press, in closed sessions, a clear transgression of norms set up by the UN General Assembly. In this context Milosevic's right to cross-examine Clark was severely curtailed, contrary to rules established by the ICTY itself. Clark, a public figure who later ran for the U.S. presi-dency, had been in charge of the NATO military action in Yugoslavia and admitted that the intervention was a "technical" violation of international law. It is difficult to imagine that Milosevic and other defendants at The Hague could ever receive a fair hearing by such a thoroughly politicized tribunal.

Meanwhile, the ICTY was regarded with contempt by large sections of the Serbian population, reflected in the fact that the status of Milosevic and other leading defendants was enhanced despite the extremely serious nature of the charges. In November 2003 elections, defendant Voijislav Seselj, representing his Serbian Radical Party from jail, won 28 percent of the parliamentary seats—a vote clearly in defiance of the NATO agenda. Both Seselj and Milosevic emerged as heroes in Yugoslavia owing to their defiance of the United States and NATO, which has imposed a harsh ne-oliberal regimen on Serbia and used financial inducements to get the gov-ernment to support the ICTY proceedings. Indeed a central plank in Seselj's campaign was full rejection of the Hague Tribunal as a kangaroo court set up to stigmatize and demonize the Serbs.

In this context the Hague Tribunal ought to be seen as nothing more than a recycled form of victor's justice, the proceedings so politically biased and legally one-sided as to deny their very legitimacy. It represents not so much a new era of international law as a great retreat from its promises and a return to the earlier colonial ethos, where the Western powers could dic-tate everything by means of crude military superiority.[18] Reflecting on the conflicted legacy of Nuremberg, Telford Taylor writes: "To punish the foe—especially the vanquished foe—for conduct in which the enforcing nation has engaged, would be so grossly inequitable as to discredit the laws themselves."[19]

CRIMES AGAINST PEACE

Even setting aside forms of intervention such as proxy wars, CIA-sponsored covert action, attempts at economic or political subversion, and blockades, the U.S. record of military aggression waged against sovereign nations since World War II stands alone for its criminality and barbaric outcomes. Im-mersed from the outset in a logic of seemingly perpetual warfare, the Amer-ican nation-state first achieved imperial status as it expanded westward and outward, and then reached maturity through development of the permanent war economy during and after World War II. Since 1945 the United States has initiated dozens of military attacks on foreign nations, resulting in a gruesome toll: at least eight million dead, tens of millions wounded, millions more made homeless, and ecological devastation impossible to measure. In the post-9/11 milieu, with the brazen military attack on Iraq and new U.S. interventions on the horizon, there is sadly no end in sight to this imperial onslaught. With just two exceptions (the UN-backed Korean venture and recent operations in Afghanistan) these interventions violated commonly held principles of international law.

At the end of World War II the Germans and Japanese were tried for "crimes against peace"—that is, unprovoked military aggression waged against sovereign nations. Eventually fifteen Germans and twenty-four Japanese were convicted of such offenses, with U.S. prosecutors the most adamant in pursuing guilty verdicts. Nazi elites were prosecuted and convicted of planning and waging war against Poland, the USSR, Norway, Denmark, Holland, Yugoslavia, and Greece. The Charter of the International Military Tribunal at Nuremberg defined "illegal warfare" as "planning, preparation, initiation, or waging a war of aggression, or a war in violation of international treaties, agreements, or assurances, or participation in a common plan or conspiracy [for war]." Drawing on the Nuremberg principles, the nascent UN banned the first use of force, stating, "All members shall refrain in their international relations from the threat or use of force against the territorial integrity of political independence of any state." According to Steven Ratner, "The illegality of aggression is perhaps the most fundamental norm of modern international law and its prevention the chief purpose of the United Nations."[20] The UN Charter provides a definitive list of acts of military aggression: invasion, occupation, bombardment, blockade, attack on a nation's armed forces, using territory for aggression, supporting groups to carry out aggression. Such prohibitions are contained in many treaties, convention protocols, and organizational charters drawn up in the several decades since Nuremberg.

At one time or another, the United States has violated every one of these principles, holding itself (then as now) above the most hallowed norms of international law. Its acts of military aggression have, for the most part, been planned, deliberate, systematic, and brutal, with its massive firepower often directed against weak, small, underdeveloped, and militarily inferior countries. Such acts have *always* been carried out in the absence of serious military threat to the United States arising from the nations targeted for attack; the United States took the first move, usually sidestepping or ignoring diplomatic initiatives. The American military has conducted both selective and strategic bombing, attacked civilian populations and infrastructures, mined harbors, invaded and occupied foreign territories, set up blockades, organized population relocation programs, and set up paramilitary groups for proxy wars on behalf of U.S. interests—and has done so across the globe. In most cases U.S. military operations have been patently unilateral, while in others they came under cover of a UN or NATO coalition where U.S. military (and political) resources were all decisive. Rhetorical justifications for military adventure are offered for public consumption with regularity— humanitarian agendas, human rights, defense of national security, protection of American lives, arrest of drug traffickers, defeat of Communism or terrorism, support for democracy—none of which, however, enjoy much credibility outside the United States. Economic and geopolitical interests have consistently driven U.S. military intervention in the postwar years.

A comprehensive list of U.S. military actions, direct and indirect, can be found in William Blum's *Rogue State*.[21] The flimsy use of a human-rights crusade to justify military aggression in the Balkans has already been mentioned. In the case of Vietnam, American leaders looked to a military solution from the first breakout of Vietnamese nationalism, purportedly to halt the spread of Communism in Southeast Asia and beyond. President Kennedy and his enlightened liberal circle (Dean Rusk, Robert McNamara, McGeorge Bundy, Walt Rostow, Maxwell Taylor, and others) set forth an ambitious war plan according to which Indochina was to be a major testing ground in the cold war. The foundation of everything that would unfold later—large-scale deployment of troops, aerial bombardments, strategic hamlets, free-fire zones, chemical warfare—was already in place under Kennedy.[22] War as counterinsurgency was immediately and energetically taken up as vital to the global contest between Communism and democracy. The logic of military intervention meant the rapid expansion of U.S. operations, starting with teams of "advisers," from South to North Vietnam by 1965 and then to Laos and Cambodia, ignoring diplomatic overtures as spelled out in the 1954 Geneva Accords, not to mention the UN Charter prohibition against military aggression. What Kennedy and his planners had set in place was pushed further along during the Johnson and Nixon presidencies, even though war was never formally declared against North Vietnam, Laos, or Cambodia. The United States mercilessly bombed North Vietnam (after 1965), Laos (after 1965), and Cambodia (1969–1970) with the deadliest aerial onslaught in history, leaving vast regions of utter destruction. For one of the most flagrant violations of international law ever, three U.S. presidents and their war managers could and should be held criminally accountable for crimes against peace just as the Nazis and Japanese were at Nuremberg and Tokyo. Christopher Hitchens has correctly identified Henry Kissinger as a mass murderer and war criminal for his role in Indochina, but Hitchens fails to explain why the list should stop with Kissinger.[23]

Turning to the Caribbean region, the United States has a long and well-known legacy of unprovoked military aggression there, designed to protect American economic and strategic interests. Leaving aside covert action and proxy wars, recent decades have witnessed one-sided warfare launched against five sovereign nations: Haiti, the Dominican Republic, Nicaragua, Grenada, and Panama. In April 1965, a popular revolt broke out in the Dominican Republic with the aim of restoring to power reformist Juan Bosch (earlier overthrown with U.S. help). The United States sent in twenty-three thousand troops to crush the rebellion and preserve the military dictatorship. As the United States waged proxy warfare in Central America for many decades, its operations became more direct at times—for example, with the mining of Nicaraguan harbors in the early 1980s. Nicaragua filed suit in the World Court in 1984 asking for relief, whereupon the court ruled (in 1986) that the United States was in violation of international law, should cease its intervention, and should pay reparations. The Reagan government dismissed the charges and the verdict summarily, refusing to accept the court's jurisdiction. In October 1983 the United States invaded tiny Grenada, killing hundreds of people (including eighty-four Cubans), with the intent of overthrowing the reformist Maurice Bishop government—ostensibly to restore democracy. A decade later, in Haiti, President Clinton sent U.S. troops to bring Jean-Bertrand Aristide back to power under the diktat (enforced by occupying soldiers) that he adopt neoliberal economic policies.

Perhaps the most brazen U.S. military attack came against Panama on December 20, 1989, when air and ground forces invaded and then took over the country, ousting supposed drug trafficker Manuel Noriega and installing its own friendly regime, at the cost of at least four thousand Panamanian lives (mostly civilians) and the crushing of opposition political groups. The working-class section of Panama City, El Chorillo, was largely demolished, with fourteen thousand left homeless. The Bush presidency justified its totally unprovoked attack on several grounds—arresting Noriega for drug trafficking, restoring democracy, protecting American lives—none of which carried much weight relative to the pull of U.S. strategic interests in the Panama Canal region. Bush never declared war, nor did he secure the endorsement of the Organization of American States or the United Nations.[24]

In the case of Iraq, United States–organized and -managed crimes against peace must be considered among the most egregious of the twentieth century—and, sadly, they are ongoing. Dismissing all negotiating initiatives after the Iraqi attack on Kuwait in 1990, the United States mobilized a coalition of military forces, largely by means of bribes and threats, to carry out a devastating technowar against Iraq, destroying the country's frail infrastructure and killing at least two hundred thousand people, including thirty thousand troops in retreat along the "highway of death" as operations were ending. The United States inflicted more damage on Iraq than on any other country in the twentieth century, aside from Korea and Vietnam. (Although the United States was able to buy the participation of coalition partners, for example by $7 billion in loans to Russia, *military* action remained mostly the province of Americans, with British help.) After the Gulf War the United States created no-fly zones over Iraq, continued regular bombing missions, and enforced draconian sanctions that UN agencies report to have cost about five hundred thousand lives.[25] While the Security Council endorsed *political* efforts to contain Iraqi foreign ambitions, there were no stipulations allowing the kind of *military* carte blanche so eagerly pursued by the United States. War crimes visited upon Iraq include some of the most barbaric in modern history. Even with the blessings of UN cover in the case of Desert Storm, the United States was clearly guilty of planning and carrying out a war of aggression. The second Gulf War, carried out essentially to finish what was begun in 1991, was never able to win UN support despite months of Bush administration maneuvering.

In the wake of the second Gulf War, the United States moved quickly and ruthlessly to secure its geopolitical advantage in Iraq, with predictably disastrous consequences. The military occupation established in spring 2003 set up a colonial regime that the United States employed to remake the economic, political, and legal structures of Iraq—a violation of international law, contained in provisions of the 1949 Geneva Conventions governing military occupation. These conventions state that any occupying power must respect the laws, customs, and institutions of the nation it controls, but the United States set out to change everything, in complete disregard of such universal principles. Thus, according to order 39, in September 2003 the Bremer provisional administration issued decrees privatizing state property and allowing foreign ownership in the economy, clearly a plan to allow heightened Western investment in and control over the Iraqi system of production. Instead of safeguarding resources and laws, as it is obligated to do, the United States moved resolutely and brazenly to secure its own interests and those of Western corporations anxious to reap huge profits during the reconstruction process. One can fairly assume that no Western government or corporate leaders will be held accountable for criminal actions in violation of the Geneva Conventions, even as Iraqis presumed guilty of war crimes (including Saddam Hussein) are destined to be brought before a politicized tribunal.

Other, less flagrant or horrendous cases of U.S. military aggression have taken place during the postwar years—for example, four aerial bombardments of Libya in the 1980s, troop deployments to Somalia in 1997, and the "war against terrorism" in Afghanistan beginning in October 2001. (The Afghan operations to destroy al Qaeda base camps and overthrow the Taliban regime might be justified as strictly *defensive* responses to 9/11, permitted under the UN Charter, but the excessive cost in human lives there, reaching well over three thousand, raises questions of proportionality.) In early November 2002, a CIA-operated, unmanned Predator aircraft struck a target in Yemen with a laser-guided Hellfire missile, killing six people in a vehicle—part of the increasingly bold military response to terrorism. This attack, coinciding with Bush's doctrine of preemptive strike, expands the boundaries of warfare: the United States has given itself the right to intervene militarily in any country, at any time, in flagrant violation of international law.[26] In these and other cases a few generalizations regarding U.S. military actions stand out: the casualty toll is mainly civilian, the military option is unprovoked, justifications are bogus, reliance on aerial technowar minimizes American casualties while creating more bloodshed on the ground, attacks are waged against rather small, weak, defenseless nations that deviate in some way from U.S. global priorities. In all cases (with the possible exception of Afghanistan) U.S. militarism stands in direct, increasingly dangerous violation of international law, the very essence of crimes against peace.

U.S. leaders often argue that a breakdown in negotiations, owing to the unreasonable stubbornness of adversaries, is enough to warrant military response. For the most part, however, U.S. "diplomacy" when confronting much weaker rivals has not been very serious, providing mainly a pretext for warfare. At no time has U.S. intervention met conditions stipulated in the UN Charter—namely, that armed attack cannot proceed except in cases of national defense, or without efforts to negotiate in good faith. Indeed the very requirement for diplomacy has typically been problematic: international "crises" are more often than not contrived phenomena, as the cases of Vietnam, Iraq, and Panama reveal. When it takes place, U.S. diplomacy usually involves laying down a set of demands treated as ironclad and nonnegotiable, presented as the basis of "agreements." The other side is naturally reluctant to concede every point or yield to every condition (such as allowing foreign occupation troops or weapons inspectors to roam freely around its country). The predictable lack of cooperation is seized on by U.S. "negotiators" as a clear sign of obstructionism, a failure to negotiate in good faith. Ultimatums are issued, followed by the massive use of firepower extending from days to months and even years. Such maneuvers are doubly criminal insofar as they are deliberately fraudulent and a cynical cover for militaristic intent.

AERIAL TERRORISM:
FROM HIROSHIMA TO BAGHDAD

Since the final months of World War II, the U.S. military has dropped tens of millions of tons of bombs on several mostly defenseless countries, with casualties (the vast majority civilian) also running into the tens of millions. Since the 1920s war managers have placed overriding faith in the efficacy of aerial warfare: at that time planes were seen as awesome destructive machines capable of bringing order to the general chaos and unpredictability of ground and naval operations. Bombing from high altitudes was indeed a nascent form of technowar. By 1944 and 1945 this faith assumed new dimensions as first Britain and then the United States embraced plans for "strategic," or area, bombing in Germany and Japan, ostensibly to end the war more quickly but in reality for purposes of revenge, weapons testing, and sending political messages. With incendiary assaults on German cities (Hamburg, Dresden, Berlin) by the Royal Air Force, U.S. General Curtis LeMay saw a new model of aerial warfare with vast possibilities for punishing the Japanese, literally burning cities to the ground, while minimizing American casualties. This legacy remains a cornerstone of U.S. imperial power to the present day.

One problem with aerial bombardment is that it obliterates the time-honored distinction between combatants and noncombatants, between military and civilian targets—a maxim especially applicable to strategic bombing, which, by definition, rains death and destruction indiscriminately across wide parcels of territory. Article 25 of the Fourth Hague Convention in 1907 states that "bombardment, by whatever means, of towns, villages, dwellings, or buildings which are undefended, is prohibited"—still a valid principle of international law.[27] Efforts to deepen and further codify these provisions have been, predictably, fiercely resisted by the United States and Britain, nations that refused to prosecute the Germans and Japanese after World War II for bombing civilian populations, knowing they were even more guilty of the same crimes. Such rejectionism continued into the Geneva Convention of 1949, with the United States especially opposed to any restraints on aerial bombing (including the use of nuclear weapons). The two countries worked diligently to block any reference to aerial "war crimes" from the convention. As Lindqvist notes: "The victorious powers could hardly forbid bombing of civilians without incriminating themselves for what they had already done and planned to continue doing."[28] Finally, in 1977 Protocol One of the Geneva Conventions was signed by 124 countries, despite continued U.S. resistance to any laws guaranteeing the protection of civilians. The basic rule states: "In order to ensure respect for and protection of the civilian population and civilian objects, the parties to the conflict shall at all times distinguish between the civilian population and combatants and between civilian objects and military objectives and accordingly shall direct their operations only against military objectives." Article 52 further states that "attacks shall be limited strictly to military objectives." Article 54 contains additional references—for example: "It is prohibited to attack, destroy, remove, or render useless objects indispensable to the survival of the civilian population, such as foodstuffs, agricultural areas . . . crops, livestock, drinking water installations and supplies and irrigation works." Article 57 warns those planning military attacks to "refrain from deciding to launch any attack which may be expected to cause incidental loss of civilian life, injury to civilians, damage to civilian objects, or a combination thereof."

If strictly adhered to, such provisions would rule out aerial warfare directed against populated areas or civilian infrastructures—precisely the methodology most favored by the Pentagon since 1945, and precisely why the war planners vehemently object to the provisions. In July 1945 American planes, with the Pacific war virtually ended, raided sixty-six defenseless Japanese cities with no military purpose in mind, burning most of them to ashes and killing up to five hundred thousand civilians. On March 9–10, 1945, hundreds of U.S. planes attacked Tokyo with incendiary bombs, killing one hundred thousand and making another one million homeless— again, without real military intent. As is well known, on August 6 and 9, 1945, the United States dropped atomic bombs on Hiroshima and Nagasaki, unprotected urban centers with little military import, killing a total of at least two hundred thousand civilians. LeMay and his aides celebrated these raids as wonderful testimonials to the awesome power of aerial bombardment. Douglas MacArthur's aide General Bonner Fuller, on the other hand, described the raids as "one of the most ruthless and barbaric killings of noncombatants in all history."[29] They were in stark violation of the Fourth Geneva Convention. From 1946 to 1948 the International Military Tribunal for the Far East tried Japanese political and military elites for war crimes, but in reality the United States was a far more serious offender. Of course, since the United States was a victor none of its officials were ever brought to justice, nor was the very *discourse* of U.S. war crimes ever broached (except by the Japanese themselves).

In 2003 the Smithsonian National Air and Space Museum in Washington, DC, opened a new annex with its centerpiece a display of the Boeing B-29 superfortress *Enola Gay*, which dropped the first atomic bomb on Hiroshima. Unfortunately, the museum provides an abundance of technical details regarding the plane but nothing about its bombing mission or its consequences. Such a lack of information, of course, could hardly amount to an oversight. The museum director, retired General John Dailey, says the public has no need for such details: "We are displaying it in all its glory as a magnificent technological achievement. . . . Our primary focus is that it was the most advanced aircraft in the world at the time." That the *Enola Gay* was responsible for the deaths of well over one hundred thousand people, 95 percent of them civilians, strikes Dailey as an irrelevant or trivial fact, but of course an objective judgment would regard the aircraft as a vehicle of massive war crimes, a conduit of aerial terrorism—its mission quite unnecessary to end the war. Any display with even a modicum of professional objectivity and ethical sensitivity would present such information as a central feature of the exhibit.

The remarkable absence of this reveals not only a keen ethos of American exceptionalism—the nation being so noble that anything it does must be regarded as acceptable—but precisely the kind of war-crimes denial for which the United States so frequently scolds other nations (above all Japan).

The end of World War II brought a new era in the history of military combat—aerial warfare without limits. Strategic bombing, with its inevitable destruction of civilian populations and infrastructures, was now (above all for the United States) perfectly legitimate, indeed preferred and celebrated. If World War II provided a testing ground for massive area bombing, for widespread use of incendiary devices including napalm, for nuclear weaponry, the Korean War offered new opportunities for refinement: aerial terrorism was pushed to new levels. In three months of 1951 alone the USAF used B-29s to systematically destroy every significant North Korean city and town, not only slaughtering hundreds of thousands of defenseless civilians but creating widespread homelessness, starvation, disease, and other miseries. No laws of warfare were adhered to. By the end of the war the Korean death toll (North and South) reached nearly three million, mostly from U.S. aerial bombardments. Visiting Korea in summer 1952, Supreme Court Justice William O. Douglas said: "I had seen the war-battered cities of Europe, but I had not seen devastation until I had seen Korea."[30] As in the case of Japan (and later Indochina), civilian populations were deliberately targeted, the massive death and destruction celebrated by its perpetrators. Referring to Korea and China, Lindqvist writes: "In American eyes, the yellow and red perils had now been united, and a half-billion people had suddenly become America's enemies."[31]

Two decades later, the United States had (between roughly 1965 and 1973) dropped eight million tons of bombs on Vietnam—by far the largest aerial bombardment in history, equivalent to one hundred Hiroshima-sized atomic bombs. The goal was to conduct massive counterinsurgency operations mainly through saturation bombing carried out by B-52s, with no attempt to distinguish between civilian and military objects. As William Gibson writes, Vietnam marked the real beginnings of technowar involving a strategy explicitly designed to minimize ground combat and U.S. casualties, though this style of war would not achieve full expression until Desert Storm in 1991.[32] Except for nuclear weaponry itself (actually considered at one point), the U.S. military employed everything in its arsenal, with the aim of bombing an underdeveloped country into total submission: saturation attacks with two-thousand-pound bombs, napalm, white phosphorous, cluster bombs, chemical defoliants like Agent Orange, sophisticated missiles, and frightening amounts of regular ordnance. Laos and Cambodia became targets of much the same strategy, in more concentrated dosages. The war left some ten million bomb craters in Vietnam alone.[33] Commenting on such aerial terrorism, Marilyn Young writes:

> In the South 9,000 out of 15,000 hamlets, 25 million acres of farmland, 12 million acres of forest were destroyed and 1.5 million farm animals had been killed; . . . all six of the industrial cities in the North were badly damaged, as were the provincial and district towns and 4,000 out of 5,800 agricultural communes. North and South, the land was cratered and planted with tons of unexploded ordnance.[34]

Waging merciless assaults against civilian targets, the United States manufactured new types of napalm designed to adhere more closely to the skin, burn more deeply, and cause more horrific injury. During World War II the United States had dropped 14,000 tons of napalm, mainly against the Japanese. During the Korean War the total was 32,000 tons. But in Vietnam from 1963 to 1971 the total was about 373,000 tons of the new, more effective napalm—eleven times the total used in Korea. Napalm was especially preferred by the military since it could destroy wide target areas while incapacitating human beings with only peripheral hits.[35]

During the first Gulf War the USAF flew 11,000 sorties that dropped 88,000 tons of bombs, more than half of them on densely populated urban centers like Baghdad and Basra. There was deliberate intent to destroy the Iraqi infrastructure, with the stated objective of leaving the country of twenty-three million people in a preindustrial state. This meant destroying targets essential to human life: water and electrical plants, transportation, communications, agriculture, factories, even residential dwellings. The United States brought debilitating aerial weapons, including 15,000-pound "daisy cutter" bombs, CBU-87 cluster bombs with random killing effects over hundreds of square meters, 2.5-ton superbombs, and a variety of bombs and missiles tipped with depleted uranium (DU). The human and ecological consequences of such weapons of wanton destruction will persist for decades, exacerbated by continued bombing raids *after* 1991, draconian economic sanctions, and the second Gulf War.[36] For acts of military aggression against Iraq the first Bush administration was charged with war crimes by the independent Commission for Inquiry for the International War Crimes Tribunal. Indictment four states: "The U.S. intentionally bombed and destroyed civilian life, commercial and business districts, schools, hospitals, mosques, churches, shelters, residential areas, historical sites, private vehicles, and civilian government offices." Indictment five adds: "The U.S. intentionally bombed indiscriminately throughout Iraq." Volumes of evidence were brought forward in support of these charges.[37] Such wanton aerial destruction violates every canon of international law and morality. As we have seen, in spring 1999 the United States and a few NATO allies initiated bombing raids over Yugoslavia that would last for seven weeks, visiting similarly terrible destruction on Belgrade and other Serb cities and towns. As in Iraq, these attacks destroyed public and residential buildings, water and electrical works, transportation, communications, bridges, hospitals, schools, and food production, as well as military targets, leaving the Serb civilian infrastructure in ruins.[38]

All this took place against a nation virtually devoid of an air force or even air defenses—that is, defenseless, as revealed by the fact the U.S. military suffered *no* casualties while producing its carnage. As in Iraq, of course, this was really no war but rather an organized, planned, criminal massacre orchestrated from the skies. Michael Parenti is correct in his observation that "such a massive aggression amounts to a vastly greater war crime than anything charged against Milosevic."[39] And indeed wanton destruction of this sort is clearly prohibited by the Hague and Geneva Protocols.

After the events of 9/11, Bush II launched a bombing campaign in Afghanistan directed against al Qaeda and the Taliban regime, resulting in at least three thousand civilian deaths. Previous missions were carried out in Afghanistan and the Sudan, with fewer casualties. Insofar as these actions can be seen as a defense against terrorism, their status as war crimes is more ambiguous—though deliberate assaults on civilian objects *under any circumstances* is a violation of international law. Other instances of U.S. aerial terrorism—for example, Panama and the more recent bombardments of Iraq—deserve more serious attention. Since World War II the United States has defended its military atrocities—including the systematic destruction of civilian objects—as a necessary means of undermining enemy morale, blunting the capacity of the enemy's workforce, creating social and psychological havoc, and destroying the basis of the enemy's arms production. Military violence directed against civilian populations for any of these reasons, however, is still unjustified and must be placed in the category of war crimes or even, in some cases, of crimes against humanity.

WARFARE AGAINST CIVILIANS

Contrary to popular mythology, civilian populations have always been the main victims of U.S. military ventures, and, more often than not, such victims were clearly *intended*. Tariq Ali is not exaggerating when he writes: "The massacre of civilian populations was always an integral part of U.S. war strategy."[40] Nor is Edward Herman overstating the case when he observes that "U.S. military policy has long been based on strategies and tactics that involve a heavy civilian toll."[41] This is patently true of aerial warfare, as we have seen, but the perpetual, bloody onslaught against civilians also includes ground operations.

The record of European settler military assaults on native peoples, as Ward Churchill documents, spans at least four centuries, part of a "vicious drive toward extermination" that killed tens of millions. Upon its founding the United States became a powerful force behind exterminism even as its military forces proclaimed civilizing agendas. Carried out within a matrix of capitalism, imperialism, and racism, massacres of Indian tribes were often systematic, planned, and accompanied by utter destruction of land and culture—war crimes and crimes against humanity by any reckoning, although such crimes were not yet internationally codified.[42] So much of the American tradition of war—savage, total, racist—was inherited from the Indian wars, then given ideological meaning through such nationalist discourses as Manifest Destiny and the Monroe Doctrine. It was a tradition that, to varying degrees, generally allowed for merciless attacks on civilian populations.[43] The legacy was continued during wars with Mexico and Spain, turning outward with colonial expansion in the twentieth century. Not surprisingly, the United States has consistently rejected international treaties and protocols for protecting civilians against the horrors of war. As Caleb Carr writes, the United States was historically adept at constructing an "evangelical military" bereft of any respect for other nations and cultures, which, thoroughly devalued as a matter of imperial arrogance, were readily demonized and offered up for destruction.[44] The United States has pursued global ambitions through every conceivable barbaric method: wars of attrition, carpet bombing, free-fire zones, massacres of unarmed civilians, support for death squads, forced relocations, the destruction of public infrastructures, the burning down of cities, and the use of weapons of mass destruction, including atomic bombs. Often propelled by imperial contempt for others and sense of moral supremacy, U.S. leaders have established themselves as beyond the reach of international law, immune to moral or legal rules of engagement.

Had such rules of engagement ever come into play historically—as seemed to be the case in World War I, when civilians were spared the brunt of the carnage—they were mercilessly transcended by the end of World War II, when large urban areas became targets of military action. In the Pacific, this was not simply a matter of aerial terrorism. Ground and naval combat was also devoid of limits, on both sides. For its part, the United States carried out military operations with unbelievable savagery: prisoners were regularly tortured and shot, soldiers and civilians were massacred by the hundreds and thousands, prisoners were buried alive in mass graves, survivors of sunken ships were strafed and killed at sea, towns and cities were annihilated with wanton disregard for human life. Savagery of this sort was hardly incidental to larger military goals and modus operandi or a simple product of "collateral damage"; it was in large part an established *pattern*, accepted within virtually nonexistent rules of engagement in the Pacific theater. Thus officers of the U.S. Army were proud to say, for example, that "the 41st [unit] didn't take prisoners."[45]

The Korean War of 1950–1953 took an even more horrendous toll on civilian life: aside from the torrent of bombs dropped by U.S. planes, ground forces conducted themselves with extreme cruelty in what became an exhaustive war of attrition. During a period of retreat in fall 1950 General MacArthur ordered a total scorched-earth campaign, whereupon the U.S. Army destroyed everything in its path—factories, homes, farms, hospitals, sources of water and electricity, irrigation dams, roads, animals. Hundreds of towns and villages were destroyed with no regard for the civilian inhabitants, who were dismissed as the enemy or otherwise useless in the anti-Communist crusade. As in the Pacific theater against the Japanese, prisoners were routinely tortured and killed. Large-scale massacres, such as the well-known incident at Nogun Ri in 1951, were as common as they had been during World War II and would later be in Vietnam. Referring to the entire debacle of Korea, Stephen Endicott and Edward Hagerman write: "American military culture accepted the World War II standpoint that mass destruction of civilians was a legitimate military target in an expanded war of attrition."[46] Flagrant war crimes were committed by the highest-ranking military officers down to the lowest ranks, but no one was ever charged with, much less convicted of, such crimes.

U.S. military policy and conduct was even more brutal throughout Indochina, spanning an entire decade rather than three years, as in Korea. Carnage in Vietnam resulted not only from aerial bombardments but from ground warfare of all types: strategic hamlets where civilians were placed in enclosed compounds, free-fire zones, search-and-destroy missions, defoliation, soldiers prepared to kill anything that moved. More than ten million persons were displaced, while hundreds of thousands were relocated in "hamlets" that served as concentration camps. Herbicides destroyed millions of acres of jungle and cropland. More than twelve hundred square miles of land was bulldozed. Towns and villages were bombed, torched, and bulldozed, their inhabitants slaughtered. Vast regions of Vietnamese society were pulverized in the name of "pacification" and "nation building," code words for the most ruthless counterinsurgency program ever undertaken.

The standard modus operandi in Vietnam, as in Korea, was to destroy *any* impediment to military success in the field—to "kill 'em all," as the title of a BBC documentary on U.S. war crimes in Korea conveys. "Search and destroy" meant attacking not only combatants but civilians, animals, the whole ecology as part of effective counterinsurgency operations. When troops came upon any village they usually began by opening fire, often with the support of helicopter gunships. U.S. troops were rewarded according to the well-known "body count," never limited to identifiable combatants. As one GI put it: "We're here to kill gooks, period." A common U.S. troop refrain in Vietnam went: "Bomb the schools and churches. Bomb the rice fields too. Show the children in the courtyards what napalm can do."[47] Still another refrain: "Kill one, they call you a murderer. Kill thousands, and they call you a conqueror, kill them all, and they won't call you anything."[48] Units that routinely engaged in murder, rape, and mutilation went out of their way to make sure that no soldier would press charges, and few did. Under these conditions prisoners were rarely taken; those who were taken were tortured and then executed. At the Dellums Committee hearings in April 1971 several veterans testified as to how military training prepared them for savage, unrestrained killing in the field: it was crucial to dehumanize the enemy so that it would be possible to "kill without mercy."

As in Korea, U.S. military forces pursued a relentless war of attrition in Vietnam, as well as in Laos and Cambodia. The use of American firepower was nothing short of frenzied, resulting in the loss of three million lives (again, mostly civilians) across Indochina. The crimes were virtually routine, carried out with a fierce chauvinistic animus, but no political officials or military personnel were ever charged—with the famous exception of Lieutenant William Calley, for his role in the My Lai massacres of March 1968, when more than two hundred innocent civilians were shot to death. Calley was court-martialed and given a light sentence, serving less than three years for crimes that obviously deserved much harsher punishment. The problem was that My Lai was hardly an aberration; massacres were common but never reported or, if reported, covered up by military personnel. As the Bertrand Russell Tribunal made clear at the time, U.S. war crimes were of such a magnitude and implicated so many high-level political and military officials that only a Nuremberg-style international tribunal could have brought justice. Since the perpetrators of mass murder and other crimes of war were able to hide under the cloak of a superpower, there was no Nuremberg and no justice. Indeed one of the leading war criminals of the period, President Richard Nixon, would have the last word: "When the President does it, that means it is not illegal"—a maxim that, in the case of Nixon, pertained only to foreign affairs.

Compared to the Indochina carnage, which continued for well over a decade, the U.S. invasion of Panama in December 1989 was a relatively minor, brief incursion resulting in only moderate casualties. Quick as it was, however, the operation was intense, high-tech, and deadly, revealing again the utter contempt of U.S. military forces for local populations. With the ostensible goal of arresting Noriega and protecting American lives, the invasion produced at least four thousand civilian deaths and fifty thousand homeless, according to the 1990 Independent Commission of Inquiry. The El Chorillo district of Panama City was mostly burned to the ground. Many oppositional groups were destroyed or banned, while people were arrested and detained for weeks, even months, with no formal charges and many others (both military and civilian) wound up "disappeared."[49] The Pentagon strategy for a rapid, total victory meant using heavy firepower over a small, densely populated territory. According to one eyewitness report: "Before reaching the street, we saw a group of some 18 U.S. soldiers coming down the street. We saw them entering each house and the residents coming out followed by the soldiers and then we saw houses one-by-one going up in smoke. The U.S. soldiers were burning our houses."[50] Commenting on the horrors of technowar in Panama, Chu Chu Martinez says: "The volume of U.S. firepower and the refinement of their weapons is incredible. They did in Panama more or less what Hitler did in Spain, using it as a practice ground for the weapons he would use during World War II."[51] In this case, the dress rehearsal happened to be for the first Gulf War little more than a year later.

It was during Desert Storm that the U.S. military was first able to unveil technowar in its full glory: Iraq became a "free-fire" zone over which 110,000 aerial sorties were flown, dropping some 88,000 tons of bombs on a country with minimal air defenses. As we have seen, the USAF was able to pulverize the Iraqi infrastructure while suffering few casualties of its own (until later, when the terrible health effects of DU and other toxic agents became visible). At the end of combat, with nothing left in doubt, U.S. planes bombed and strafed retreating Iraqi troops, killing at least thirty thousand—clearly a violation of the Hague and Geneva protocols. The bombings continued regularly after the main warfare concluded. The United States employed thousands of weapons tipped with DU, ensuring that radioactive substances would be left in the water, soil, and food chain for decades.[52]

The harshly punitive regimen of economic sanctions against Iraq, enforced mainly by the United States and Britain under UN cover, led, according to most estimates, to at least five hundred thousand civilian deaths. Sanctions were based on the hypocritical insistence that Iraq dispose of its weapons of mass destruction. The embargo cruelly blocked vital imports such as medical supplies, water-treatment technology, even certain foodstuffs that, under the excessively broad definition of "dual use," might have been considered useful to the military. Sanctions policies have been employed regularly by the United States, which has been using its economic clout as a foreign-policy tool since the 1950s. The main victims have been civilians, a large percentage of them children. The 1977 Additional Protocols to the Geneva Conventions prohibit measures that deprive the civilian population of goods indispensable to survival, with article 18 mandating *relief* operations to aid a civilian population suffering "undue hardships owing to lack of supplies essential for its survival, such as foodstuffs and medical supplies." In fact the United States alone had obstructed every humanitarian effort, mounted by NGOs as well as members of the UN Security Council, to lift the sanctions. Writing in *Harpers*, Joy Gordon characterizes the sanctions as a "legitimized act of mass slaughter." She adds: "Epidemic suffering is needlessly visited on Iraqis via U.S. fiat inside the U.N. Security Council. With that body, the Untied States has consistently thwarted Iraq from satisfying its most basic humanitarian needs, using sanctions as nothing less than a deadly weapon."[53]

As the U.S. military theoretically enters an era of "safe wars," a profound "asymmetry" of warfare emerges, meaning that a superior force can expect fewer risks and casualties while inflicting even greater damage on targeted foes. The atrocities likely to result from such warfare will go largely unreported in the United States or, if reported, will be quickly swept aside in the midst of wartime media superpatriotism. Thus in Afghanistan it became known that U.S. planes frequently attacked and destroyed civilian targets: bombers saturated large areas with devastating impact, while heavy AC-130 gunships armed with howitzers, cannons, and machine guns had carte blanche throughout the country. The main targets were al Qaeda base sites, Taliban military positions, and bunker hideouts, yet civilian areas were hit, with the loss of life estimated (by the Red Cross) to be upwards of three thousand. On December 29, 2001, U.S. aircraft destroyed an entire village, killing dozens of civilians and injuring many more, after flying several quick sorties in early-morning darkness. Taliban leaders were said to be concealed in the village of Qalaye Niazi, but most of the people hit were involved in a large wedding party. According to the UN, unarmed women and children were chased and killed by helicopters as they fled to shelter or tried to rescue survivors.[54] After nearly three months of sustained bombing over one of the poorest countries on earth, various aid agencies made desperate pleas for a bombing halt so that food and medicine could be delivered to hundreds of thousands of refugees, but the United States flatly refused. The United States may have been involved in the mass murder of Taliban prisoners (reportedly more than a thousand) rounded up by the U.S. and Northern Alliance forces near Konduz in late November 2001. According to many reports from different sources, prisoners were herded into container trucks on the journey from Konduz to Sheberghan, condemned to a slow and painful death, and then dumped into mass grave sites, all while U.S. Special Forces—working closely with the ruthless General Abdul Rashid Dostum—remained in the area. As Red Cross and UN representatives expressed "grave concerns" about the atrocities, the Pentagon stonewalled any investigation.[55] If a cardinal principle of international law is to protect both civilians and prisoners of war from random or indiscriminate military attack, the United States has failed this test in most cases where it has intervened militarily.

The long U.S. record of war crimes against civilians, including episodes that go far beyond combat miscalculations or "collateral damage," can be attributed to several combined factors: unprecedented global reach and ambitions, the widespread application of technowar, a deepening culture of violence and militarism, a xenophobic patriotism and ethnocentrism devaluing the lives of human beings from other (especially non-European) territories and cultures. These factors take on greater weight in the context of yet another condition—the elite psychology of sheer imperial arrogance. As Phyllis Bennis comments: "This American-style law of empire exuded extraordinary arrogance, the arrogance of absolute power unchallenged by any other global force."[56] Viewed in cultural terms, this enters into the "sacralization of war" within what Barbara Ehrenreich characterizes as a "burst of nationalist religiosity," where foreign populations become faceless, dehumanized, and demonized, always with a powerful assist from the jingoistic mass media.[57] Military training stresses all this and more, producing a kind of conversion process leading to what Richard Rhodes defines as a "brutalization ethos" marked by a quick willingness to kill, especially from a distance. Such killing is often accompanied by pleasure, even celebration, resembling ancient Roman spectacles.[58] Here the military prepares its recruits for a comfortable escape from all moral restraints, where the harsh consequences of militarism become more or less normalized. This helps explain why the long U.S. legacy of war crimes—repeated with callous indifference throughout the postwar era—has been so widely ignored, denied, and (when necessary) covered up. The legacy meets with silence even from reputed ethical agents that one might expect to speak out: religious leaders, political officials, intellectuals, the mass media. Silence is made all the easier when even the most horrendous crimes are carried out under cover of "democracy," "human rights," and "social progress."

WAR CRIMES BY PROXY

An especially common U.S. violation of international law and human rights principles has been its support of terrorist regimes and paramilitary groups around the world since the late 1940s, often with the aim of setting up proxy wars, insurgencies, and other forms of mayhem to advance imperial designs. Brutal governments have been given substantial aid in Israel, Colombia, Turkey, Chile, and Indonesia; rebellions have been financed in Nicaragua, Yugoslavia, and Afghanistan; and death squads have been created as in El Salvador and Guatemala. Governments have been overthrown by means of covert and/or direct intervention, as in Chile and earlier in Iran and Guatemala. Proxy activities, where U.S. military forces remain in the background while atrocities are carried out mainly by local groups, are often the preferred method. Support has taken many forms: direct material assistance, military equipment and weaponry, training and recruitment, intelligence, and political supports within international bodies like the UN. For many decades the United States has trained thousands of operatives within the country who would later become members of governments, militias, and death squads complicit in various war crimes. Countries that commit such crimes by proxy—that knowingly and deliberately provide perpetrators with the resources to carry out their barbaric deeds—are just as guilty as the perpetrators and ought to be held just as accountable. Within international law this is known as "aiding and abetting war crimes." Indeed this is one of the major charges against Milosevic at the Hague Tribunal, where he is accused of helping paramilitary groups in the Balkans (Arkan's Tigers, for example) by means of financial aid, training, weapons shipments, and logistical support. Prosecutors argue that Milosevic is just as culpable of the war crimes perpetrated by the groups involved as if he had taken over their formal leadership.[59] Such a proxy relationship to regimes and organizations has been a stock-in-trade of U.S. foreign and military policy since World War II—yet no U.S. leader has ever been held accountable.

From 1980 to the mid-1980s the CIA recruited, trained, and supported a well-armed Contra network, a made-in-America insurgency set up to overthrow the reformist Sandinista government in Nicaragua. Based in Honduras, the Contras did everything possible to destabilize the system: economic sabotage, mining of harbors, assassination of political officials, above all the large-scale massacre of civilians as part of subverting public morale. The death toll will never be known, but probably ran well into the thousands.[60] Later, during the 1990s, the United States helped recruit, train, and equip local rebellions in Yugoslavia—most notably the right-wing Kosovo Liberation Army (KLA)—operating alongside fascistic groups, as in Croatia and Bosnia, intended to destabilize the elected leaders of Serbia. During 1995–1998 the KLA moved freely throughout Kosovo, killing hundreds of local Serb officials with the goal of liberating the province from Serb control. (The Serb military response to KLA actions was defined as "ethnic cleansing," but the KLA was naturally exempted from such labels in the United States.) In early August 1995, Croatian military forces, armed by the United States, launched what turned out to be the most brutal offensive of the Balkans civil wars, destroying large Serb areas in the province of Kraijina, killing several thousand civilians and forcing more than two hundred thousand from their homes. Trapped Serbians pouring into Bosnia were massacred in large numbers by Croatian and Bosnian military troops that were supported by Germany and the United States. It was a bloody offensive that Clinton's secretary of state, Warren Christopher, had openly endorsed.[61] While the Hague Tribunal was quick to charge Milosevic and other Serb leaders with "ethnic cleansing" and war crimes, nothing was said about this criminal military aggression directed against civilians, nor about U.S. involvement in the very type of proxy war crimes laid at the doorstep of Milosevic.

The United States has supported, indeed *created,* dozens of paramilitary terrorist groups in Latin America alone since the early 1980s. At the School of the Americas (SOA), renamed the Western Hemisphere Institute for Security Cooperation, located in Fort Benning, Georgia, the U.S. military has trained thousands of terrorists in methods of bloody guerrilla warfare directed at legitimate nation-states and local civilian organizations—methods including assassination, torture, murder, and death-squad actions directed against specific targets. Graduates of SOA include Roberto D'Aubuisson, who organized a death-squad network in El Salvador during the 1980s, reportedly killing upwards of ten thousand people as part of U.S. and Salvadoran elite campaigns to destroy leftist and popular organizations. Massacres were common, with scores of villages burned to the ground. Death squads were comprised of both civilians and members of the armed forces, trained and supported by the United States. According to the UN Truth Commission on Salvadoran Death Squads, former major D'Aubuisson helped organize and maintain the paramilitary groups, bringing together American interests, Miami-based exiles, and right-wing Salvadoran forces. In Guatemala, the CIA and Pentagon have supported death-squad activity and governmental repression since the United States engineered the overthrow of Jacobo Arbenz in 1954. The killings, presided over by a series of brutal United States–backed dictators, have been estimated at over two hundred thousand—all made possible by American weapons, equipment, training, money, and logistical aid. Throughout the 1980s and 1990s the Guatemalan death squads were organized primarily by two organizations, the G2 and Archivo, both funded by the CIA and run by CIA-paid Guatemalan military and police officers trained at the SOA and elsewhere. According to witnesses, the G2 has maintained a web of torture centers, secret body dumps, and crematoria.[62] This is nothing less than an ongoing terroristic U.S. military action by proxy.

U.S. assistance to regimes guilty of long-term war crimes against targeted civilian populations struggling for independence and/or human rights has been one of the darkest features of American foreign policy. The Guatemalan repression and murder of tens of thousands of indigenous peoples is just one of the more egregious instances of such policy. The arming and financing of the Iraqi military throughout the 1980s during its brutal war with Iran, including the use of chemical weapons, provides another example. Between 1965 and 1969, the Indonesian military regime massacred some five hundred thousand people, including virtually anyone linked to the left opposition, with full U.S. diplomatic and military support—surely one of the great atrocities of the postwar years, but one that was met with silence in the Western media. A decade later Indonesia invaded East Timor, killing perhaps another one hundred thousand people for the sin of wanting national self-determination, all while the United States continued to arm the regime and block UN measures to halt the carnage. The Suharto regime was for many years one of the favorites of the CIA and Pentagon, owing to its ruthless efficiency. After the 1975 invasion of East Timor U.S.

weapons sales to Jakarta exceeded $1 billion. In the case of Turkey, its harsh treatment of the large Kurdish population has continued for decades while the nation remains a close U.S. ally and a major recipient of U.S. financial and military aid. Repression worsened throughout the 1990s as the Turkish army devastated Kurdish regions, sending hundreds of thousands of poor civilians into flight. Perhaps two million were left homeless, while death squads murdered thousands more. Napalm was used on villages, dropped by United States–made planes. By the year 2000 Turkey had become the single largest importer of U.S. military goods, including F-16 fighter bombers, M-60 tanks, Cobra gunships, and Blackhawk helicopters in substantial numbers, all used against the mostly defenseless Kurds.

The Israeli occupation of Palestine, with its ruthless political and military actions over several decades, is perhaps the most visible case of U.S. war crimes by proxy. In many respects the state of Israel has been an American outpost in the Middle East, replete with every conceivable form of financial, political, diplomatic, and military backing; it is indeed a relationship sui generis. Israel has the fourth largest army in the world, and its militarism has ensured the perpetuation of something resembling an apartheid system marked by ongoing violations of international law: forced settlement of the land, illegal arrests, torture, the relocation of civilian populations, massacres, harsh curfews, assaults on cultural institutions, the wanton bulldozing of homes and property, depriving people of basic services. These actions involve ongoing violations of the Fourth Geneva Convention, along with the UN Charter, but efforts to hold the Israelis accountable have been blocked by the United States, which helps guarantee Israeli occupation of Gaza and the West Bank through its repeated vetoes of UN resolutions. Further, there are 5.5 million Palestinian refugees housed in fifty-nine camps, denied the right to return to their homes in contravention of UN Resolution 194 and international law. The issue of war crimes here cannot be addressed in the United States since, as Edward Said notes, "the systematic continuity of Israel's 52-year-old oppression and maltreatment of the Palestinians is virtually unmentionable, a narrative that has no permission to appear." It is the "last taboo."[63] From 1949 to 2000, the United States gave more than $90 billion in foreign aid and other grants to Israel, including $5.5 billion in 1997 alone. There were eighteen arms sales to Israel in just the year 2000. Thanks to American largesse, the Israelis have the largest fleet of F-16s outside the United States, which forms an integral part of their sophisticated war machine. The regime of Ariel Sharon is fully backed by the United States, although Sharon was held responsible for horrific attacks against Palestinians, including the 1982 invasion of Lebanon and the massacre of several thousand unarmed civilians in the refugee camps of Sabra and Shatila in September 1982, clear violations of international law.

The very charges leveled against Milosevic at the Hague Tribunal—the aiding and abetting of war crimes—could be brought against the United States hundreds of times over, as it uses its supreme economic, political, and military power to wage extended proxy wars around the globe.

THE ROUTINIZATION OF MASS MURDER

One of the more tragic parts of the U.S. war crimes legacy has been its almost total absence from the public discourse: mass media, politics, academia, intellectual life. This can be understood as the result partly of civic ignorance, partly of collective denial, partly of what Gilbert Achcar refers to as "narcissistic compassion," indifference to the suffering of others.[64] However understood, there is little question about the degree to which the horrible costs and consequences of American Empire have become largely routinized within both elite and popular consciousness; the very idea of U.S. culpability for terrible atrocities, including war crimes, human rights violations, and crimes against humanity, is generally regarded as too far off the normal spectrum of discourse to be taken seriously.

Given the postwar historical record, we are dealing here with nothing less than large-scale insensitivity to mass murder. The United States has become such a dominant world superpower that its crimes are more or less invisible, that is, they appear as an integral, acceptable, indeed predictable element of imperial power. Rarely a loser in war, the United States has never had to confront the grievances of those who have been wronged. This condition is exacerbated by the phenomenon of technowar, which, since World War II, has increasingly removed any sense of immediate *personal* involvement in warfare, meaning that feelings of guilt, shame, and moral outrage that might be expected to accompany killing, and especially acts of mass murder, are more easily sidestepped, repressed, forgotten—more easily yet where such acts are carried out by proxies. Long experience tells us that ordinary people, once having completed military training, can all too often calmly plan and implement the killing of vast numbers of unknown, faceless, innocent, defenseless human beings, whether by firing missiles, dropping bombs from thirty thousand feet, shooting off long-distance artillery shells, or engaging in traditional ground combat (increasingly rare for the U.S. military). Once the enemy is portrayed as a sinister beast and monster, dehumanized as a worthless other, then the assault becomes a matter of organization, technique, and planning, part of the day-to-day routines of simply obeying commands, carrying out assigned tasks, fitting all activities into a bureaucratic structure. Within this universe the human targets of military action are regularly defined as barbaric, subhuman, deserving of their fate and possibly even complicit in it: Native Americans, Filipinos, Japanese,

Guatemalan peasants, Koreans, Vietnamese, Iraqis, Serbs. As on the frontier, mass killing may be understood as necessary, a moral imperative to ensure human survival and save "civilization." Viewed accordingly, forces giving expression to racial supremacy, imperialism, and xenophobia converge with a cult of violence (like that discussed in chapter 4) to form an ideological cauldron where crimes of war may come to seem natural, logical.

Within the culture of militarism, large-scale massacres, authorized and legitimated by political and military commands, take on the character of the *ordinary*, where guilt and culpability are routinely evaded.[65] Actions viewed from outside this culture as heinous and criminal appear rather normal, acceptable, even praiseworthy *within* it, part of a taken-for-granted world. Ethical discourses are roundly silenced, jettisoned. Surveying U.S. war crimes, one can see that taken-for-granted barbarism takes many forms: the saturation bombing of civilian populations, free-fire zones, chemical warfare, relocations, search-and-destroy massacres, the torture and killing of prisoners—all sanctioned through an unwritten code of regular military operations. In technowar especially, all human conduct becomes managerial, clinical, distant, impersonal, rendering the carnage technologically rational; individual emotional responses, including the pain and suffering of victims, disappear from view. Even the most ruthless, bloody actions have no villains, insofar as all initiative vanishes within the organizational apparatus and the culture supporting it. War managers' ideology contains specialized military/technical discourses with their own epistemology, basically devoid of moral criteria. As Gibson writes in the context of Vietnam: "Technowar as a regime of mechanical power and knowledge posits the high-level command positions of the political and military bureaucracies as the legitimate sites of knowledge."[66] Here bureaucratic jargon conveniently serves to obscure militarism and its victims with familiar references to the primacy of "national security," the need for "surgical strikes," the regrettable problem of "collateral damage," and "self-inflicted" casualties. Words like "incursion" substitute for real armed attacks, "body counts" for mass slaughter, "civilian militias" for death squads. The very structure of language helps to establish a moral and political gulf between perpetrators and victims, between war criminals and the crimes they commit. In general those who plan do not kill, and those who kill are merely following orders—and they too are usually shielded from psychological immediacy by the mechanism of technowar.

Yet not all war crimes are extensions of technowar: in Vietnam and other locales massacres were indeed authorized and carried out in the midst of ground combat. The My Lai atrocities are well known, but others like them occurred with some frequency in Vietnam and elsewhere. My Lai in fact was part of a much larger search-and-destroy mission by U.S. troops, whose standing orders were to obliterate any resistance or "suspicious" activity and whose well-known incentives were high body counts. After troops used machine guns and grenades to slaughter innocent people in the village, the operation was defined as a "great victory" for Charlie Company. It is a matter of record that neither Lieutenant Calley nor any of the other participants expressed much regret for what they did, echoing previous responses of U.S. military personnel after such atrocities as Wounded Knee and Hiroshima. Said Calley: "I was just ordered to go in there and destroy the enemy. That was my job on that day. That was the mission I was given."[67] Similarly, former U.S. senator and now president of the New School University in New York, Robert Kerrey, expressed few misgivings over having led a commando raid that slaughtered fourteen unarmed civilians in the hamlet of Thanh Phong in February 1969. When finally compelled to face the atrocity twenty-two years later, after reports began surfacing in the media, Kerrey expressed some anguish over his involvement but refused to accept moral accountability, pleading a bad memory.[68] Kerrey, of course, remained on as president of a major American university while life on campus routinely went on (after the Faculty Student Union unsuccessfully called on Kerrey to step down), and the mass media largely ignored the charges in question while sympathizing with Kerrey's own emotional travails.

In the end, the normalcy of Kerrey's life was hardly disturbed, consistent with the embellishment of his persona as just another dedicated, hardworking, distinguished American citizen who fought for his country and might have made some mistakes along the way—far from the image of war criminal. Kerrey looks and acts "normal" enough. So too do the vast majority of U.S. political and military elites who in some way were involved in the crimes of war discussed in this chapter: the Pentagon war machine is led and staffed by ordinary folks with good educations, solid family backgrounds, nice manners, elevated cultural tastes, and benevolent ways. Indeed the Vietnam War itself was the product not of revolting thugs or Hannibal Lecter–type maniacs—or even xenophobic right-wingers—but mainly of liberal, highly educated, literate, humane government officials, many of them celebrated academics, like McGeorge Bundy, Walt Rostow, and Henry Kissinger. Joseph Persico writes that the Nazi defendants at Nuremberg looked and acted in ever respect "ordinary," with the exception of the massive, gruff, red-faced Ernst Kaltenbrunner, a Nazi from central casting. Few Nazis looked like sadistic monsters. "It would be hard to pick out most of these men as war criminals from a gathering of Rotarians or accountants."[69] In fact Albert Speer came across as just another intelligent, successful businessman, someone who could have been an executive at General Motors—although Speer at least confessed to war crimes.

Given the immense size and scope of the U.S. war machine, no one should be surprised to find the most terrible human deeds engulfed and camouflaged by bureaucratic structures that seem ordinary and rational enough on the surface. Obedience, violence, imperial arrogance, even racism are built into the logic of the system—and effectively covered up by that same system. This recalls Hannah Arendt's famous analysis of the Eichmann trial and Nazism. The Nazis too were viewed as "normal" in their killing operations, and most indeed led "normal" lives. Writes Arendt: "The trouble with Eichmann was precisely that so many were like him, and that the many were neither perverted nor sadistic, that they were . . . terribly and terrifyingly normal."[70] As would later be the case in Hiroshima, Vietnam, Panama, Iraq, and other theaters of U.S. war crimes, the people committing atrocities, from top to bottom, with very few exceptions believed they were doing the right, patriotic thing—scarcely giving a second thought to their actions.

CONCLUSION

The experience of two disastrous world wars produced a global commitment to international law that would presumably curtail the worst features of human warfare. This commitment is reflected in the Nuremberg and Tokyo Tribunals, the UN Charter, the Geneva Protocols, and more recently the International Criminal Court set up in Rome. All states and political actors would have strict obligations to follow moral and legal principles, including definite rules of engagement in warfare. The UN Charter, above all, prohibits military force as an instrument of statecraft except in cases of a clear-cut need for self-defense. Of course the very notion of such a paradigmatic shift in relations among nations always depended on the emergence of an international community of interests. Despite references here and there to a growing "culture of human rights," however, this pacifistic dream has turned into a Hobbesian nightmare, as imperial aggression and armed violence have come to dominate the global scene. In such a milieu, moral and legal criteria, following the "realist" outlook championed by Western powers, have seemingly vanished from the political landscape.

There can be no universally valid tenets and practices of international law so long as the United States carries out its relentless pursuit of global domination to further its economic and geopolitical interests. The expansion of U.S. militarism into every corner of the globe, as well as space, is incompatible with a regimen of international law and human rights—as is the neoliberal corporate order that militarism sustains.[71] We are at a point where U.S. global ambitions supersede all hope for shared norms, laws, customs, and treaties.[72] The deadly cycle of militarism and terrorism, involving perpetual war waged from the White House and Pentagon, can only exacerbate this predicament. Increasing awareness concerning U.S. blueprints for full-spectrum world domination, for an extended global Pax Americana, are scarcely reassuring. Strategic departures by the Bush clique make it clear that the United States will tolerate no powerful rival and, to that end, has followed the neocon prescriptions for gaining control of the Gulf region that go back to well before the 2000 election.

The implications of current American foreign and military policy for the future of international relations are therefore depressing indeed: as an imperial rogue state with few constraints on its power, the United States will no doubt be further emboldened to subject the world to its ruthless economic and military agendas. Now more than ever, American elites will feel empowered to disregard and then violate laws and treaties, even as they proclaim their allegiance to human rights and the peaceful resolution of conflicts—all the while expecting other nations to obey those same laws and treaties. As in the scandalous U.S. rejection of the International Criminal Tribunal, the U.S. posture today remains one of exceptionalism, of moral supremacy, placing the most powerful, aggressive military force on earth beyond the reach of controls and sanctions. This is hardly shocking, for, as Chomsky writes: "Contempt for the rule of law is deeply rooted in U.S. practice and intellectual culture."[73] Meanwhile, as U.S. imperial domination expands (at least for the moment) in the face of shrinking obstacles, thriving on the cycle of militarism and terrorism, the superpower capacity to wreak havoc across the globe increases menacingly. A frightening world, given new life by U.S. policies and actions, feeds into the militaristic impulse. Writing even *before* the events of 9/11, Lindqvist observes: "Wars will not disappear—instead they will be longer, bloodier, and more terrible."[74] The refinement of technowar, while perhaps shortening military episodes, is bound to make them ever more terrible. For the American public, however, warfare visited on other countries has become an entertaining spectacle, profitable and at the same time a mechanism for satisfying masculine power and imperial egos.[75]

As for the legacy of war crimes, its very discourse has become obliterated under the weight of U.S. imperial and military power. The Nuremberg principles, adopted by the UN in 1950, state that any person committing an act that constitutes a war crime under international law is legally accountable and subject to punishment, as was the case with the postwar German and Japanese defendants. Such principles were regarded as universal, transcending national laws, traditions, and ideologies, binding for all persons whatever their place in the chain of command. No heads of state, no political or military officials, were seen as immune to criminal prosecution. Over the past several decades, unfortunately, the United States has done everything possible to subvert the Nuremberg principles, with the result that its ringing endorsement of human rights and rule of law is rendered abstract, hypocritical, meaningless. The legacy of war crimes and human-rights abuses stemming from unfettered U.S. global power goes even deeper, however, with its extended roots in historical *continuity*, the result of a deliberate, planned, and systematic pattern of imperial aggrandizement. From this standpoint, war crimes have been a predictable outcome of the U.S. relationship to other nations and the world, virtually a matter of institutional necessity—easy to get away with, moreover, in the absence of media, political, or intellectual scrutiny. Hiding behind the veneer of "democracy" and "human progress," American ruling elites have never come to grips with this criminal history: no apologies, no self-reflection, no reparations, no sense of accountability. The superpower accepts no moral or legal and few political restraints on its grandiose ambitions. It would be foolhardy to expect otherwise so long as the U.S. imperial behemoth, championing doctrines of "humanitarian intervention" and "preemptive strikes," continues to seek world domination.

6

THE ECLIPSE
OF U.S. HEGEMONY?

The new militarism refers to far-reaching changes in the U.S. armed forces and their role in the world: RMA high-tech innovations, the weaponization of space, new global flexibility, the overall growth of the war economy, a bolstering of Empire through economic globalization. More crucially, it is the product of a specific conjuncture in the post–cold war era where the United States has emerged as the lone superpower and the Pentagon has forged more aggressive strategies in the context of international terrorism, 9/11 and its aftermath, a flexible nuclear doctrine, the concept of preemptive strike, and the urgency of resource wars presently focused on the Middle East and Central Asia. U.S. willingness to subvert or bypass international treaties, conventions, and laws, including those embedded in the UN Charter, though hardly novel, when taken together also correspond to a new phase of militarism. The increasing American obsession with military power as a means of asserting national interests, taken to new levels with the presidency of George Bush II, has opened up a potentially ominous new era of world politics. A question that needs to be posed here is: Can the United States sustain long-term global domination mainly on the basis of the deployment of overwhelming force? Are there modes of ideological legitimation available to American ruling elites that could help solidify their supremacy in the face of mounting contradictions and dispersed forms of resistance, both domestic and worldwide?

The resurgence of military priorities and agendas in the service of U.S. global domination hangs over the world like a horrific nightmare that promises never to go away. Over a period spanning many decades American superiority has been reached through a combination of economic, political, diplomatic, and cultural, as well as military, power, but in the post–cold war period the *military* dimension has taken on new significance. Of course there is little that is absolutely novel about an aggressive U.S. foreign and military policy: it has been central to the imperial legacy from the very outset. Owing to some powerful domestic and international trends at work, however, we are witnessing something of a historical turn in the scope, intensity, and probable long-term consequences of Pentagon interventionism. Old limits and restraints are superseded by continuing expansion of the war economy, mounting resource pressures, the informational revolution, and the plain hubris of imperial power. The result could be new levels of military violence that the planet will not be able to withstand.

The fusion of capitalism, racism, and imperial power is deeply rooted in U.S. history. Recent developments have brought not so much a loss of national innocence or betrayal of democracy, much less any departure from "American values," as an intensification of old patterns in a profoundly changed historical matrix. Traditions and ideals frequently associated with the American experience—democracy, freedom, rights, and so forth—appear at the start of the twenty-first century in largely truncated, distorted, partial form, eroded by the harsh effects of corporate, government, and military power swollen by the dictates of Empire. Such traditions and ideals, assimilated by large sectors of the population, can be viewed as sources of legitimation that help sustain unprecedented concentrations of wealth and power. As in the past, Empire cannot long survive without mass belief systems (nationalism, religion, political ideologies) that justify burdensome adventures and deflect public attention away from the terrible costs, pain, and material hardships that inescapably accompany war making. For most of U.S. history, in fact, widespread acceptance of hegemonic discourses and practices—involving an organic linkage between elites and masses—has endowed the imperial project with considerable popular energies. In foreign policy more than other realms, U.S. political leaders have enjoyed a great measure of autonomy, latitude, and credibility even in the face of costly failures like Vietnam.

An urgent question for the fate of the planet is whether U.S. ruling elites can for long sustain their drive toward global domination—that is, whether they can prevail in an arena where military force and political coercion have become the chosen methods of achieving strategic goals. We know that what governing regimes may require for popular support *domestically* may not readily extend to the sphere of world politics, where Hobbesian chaos so often blocks the normal mechanisms of legitimacy and order. U.S. efforts to impose corporate and geopolitical agendas through military power, which it possesses in great abundance, will depend on conditions of effective popular mobilization, needed to justify the costs and sacrifices of Empire. But those very conditions (e.g., patriotism and sense of national exceptionalism) quickly lose their ideological rationale beyond the national territory. Such conditions are more likely to breed opposition and resistance to Empire, including diverse expressions of blowback. Signs of intensifying opposition to Empire have become increasingly visible: global terrorism and the events of 9/11, the flourishing of an international antiwar movement during 2002 and 2003, the growth of antisystem forces such as the World Social Forum, the diffusion of anti–American sentiment in Europe, the Muslim world, Asia, and elsewhere. To the degree those ideological factors generating legitimacy for a new *American* militarism are destined to be counterproductive *globally*, imperial stability will more likely be reinforced by postmodern conditions involving widespread depoliticization, mass apathy, and privatized retreat, and these conditions are bound to ensure greater elite autonomy.[1] No doubt the rulers of Empire would prefer a quieter, more atomized, more depoliticized universe smoothly governed by routine economic transactions, the market, and consumerism, the ideal of an American-managed neoliberal hegemony grounded in a peaceful, more or less consensual imperial order. The problems here are twofold—the neoliberal model itself generates massive social contradictions, while globalized, aggressive U.S. military power ironically works against the trajectory of orderly corporate globalization. As the United States consolidates its status as single world hegemon, hoping to extend its rule over the international system, these contradictions can only significantly worsen.

The global system, now more than ever the product of U.S. economic and military supremacy, requires a strong component of ideological hegemony to reproduce the conditions of that supremacy: "automatic" mechanisms of corporate globalization, a relatively open network of communications and trade, "free markets," consumerism, sufficient popular apathy to permit elite flexibility in its decision making. Widespread chaos and disorder endemic to the ongoing cycle of militarism and terrorism, while no doubt favorable to the power aspirations of a small circle of elites, ultimately works against the smooth functioning of the New World Order, including any system of consensual governance. Alternatives to a Hobbesian scenario look bleak in the post-9/11 setting, in the wake of U.S. military interventions in Afghanistan and Iraq, and with the ever-present likelihood of new military ventures—during what promises to be an endless war on terrorism. As noted, moreover, hegemonic discourses readily available to elites on the home front will be ineffective outside American borders; they will tend to *subvert* hegemony as the United States mobilizes its resources to shore up the foundations of its global supremacy. In the postwar years the United States has enjoyed something of a precarious hegemony, built on liberal democracy, economic successes, consumerism, and the diffusion of its cultural products, but in recent years these tried-and-true sources have begun to atrophy. At the same time, to ensure world *domination* in the post–cold war setting the United States retains a wide repertoire of ruling devices—not only its military superiority but its corporate and financial power and capacity to manipulate international structures like the UN, World Trade Organization, World Bank, and International Monetary Fund. The current predicament derives from the fact that such *domination* does not inevitably translate into much-needed *hegemony*.

The concept of ideological hegemony does not exclude the reliance of a power structure on force, but rather indicates that two elements—force and consent—develop within some measure of equilibrium. The issue is not military power as such but the degree to which its exercise can be legitimated by a variety of social and political arrangements and through popular support. Hegemony is reproduced across multiple venues: education, religion, laws, the political system, mass media, culture. Effective power is established largely within the political arena, where legitimating mechanisms are typically formed and crystallized. Such mechanisms can scarcely be anticipated on the global terrain, however, insofar as distinctly political structures are weak or absent, lacking in effective universality.

For Antonio Gramsci, as for Machiavelli before him, dynamic leadership is always emphatically *political* in character. It is politics that has the special capacity to mobilize popular consent behind generalized ideals and objectives, as in the process of Italian unification, which transcended the limits of social fragmentation and cultural provincialism while creating the foundations of a cohesive, stable nation-state. Here visionary leadership resorts to force only where consensual supports are already widespread, where political goals have been assimilated by large (or at least strategically central) sectors of the population. Where such conditions are absent, reliance on military force exhibits weakness, not strength, which means that the *political* agenda is doomed. For both Machiavelli and Gramsci, viable military operations demand a strong ideological bond between leaders and led, rulers and masses, the state and popular strata. Gramsci's schema in the *Prison Notebooks* indicates the formation of a powerful "moral-intellectual" leadership grounded in widely shared beliefs and values associated with an *emergent* hegemony. Even the most awesome military machine requires this kind of consensual support to forge its own brand of order and discipline and carry out battlefield victories—a case in point being the rise and consolidation of Italian Fascism, which in the 1920s and 1930s legitimated hierarchical rule through its capacity to mobilize a powerful ensemble of nationalist, religious, and political beliefs.[2]

In the tracks of Machiavelli and Benedetto Croce, Gramsci writes that power structures need a supportive "ethico-political" element in order to sustain effective governance. Coercive methods can occasionally work in the short term, but *durable* order necessitates a shift to popular, consensual footing, an equilibrium of force and consent. As for Machiavelli, "politics" for Gramsci involves the winning of popular support that will endow leaders with the two crucial resources of stability and flexibility. Thus: "But to fix one's mind on the military model is the mark of a fool: politics here too must have priority over the military aspect, for only politics creates the possibility for maneuver and movement."[3] Such resources are never available to military power alone, whatever its might and scope, because it can never establish a firm hegemony. At the same time, to create and sustain legitimacy a power structure must achieve not only consensual but a "national-popular" presence, sinking roots in particular (that is, national) traditions, myths, and ways of life. Thus only *politics*, here regarded as the distinct sphere of creative action, historical vision, and legitimation, can organize and manage the various complex expressions of social life—the "ensemble of relations." It follows that in matters of governance military power is usually trapped within the limits of its own authoritarian rigidity, its deep attachment to discipline and rules, its penchant for violent solutions. The eclipse of hegemony presupposes a severe crisis of authority, an erosion of governing capacity that no amount of coercive power or bureaucratic control can reverse. Imposition of dictatorial or military rule in the absence of consensual supports—Gramsci refers at different points to "Caesarism," "Bonapartism," and "Cadornism"—is almost certain to be counterproductive, leading to dysfunctions, breakdowns, and resistance.[4] In the case of present-day capitalism, hegemony serves to compensate for systemic contradictions in the economy: nationalism, religion, Fordism, and consumerism, for example, furnish ideological cohesion in a world where people face terrible material hardships, dislocations, and a sense of powerlessness. A strong consensual base, moreover, reduces the need for political coercion and military violence, precisely what Machiavelli anticipated—contrary to the common misconceptions about his work.

Gramsci argues what for him was a simple truism—that military leadership must be subordinated to politics, a maxim that Napoleon, among others, failed to recognize, to his great undoing. Of course the military usually has the capacity to impose a regime of order and discipline within its own domain—perhaps even briefly outside it—but it lacks the resources to generate ideological or cultural unity over broad expanses of time; it can win "battles" but rarely "wars" in the larger historical sense. The temptation of leaders to seek military solutions at moments of crisis is grievously mistaken insofar as "only a very skillful political leadership, capable of taking into account the deepest aspirations and feelings of the human masses, can prevent disintegration and defeat."[5] Put differently, as power arrangements require integration and coordination they also demand *legitimation* based in an "organic relationship between leaders and led," beyond the rigid, hierarchical, instrumental outlook of military elites.

While Gramsci never systematically brings the concept of hegemony into the realm of international politics, insights can be gleaned from several passages in the *Prison Notebooks*, including those referred to above. Of course the global terrain, with its vast mélange of competing nation-states, expansive scope, and virtual absence of governing mechanisms, differs radically from the state system that commanded most of Gramsci's attention and survives into the present epoch. Yet it is not too difficult to see how the unique conditions of *domestic* support for U.S. worldwide economic and military power might run counter to requirements for *global* hegemony. The strong elements of "national-popular" consent underlying U.S. Empire, rooted above all in a virulent patriotism, will sooner or later conflict with the multiplicity of competing interests and wills across the globe—interests and wills leading to anti-imperial resistance and opposition as predictably as if compelled by a law of physics. A system of global domination resting largely on military force, or even the threat of force, cannot in the greater scheme of things consolidate its rule on a foundation of legitimating beliefs and values. Nor can it smooth over the harsh dysfunctions and conflicts endemic to the corporate world economy by mobilizing forms of hegemony such as nationalism and consumerism, that work so fluidly in domestic politics. As the lone superpower with a huge, seemingly invincible military apparatus and dedicated to ruling the globe by force, the United States has already lost much of its room to maneuver, even as it wins immediate victories by means of economic and diplomatic leverage combined with military power—the same power that may soon become a double-edged sword.

The long history of empires aspiring to tyrannical rule over mass populations, hoping to expand their domain through overwhelming political coercion and military force, has been saturated with fierce resistance, deep quagmires, and humiliating failure: Rome, Spain, France under Napoleon, England, the brief twentieth-century global ventures of Nazi Germany and Imperial Japan. All at some point combined an unshakeable political hubris with faith in armed violence as a means for building Empire—and all had dazzling periods of success before eventually disintegrating or being vanquished. Previous imperial regimes violated the basic Machiavellian (and later Gramscian) premise that power without broad popular consent is destined to either implode or be overthrown. A corollary is that imperial domination by its very logic cannot easily secure much popular legitimacy, if any. By the 1950s the very idea of imperial control based on foreign occupation had become historically obsolete, swept away by a series of postwar (and earlier) anticolonial struggles. The French colonial wars intended to retain control of Indochina and parts of Africa amounted to a final desperate reliance on brute force as the famous European "civilizing" mechanisms of religion, culture, and legal codes met with increasingly violent resistance. Dien Bien Phu and the Battle of Algiers symbolized the final eclipse of a colonial era in which European powers had recognized few limits to the use of military violence, much of it directed against civilian populations. The very *ideology* of imperial domination had been assaulted and destroyed in the name of ideals mainly imported from Europe itself—national self-determination, cultural autonomy, democracy.

If there had been an overriding logic to European colonization, there was an equally powerful logic underlying its negation and demise, identified by such diverse theorists as J. A. Hobson, Rosa Luxemburg, V. I. Lenin, Albert Camus, and Frantz Fanon. As a general statement one could say that the more militarized the system of rule, the more coercive and bloody the foreign domination, the more widespread and successful the resistance— leading to a pattern of nationalist mobilization against the hated presence of a foreign power. This dynamic produced the major Communist and radical-nationalist revolutions of the twentieth century: Mexico, Russia, China, Algeria, Yugoslavia, Vietnam, Cuba, Nicaragua. Eric Wolf points to the vast political turbulence, social dislocations, and armed violence experienced by mostly peasant local populations that were essentially *forced* to oppose the foreign occupiers and their local clients. Large-scale military operations gave rise to a multitude of antisystem movements, community organizations, and political parties with enough structural and ideological cohesion to win state power in a milieu where the imperial forces could never win much popular legitimacy.[6] Valiant attempts by the leading powers to dismantle indigenous social structures, community networks, and political groups, while often all too successful, were ultimately counterproductive, owing precisely to their lack of legitimacy. As the old control systems broke down or were destroyed, new, more oppositional ones generally emerged in their place.

It was in such circumstances that mass-based revolutionary movements, armed in the fight against a militarily superior colonial force, achieved sufficient legitimacy and then power to overthrow the imperial regime. The greater and more bloody the militarism of the dominant power, the more generalized and militant the resistance. In Russia, prerevolutionary colonialism was largely a matter of European (mostly French) economic penetration, but it was the protracted and costly military encounters of World War I, followed by the armed interventions of several capitalist powers, that set the stage for a *successful* Bolshevik Revolution. The Yugoslav partisans mobilized popular insurgency against a brutal Nazi military occupation in the early 1940s—a pattern of resistance duplicated in France, Italy, Greece, and Czechoslovakia—leading to consolidation of a Communist regime after the war. The Algerian revolution of 1962 marked the culmination of decades of opposition to militarized French rule. In Vietnam, the struggle for national independence mixed with radical goals produced a mass-based guerrilla insurgency against a series of occupiers—Japan, Britain, France, the United States—that had for decades brought unspeakable devastation to the country. The Cuban situation departed somewhat from this pattern: U.S. domination was primarily economic and political, its exercise more indirect, but the ceaseless authoritarian controls, as well as Cuba's close proximity to the United States, could be said to have approximated militarized rule.

The Chinese revolution offers perhaps the best historical evidence of the dynamic play of harsh contradictions resulting from military-driven imperial domination. Japanese invasion and occupation, beginning in 1937, wrought massive destruction and hundreds of thousands of casualties across several Chinese provinces, in large part the result of scorched-earth policies carried out deliberately to subdue the peasant population. The Japanese army laid waste to vast areas, in the process brutalizing the local inhabitants. Rather than becoming subdued and defeated, however, great masses of people rebelled and joined the anti-imperialist insurgency, which included Mao's Communist Party, as their hatred of the brutal occupier intensified; barbaric levels of military violence brought unprecedented chaos, out of which popular struggles mushroomed. According to Chalmers Johnson, it was precisely Japanese militarism that stimulated a merger of nationalist and Communist rebellion, leading to the 1949 Maoist triumph. Johnson writes:

> Prior to 1937, the peasants were a passive element in politics; even the earlier Communist bid for power, based on an appeal to peasant economic interests, was a conspicuous failure. The prewar peasant was absorbed in local matters and had only the dimmest sense of "China." Japan's invasion changed this condition by heightening the peasant's interest in such concepts as national defense, citizenship, treason, legitimacy of government, and the long-range betterment of the Chinese state.... Although the peasantry, on the eve of war, was no more opposed to the Japanese than it was to other authorities, it acquired anti-Japanese attitudes as a result of the behavior of Japanese troops and the failure of Japanese leaders to offer a better alternative than resistance or slavery.[7]

Where does a resurgent U.S. militarism today fit into this historical picture? We have seen how earlier forms of American global domination—economic, political, cultural—have become increasingly fragile, while the military dimension has grown in importance. Assuming continuation of this trend, fueled by the war on terrorism, mounting resource pressures, and simple geopolitical ambitions, crucial questions arise about the precise *modalities* of American power—namely, the degree to which military solutions might be compatible with the requisites of global domination. Viewed from yet another angle, in what manner would it make sense to apply Gramscian discourses of ideological hegemony to a global scene that appears more Hobbesian with each passing day? So long as U.S. ruling elites seem determined to solidify their global supremacy at whatever costs it takes, will existing international conditions ensure a trajectory of militarization, and, if so, is the United States destined to follow the historical pattern of crumbled, humiliated, failed imperial projects? Is a consensual Empire even possible?

One possible answer is that American power will sooner or later disintegrate from the weight of its own contradictions—so long as in decline or defeat it does not initiate a nuclear holocaust that would render discussion of future Empire meaningless. The U.S. imperial domain, despite appearances of insurmountable strength, is in many ways fragile and vulnerable. If the prescriptions for consensual power set forth by Machiavelli and Gramsci cannot be automatically extended from national to global politics, the theoretical insight nonetheless remains compelling, especially when a brazen resort to military force by the United States has become a more durable feature of international relations. The severe consequences of this epochal shift in both imperial capabilities and designs are increasingly visible: an upsurge in worldwide military conflict, the growth of civic violence, greater blowback, the eclipse of legitimating mechanisms, elevated challenges to the neoliberal economy.

A potentially explosive contradiction of Empire is the built-in conflict between global dimensions of power associated with the world hegemon and a range of distinctly *national* interests and agendas that elites want to pursue—a predicament embedded in the Middle East cauldron today. A strong patriotic mobilization that feeds into domestic legitimation needs quickly evaporates beyond American borders, where it breeds contempt, hostility, and resistance; nationalism by its very logic cannot serve *general* interests on the global terrain, even as it seeks universal justification. The single hegemon predictably works against diversity, independent centers of power, and peaceful balance, favoring coercive methods in support of a single neoliberal order, enforced along lines of an American-style fundamentalism. Empire rests on a logic of perpetual expansion: the global managers can never accrue sufficient power or enough mastery of the universe, just as billionaires seemingly can never accumulate enough wealth. Despite the onset of a supposedly postnational globalization, distinctly *national* agendas lie behind the U.S. pursuit of international power with its inevitable double standards: broken treaties, violations of the UN Charter and international law, refusal to accept inclusive disarmament processes, rejection of the World Criminal Court, seizure of space militarization for itself, preemptive wars, hectoring of other nations for human-rights abuses the United States itself commits on an even larger scale (and more regularly) around the globe. Further, to even speak of globalization as an objective, abstract, benign historical process is mystified nonsense, largely a cover for American corporate, geopolitical, and military interests that have little in common with a balanced, multipolar globalism that renders single-power domination obsolete.

As the cycle of militarism and terrorism intensifies—as the world moves ever closer to barbarism—the very premise of warfare as a method for advancing national goals must be regarded as bankrupt and irrational, for reasons having less to do with democracy or the worldwide diffusion of liberal values than with the brutal, in many ways unpredictable nature of contemporary warfare itself. The proliferation of WMD—and with it the growing prospect that such horrific weapons will be used—only underscores the insanity of militarism in a world where deep social polarization is the norm and *universal* disarmament seems a distant fantasy. Put differently, American designs for implementing "full-spectrum dominance" across a global system where strong anti-U.S. feelings prevail can only jeopardize planetary survival. We stand at a juncture where large-scale military action serves to aggravate national, religious, and other conflicts, a point doubly applicable to the lone superpower as it takes measures to secure global domination. The classic strategic view that war unfolds as an extension of politics thus makes no sense for twenty-first-century realities. As the Iraq disaster shows, war (and its aftermath) is more than anything a mechanism of senseless death and destruction, destroying civilian infrastructures, violating established rules of engagement, and destabilizing countries and entire regions. Civilian populations are deeply and irrevocably drawn into the horrors of modern warfare. As Istvan Meszaros argues, if the efforts of the only superpower to maintain total armed supremacy persist long into the future, the result is destined to be a "recipe for military suicide."[8]

As the militarization of American society proceeds, the confluence of the domestic war economy and global Empire generates popular attitudes inconsistent with a vibrant, democratic public sphere: fear, hatred, jingoism, racism, and aggression. We have arrived at a bizarre mixture of imperial arrogance and collective paranoia, violent impulses and a retreat from the norms of civic engagement and obligation that patriotic energies furnish only falsely and ephemerally. Further: the celebration of guns and violence in American society, cavalier attitudes toward war and military escapades abroad, and widespread indifference to established moral and legal codes gives elites wider autonomy to pursue their global schemes. As war becomes more acceptable to elites, often the preferred instrument to fight ubiquitous enemies, we can expect further erosion of the domestic infrastructure and culture. For many in the upper echelons of power this could well be tolerable, but the long-term consequences for U.S. imperial hegemony—both domestically and globally—are certain to be disastrous.

Corruption of the public sphere, hastened along by militarism and imperial overreach, is easily enough detected across the political landscape, perhaps nowhere more than in the remarkable deceits and criminal conduct of the Bush presidency itself. Bush's long parade of lies and schemes used to justify an illegal and immoral war against Iraq have brought political discourse to a new low, evidence of a corrosive leadership with few parallels in U.S. history. Lies have become a recurrent feature of Bush officialdom, put forward with sheer contempt for public opinion and democratic politics. Such behavior in high places counters all the platitudes about American democracy, devaluing citizenship and public life while further delegitimating U.S. international power, already compromised by the hubris of an aggressive Empire.

We have seen how one anticipated outgrowth of imperial power is blowback, which has numerous points of origin and takes just as many forms. At work here is a sort of Newtonian law of motion: power begets opposition, violence gives rise to anger, force generates counterforce. The concept of blowback speaks to the far-reaching anger and hatred that U.S. economic and military power breeds over many decades, resulting not just in widespread acts of terrorism but in local resistance, popular movements, guerrilla insurgency, and rival national alliances. As Johnson succinctly puts it: "Blowback is simply another way of saying that a nation reaps what it sows." Invincible as U.S. Empire might now appear, it cannot effectively control the long-term effects of its policies and actions, so that "future blowback possibilities are seeded into the world," where "blowback itself can lead to more blowback, in a spiral of destructive behavior."[9] This deadly logic is exacerbated as U.S. leaders continue along a militaristic path, justified by the omnipresent terrorist menace. Recent American moves to "remap" the Middle East, inspired by the designs of neocon ideologues, provide a case in point—the perfect recipe for new cycles of terrorism, local insurgency, and other modes of opposition. As the superpower behemoth extends its global reach, blowback correspondingly spreads, precisely as the Japanese and Germans learned from their military overextension, fueled by similar imperial delusions, in the period before and during World War II. One of the great ironies here is that militarism eventually renders imperial power somewhat *weaker*, more vulnerable to delegitimation and counterforce as it relies on a stronger military presence to assert its expanding geopolitical interests, spanning such regions as Indochina, the Balkans, Central America, and now both Central Asia and the Middle East. Although global terrorism constitutes a uniquely threatening instance of blowback, one can also speak of different forms of *political* blowback—as with the international backlash against U.S. military action in Iraq, Bush's subversion of the UN, repeated U.S. violations of international treaties, and stepped-up American development of nuclear weapons and Star Wars. It follows that the very conditions needed to maintain imperial power could simultaneously militate against its legitimation.

The very idea of global hegemony exercised by a lone superpower turns out to be problematic, given the inherent conflict between general and particular interests not to mention the severe dysfunctions of neoliberal globalization itself: class polarization, growing world poverty, the decline of public services, the coercive practices of international agencies, recurrent financial crises. The nearly total absence of governing or planning mechanisms, usually available to national elites, permits these contradictions in the global system to veer out of control. Elites may be tempted to "resolve" conflicts through military force, a frequent modus operandi of post–cold war U.S. foreign policy. Under these circumstances, U.S. attempts to contain anarchic features of the world system are likely to aggravate the dialectic of militarism and terrorism, as increasing superpower reliance on force simultaneously reflects and intensifies the superpower *weakness* in other spheres. Along these lines Giovanni Arrighi and Beverly Silver write: "The declining hegemon is thus left in the anomalous situation that it faces no credible military challenge, but it does not have the financial means needed to solve system-level problems that require system-level solutions."[10] One might add that the deficit involves not only financial but political and ideological resources as well. Meanwhile, the incessant militarization of both American society and the world is destined to breed chaos and disruption, which can only destabilize a global economy dependent on the smooth flow of capital, materials, and information. In this context the Bush II foreign policy, with its emphasis on patriotic mobilization and U.S. exceptionalism, could subvert its own global agendas, weakening the very international system over which it rules, or presumes to rule.

The *domestic* harm that can be attributed to Empire, the Pentagon having consumed up to $15 trillion in public revenues during the postwar years, has left a declining social infrastructure, decaying cities, and depleted public resources. Contrary to a widely entertained myth, war and preparations for war have not elevated industrial growth or living standards, as Seymour Melman, among others, has shown.[11] Enormous human, technical, and natural resources continue to flow into the war economy, as the Pentagon remains the biggest exception in a period when politicians argue for cutbacks in public spending; the huge and efficient military lobby exerts almost mystical influence on members of Congress, and will do so as long as the war on terrorism continues. With augmented U.S. military deployments around the globe, future operations and weapons programs will be far more costly, boosting Pentagon revenue to well over $500 billion yearly by 2006. The occupation of Iraq, which under Bush promises to be a long-term nightmare, alone could amount to more than $300 billion, and considerably more as the quagmire deepens. The war on terrorism likewise figures to run into hundreds of billions of dollars. The pressing question here is: To what degree, and for how long, will American citizens be willing to make these kinds of sacrifices, both human and material, on behalf on an Empire that satisfies mainly elite interests? Can the power structure, whether managed by Republicans or Democrats, adequately defend and legitimate such demands over time? At issue here is not merely costs but the entire ideological paradigm through which costs and sacrifices are perceived by the general population. Cracks in the ideological edifice were starkly visible during the large antiwar mobilizations that preceded the war against Iraq, surpass-

ing even those of the Vietnam era. If future military interventions give rise
to larger, more sustained movements against the war machine, more severe
legitimation crises (both global and domestic) can be expected.

As the new militarism reshapes the contours of imperial strategy, the
American political system and media offer more glowing celebratory images of modern warfare, which have the intended effect of loosening restraints on U.S. global behavior. By the 1990s the United States had indeed
become a rogue nation, a status already in place before Bush II, as it trampled on arrangements and rules established to keep the fragile international
order from unraveling. The invasion and occupation of Iraq demonstrates
this paradox in all its clarity: anxious to secure its purported geopolitical and
economic interests in the Middle East, the Bush administration worked
overtime to bribe and coerce UN members, lied and forged documents to
contrive a pretext for military action, violated the UN Charter, broke international law, dismissed the court of public opinion, and seemed clueless
regarding any long-term consequences of its policies. For many years the
United States has paid little heed to global arrangements and treaties it
viewed to be in conflict with its national interests. Even the famous U.S.
"crusade" against WMD is hypocritical in the extreme, as the United States
reserves for itself the right to manufacture and deploy far more WMD than
all other nations in the world combined. Invoking the rhetoric of democracy and human rights, U.S. leaders have made a mockery of international
order, helping reinforce an anarchic state of nature that would seem to be
fully at odds with all their stated intentions. The longer such conditions persist, the more the United States relies on military force to ensure its global
domination, the more precarious becomes its legitimacy within the world
system.

As the war machine strengthens its hold over American society, political elites face mounting global hostility, trapped in a predicament where
massive power begets equally massive countervailing forces: terrorism and
sabotage; guerrilla insurgencies, as in Iraq and Afghanistan; nation-state rivalries; hostile groups or nations laying hold of WMD; popular movements
against corporate globalization and U.S. imperialism. These developments,
taken together, work powerfully against U.S. efforts to maintain global supremacy, all the more so with each resort to military action. Moreover,
hopes for sustaining hegemony by means of economic success and cultural
influence—historically a strong suit for U.S. leaders—will flounder in the
world of neoliberal excesses, U.S. militarization, and imperial overreach.

With an escalating mood of anti-Americanism across the globe, the
State Department and a number of federal agencies have enlisted Madison
Avenue public-relations firms to help refurbish the national image abroad,
guessing that international public opinion would go along with the tired
mythology of freedom, democracy, abundance, and peace that serves to cloak

U.S. interests and obscures the actual legacy of authoritarian rule, exploitation, and violence known well by most of the globe. By 2002 Washington
had erected a sophisticated propaganda machine geared to Middle East issues,
looking to sell this romanticized version of "America" to Arab and Muslim
populations. One instrument of this ideological crusade is the Office of Public Diplomacy, an arm of the State Department. Against the backdrop of U.S.
support for Israel, wars in Afghanistan and Iraq, and the American struggle
to gain control of the Middle East, the public-relations apparatus works to
cosmetically remake the U.S. image in the absence of real changes in policies
or actions. The guiding premise is that once people of the region truly understand U.S. motives and interests they will naturally arrive at a more benign view of America—a rather far-fetched assumption given the daunting
reality of economic, political, and military power flexed by the superpower.
The Office of Public Diplomacy produces TV, radio, and print advertise-
ments showing idealized images of American life that, along with ambitious
educational, technical, and cultural exchange programs, are meant to create
an atmosphere of goodwill toward the U.S. government. But festering popular anger toward the United States in Arab and Muslim parts of the world
is so firmly grounded in actual lived experience that such propaganda overtures are futile, yet another telling reflection of the deepening crisis of U.S.
global legitimacy. It is well known that the vast majority of people in Egypt,
Iran, Syria, and even Iraq admire the United States for its science, technology, consumer goods, and culture while detesting its leaders for their ex-
ploitative and militaristic behavior. Propaganda methods are bound to fail in
a context where too much history is left to be explained away.

   The main counterforces to Empire have been explored more fully in
previous chapters. Two of them, however—possible rival national alliances
and resistance to occupation—deserve further mention here. The U.S.
buildup to war against Iraq gave rise to implacable opposition from several
countries, including Russia, France, Germany, and China, that is sure to have
lasting repercussions. Sentiment against U.S. militarism and superpower arrogance runs deep in these and other nations, among both the masses and
elites. The outlook of the Bush enclave toward countries that refuse to obe-
diently follow the Washington line has been nothing short of contemptu-
ous, evident in snide references by Cheney and Rumsfeld to the "old
Europe" (France, Germany) and to Turkey's stubborn refusal to cooperate
fully with U.S. military plans. As Washington continues to bask in its global
supremacy, one potential countervailing response is an emergent alliance
that in the near future could achieve economic and political parity with
the United States. Immanuel Wallerstein predicts the rise of a Paris-Berlin-
Moscow axis capable of mobilizing power on behalf of its own (hardly negligible) global interests.[12] Perhaps more ominous for the United States is the
specter of a rapidly developing China aligning with Japan or a reunified Ko-

rea, or both, to create the world's largest economic bloc. Indeed China *alone* represents a possible future alternative to the (increasingly fragile) neoliberal model and perhaps could even emerge as a challenge to existing U.S. imperial power. Such rival alliances would compete with the United States in the global struggle over resources, conceivably militarizing to the point where they could match U.S. armed strength. Whatever the constellation of forces, we can expect a powerful regional counterforce to American interests that is bound to further erode the legitimating mechanisms, in the process adding new fuel to the military side of Empire.

To the degree military force serves as the cornerstone of U.S. global strategy, imperial power grows paradoxically ever more fragile as the world system faces mounting dysfunctions: economic breakdown, political instability, terrorism, urban chaos and violence, the spread of weapons of mass destruction. Global decline can be expected to have immediate carryover into the *domestic* realm because the American economy (and society) is so fully intertwined with the world capitalist system. While militarization appears to demonstrate national strength, and surely does so in a variety of combat situations, in reality it only masks or deflects these dysfunctions: armed supremacy ironically works to compensate for imperial *weaknesses*, not only economic decline but, more crucially, the erosion of ideological hegemony. U.S. competitive advantage relative to Europe and Asia—both materially and *politically*—has been sliding for some time, even as the United States retains its superpower *military* status. So too has the domestic infrastructure of American society gone into decline, owing in part to the burdensome costs of global expansion and the dysfunctions of its grand strategy. The war on terrorism, certain to be a durable feature of American political life for decades, can only reinforce this trajectory, pushed along by the quagmire in Iraq and, more generally, the Middle East. If global domination requires broad and firm popular support within the matrix of a stable (administered, multinational) corporate economy, then heavy reliance on military force—affirming coercion over consent—is ultimately counterproductive. If demilitarization of U.S. foreign policy (and society) is the more rational strategy, the problem is that militarism has become so endemic to American society as a whole, creating an inbred way of life within the economy, politics, and culture (just as President Eisenhower said he feared in 1959), that it will be very difficult to reverse.

Since the Vietnam debacle a recurrent theme in American political culture has been the search for decidedly "good wars"—heroic military operations that could finally extinguish the national mood of humiliation, impotence, and pessimism that grew out of the Vietnam syndrome. Such good wars, of course, ideally possess all the glorious features of World War II: an obviously diabolical enemy, a clear distinction between good and evil, feverish patriotic mobilization, great deeds of heroism that propel dramatic military victories. The *Rambo* films of the 1980s capture precisely this dimension of the Vietnam syndrome and valiant struggles to conquer it, while Steven Spielberg's *Saving Private Ryan* (1998) is one of several major cinematic attempts to recover the historical sense of a "good," even romanticized, World War II for the American mass public. The Indochina disaster was, of course, an entirely different kind of story—endless guerrilla warfare in a distant Third World country, widespread opposition at home extending to the military itself, massive casualties on both sides, U.S. atrocities that were widely reported in the media, and in the end terrible defeat.

For the past decade or more American opinion makers have sought to portray U.S. military interventions in light of the World War II experience, hoping to extirpate anything resembling the Vietnam syndrome: logistical morass, unpopular military draft, open media battlefield access, terrible casualties, protracted warfare. The ideal of course would be something akin to another Normandy invasion, this time with many fewer American dead and wounded—or at least quick military victory over a weak, rather defenseless, overmatched foe. Crucial to such a Pentagon stratagem, as we have seen, is full-spectrum technowar, referred to during the beginning stages of the Iraq invasion as a "shock and awe" campaign. The American public is bombarded with World War II metaphors, starting with demonic references to a new Hitler, a mad tyrant who must be defeated before he goes on a Nazi-like rampage for world conquest—Noriega in Panama, Milosevic in Yugoslavia, Hussein in Iraq. Those protesting military action are labeled "appeasers" or enemy sympathizers, recalling the 1938 British pact with Nazi Germany at Munich. Targeted foreign leaders are painted as horrible monsters, architects of "ethnic cleansing," "genocide," even a new "holocaust," as in the case of Milosevic and other Serbs during the 1990s. They possess unspeakably horrible weapons, along with an irrational penchant for using them (Hussein). As warfare unfolds the public hears constant talk of trusted "allies" (Britain and a few others) ready to fight noble battles against the forces of darkness and primitivism, recalling heroic U.S.- and British-led invasions of Europe to liberate the continent from the Nazis. Finally, with invasion completed and occupation begun, as in Afghanistan and Iraq, the good-war parallels continue: we have a replay of 1945, when the U.S. military established occupation regimes in Germany and Japan, leading to a return of market capitalism and democratic politics. This exact theme was reiterated by National Security Advisor Condoleezza Rice and pro-Bush pundits as a move to situate U.S. military operations in Iraq within the proper "historical context," where dissent and protest could easily be stigmatized as unpatriotic, anti-American.

Such recycling of good-war motifs is intended to help legitimate U.S. imperial ambitions by dressing them up in ultrapatriotic, heroic garb and linking them to epic historical moments. War, no matter how distant, costly, and seemingly irrational, is made palatable to the mass public by means of evoking dramatic historical parallels. As a legitimation strategy for domestic consumption this ploy has often met with resoundingly positive results; media audiences are often receptive to good-war overtures. Opinion polls in 2002 and early 2003 showed overwhelming popular support for the invasion of Iraq, no doubt inspired by widespread belief in fraudulent claims made by the Bush administration to justify the attack. Meanwhile, antiwar sentiments, though loud and persistent, scarcely made a dent in the public sphere, thanks largely to an almost monolithic corporate media—at least until the massive contradictions of U.S. strategy began to surface in late 2003. Well-known American dissidents including Susan Sontag, Bill Maher, Tim Robbins, Susan Sarandon, Linda Ronstadt, and Sean Penn were sternly rebuked in the media, and fiercely attacked by the right, for raising even the most tepid criticisms of Bush's war policies. Yet the deeper currents of opposition, as reflected in the antiwar movement, scarcely vanished and figure to reappear with future U.S. armed interventions. On the global terrain, however, the situation for U.S. leaders is far less encouraging: legitimation devices have for the most part failed miserably as the credibility of the lone superpower increasingly suffers. Outside such friendly countries as Britain and Israel, crude American discourses comparing military actions against poor, weak, Third World nations with the epic struggle to defeat Nazi Germany are met with ridicule. The unique confluence of factors at work during World War II has not, and surely cannot, be reproduced in the contemporary post–cold war world. And the flagrant lies and myths perpetrated by the Bush regime, which exercises relatively little control over the global media system, contribute to a further disintegration of the U.S. standing internationally.

If one can point to a growing crisis of U.S. global hegemony, that crisis is nowhere more visible than in the nightmare of a failed military occupation in Iraq, the result of arrogant superpower initiatives that went awry the very moment the Bush administration so brazenly violated international law and provisions of the UN Charter. Far from the idealized modality of World War II, opening U.S. battlefield successes were almost immediately followed by an economic, political, and military catastrophe that (as of summer 2004) appears to have no end in sight—a catastrophe that undermines the very claims of Iraqi "liberation" (another good-war theme) while calling into question the various false justifications for the imperial gambit. What by late summer 2003 was already being defined as "classic guerrilla warfare" had gathered momentum throughout the year, marked by daily acts of sabotage, assaults on U.S. and British troops, bombings, disruptions of civil authority, and other dispersed forms of resistance. Occupation brought untold thousands of Iraqi casualties, the incarceration of thousands more, troop incursions into people's daily lives, a trampling on cultural and religious customs—in other words, a foreign-imposed regime of terror and repression. Under conditions of insurgency and sabotage, the prospects of any United States–engineered reconstruction of Iraq would appear fanciful at best. As predicted by preinvasion critics, the proclaimed goal of democracy turned out to be a cruel sham: the American leader of the occupation authority, L. Paul Bremer III, was running the country as an autocrat, tolerating few challenges to his power while issuing decrees to outlaw the Baath Party and other "subversive" groups, dismantle the Iraqi army, impose strict controls over the media, revamp the education system to fit U.S. ideological biases, and establish foreign control over oil facilities. The Iraq National Council, set up to replace the Hussein regime, was recruited from a circle of trusted elites, many of them exiles and handpicked by the United States and Britain. The "transfer of sovereignty" promised by the United States and planned to go into effect by July 1, 2004, was not expected to fundamentally transform this state of affairs. U.S. military occupation, according to Bush, will not come to an end with this new Iraqi regime.

U.S. ambitions to "remap" the Middle East by means of stepped-up economic, political, and military domination of the region have generated large-scale countervailing forces and threats, amounting to yet another recipe for blowback. More than two years after 9/11, the United States was more vulnerable than ever, its power increasingly subject to challenge, its weakness in the face of possible new terrorist attacks infinitely greater than before the Iraq operation. An upsurge in terrorism in the Middle East and beyond is sure to be devastating not only for national security and political stability in the region but for a corporate economic system strongly dependent on Middle East oil imports and geopolitical dominance. The site of the world's second largest petroleum reserves, Iraq was turned into a fierce battleground where terrorism was directed against, among other things, the vast oil infrastructure (production facilities, refineries, pipelines), which is highly vulnerable to sabotage. Given the Iraqi capacity to produce between five and seven million barrels of oil daily, any prolonged cutoff or even severe reduction could eventually plunge the United States (and world) into a downward energy spiral with disastrous economic consequences. Well-planned attacks on the Iraqi oil infrastructure began with the onset of the U.S. occupation, the large, mostly undefended targets easy to locate and hit; Saudi Arabia and Kuwait could be equally vulnerable. A strike at the massive Abqaiq complex in Saudi Arabia would reduce the world's oil flow by more than four million barrels a day for several months. With most industrialized nations increasingly reliant on Middle Eastern oil imports, the capacity of terrorist groups—activated and emboldened by the U.S. military presence—to damage vital firmaments of the New World Order is correspondingly heightened.

The Iraq venture, motivated by long-standing U.S. geopolitical and economic interests, has turned into the sort of disaster the Bush presidency and the Pentagon, blinded by imperial hubris and likely misled by their own propaganda, seemed unable to anticipate. The attack and occupation have turned out to be even more counterproductive than predicted by even the harshest critics. With 135,000 troops in place (as of June 2004) and confronting new and more terrifying assaults daily, the United States, having already snubbed the UN and violated its charter, began to call for international assistance to help manage an ungovernable situation; predictably, few countries offered much in the way of troop or police deployments, while some (Spain, for example) planned to withdraw their contingents. As the occupation force moved to consolidate its power, however, even more intractable problems arose: in Iraq, as throughout the Arab and Muslim world, the UN status had sharply deteriorated. Understandably, the international body was widely perceived to be yet another extension of American power, reflected by its inability to stop the war and its blatant use as a U.S. intelligence operation during the protracted weapons inspections of the 1990s. The bombing of the UN compound in Baghdad in August 2003 came as no surprise to Iraqis or anyone else in the region, since by then the UN was generally understood to be an agent of the occupying powers. Any move to internationalize the occupation with the aim of legitimating U.S. control would therefore seem destined to fail. The fundamental problem here is that neither the United States nor the UN has legitimacy owing to the historical role they have played, no matter what kind of cosmetic treatment or rhetorical flourishes are invoked to conceal the brute realities of militarism and imperial domination. If ideological hegemony requires effective moral and intellectual leadership, as Gramsci stressed, and if such leadership is to constitute a universal model to be emulated by others, then the U.S. pursuit of distinctly *national* interests in a global setting, largely through military force and secondarily through economic manipulation, will be self-defeating.

The U.S. "preemptive" move into Iraq has ironically shown the entire world just how fragile the military juggernaut, with all of its logistical and technological advantages, can be. The historical record is clear: armed force can achieve a string of military victories, but it cannot sustain *legitimacy* in the form of popular support for imperial ambitions, especially the kind of grand ambitions embraced by American elites today. Even the most sophisticated forms of technowar, moreover, cannot serve as a viable instrument of occupation by a foreign power within an intensely nationalistic milieu. When the Soviet Union invaded Czechoslovakia in 1968, hoping to quell unrest and an upsurge of anti-Communist ferment—in other words, to maintain its great-power control—the aggression backfired terribly, doing egregious damage to Soviet interests. The superpower could impose its coercive rule briefly, but the action was internationally condemned, the Brezhnev regime emerged from the crisis as a pariah state, and the USSR suffered a loss of legitimacy across Eastern Europe from which it would never recover. In the 1980s the Afghanistan quagmire turned out to be the final blow against Soviet bloc hegemony. As with the French in Algeria, the Japanese in China, the Nazis in Russia, and the Americans in Vietnam, national chauvinism combined with militarism and imperial overreach turned out to be brutally self-defeating. Of course the American political and media systems work indefatigably to convince the nation and the world that the U.S. brand of imperial and military power is fundamentally *different* from anything in the past, embracing the most noble, democratic ends possible, and that wars to secure global domination are just replays of the good war. As Edward Said writes:

> Every empire tells itself and the world that it is unlike all other empires, that its mission is not to plunder and control but to liberate. These ideas are by no means shared by the people who inhabit that empire, but that hasn't prevented the U.S. propaganda and policy apparatus from imposing its imperial perspective on Americans, whose sources of information about Arabs and Islam are woefully inadequate.[13]

Such an apparatus, however, will never be enough to guarantee the kind of ideological hegemony the United States will require to sustain its global domination over the coming decades.

NOTES

PREFACE

1. Chris Hedges, *War Is a Force That Gives Us Meaning* (New York: Public Affairs, 2002), 22.

INTRODUCTION

1. C. Wright Mills, *The Power Elite* (New York: Oxford University Press, 1956), 4.
2. Mills, *Power Elite,* 184.
3. Mills, *Power Elite,* 223.
4. Noam Chomsky, *Turning the Tide* (Montreal: Black Rose, 1987), 211.
5. G. William Domhoff, *Who Rules America?* (New York: McGraw-Hill), xi.
6. Domhoff, *Who Rules America?* 181.
7. Robert Jervis, "Theories of War in an Era of Leading-Power Peace," *American Political Science Review,* March 2002, 9.
8. Jervis, "Theories," 8.
9. Jervis, "Theories," 9.
10. Jervis, "Theories," 10.
11. Jervis, "Theories," 2.
12. Jervis, "Theories," 7.
13. Jervis, "Theories," 10.
14. William I. Robinson, "Social Theory and Globalization: The Rise of a Transnational State," *Theory and Society* 30 (2001): 159–60.
15. Robinson, "Social Theory," 164–65.
16. Robinson, "Social Theory," 167.
17. Leslie Sklair, *The Transnational Capitalist Class* (Oxford: Blackwell, 2001), 4, 6.

18. See Thomas I. Friedman, *The Lexus and the Olive Tree* (New York: Farrar, Strauss, and Giroux, 1999), and Michael Hardt and Antonio Negri, *Empire* (Cambridge, MA: Harvard University Press, 2000).

19. See, for example, Murray Bookchin, *Ecology and Freedom* (Palo Alto, CA: Cheshire Books, 1982).

20. See Alvin and Heidi Toffler, *War and Anti-War* (New York: Warner Books, 1993); Friedman, *Lexus*; Samuel Huntington, *The Clash of Civilizations and the Remaking of the World Order* (New York: Touchstone, 1996); and Francis Fukuyama, *The End of History and the Last Man* (New York: Free Press, 1992).

21. Fukuyama, *End of History*, xx.

22. Fukuyama, *End of History*, 260.

CHAPTER 1

1. Howard Zinn, *Howard Zinn on War* (New York: Seven Stories, 2001), 153.

2. Chalmers Johnson, *Blowback* (New York: Henry Holt, 2000), 5.

3. Theodore Roosevelt, quoted in Howard Zinn, *A Peoples' History of the United States* (New York: HarperCollins, 1995), 290.

4. Takis Fotopoulos, "The First War of the Internationalized Market Economy," *Democracy and Nature*, July 1999.

5. See Douglas Kellner, *The Persian Gulf TV War* (Boulder, CO: Westview, 1992), ch. 1.

6. John W. Dower, *War without Mercy* (New York: Pantheon, 1986), 300–301.

7. See Hans Magnus Enzensberger, *Civil Wars* (New York: New Press, 1993), ch. 1.

8. See Carl Boggs, "Economic Globalization and Political Atrophy," *Democracy and Nature*, March 2001.

9. Noam Chomsky, *A New Generation Draws the Line* (London: Verso, 2001), 1–4.

10. Colin Powell, quoted in *Los Angeles Times*, January 22, 2001.

11. Michael Klare, *Resource Wars* (New York: Henry Holt, 2001), 213.

12. On neoconservative thinking regarding foreign policy, see Robert Kagan, *Of Paradise and Power* (New York: Knopf, 2003), and Michael A. Ledeen, *The War against the Terror Masters* (New York: St. Martin's, 2002).

13. See Roger Griffin, *The Nature of Fascism* (London: Routledge, 1991), ch. 1.

14. Hardt and Negri, *Empire,* 393.

15. Karl Marx and Friedrich Engels writes: "The need of a constantly expanding market for its products chases the bourgeoisie over the whole surface of the globe. It must nestle everywhere, settle everywhere, establish connections everywhere." *The Communist Manifesto,* in *The Marx-Engels Reader*, ed. Robert C. Tucker (New York: Norton, 1972), 338.

16. Sklair, *Transnational*, 1–2.

17. Sklair, *Transnational*, 5–6.

18. Robinson, "Social Theory."

19. Hardt and Negri, *Empire*, xii.
20. Hardt and Negri, *Empire*, xiv.
21. Hardt and Negri, *Empire*, 181.
22. Hardt and Negri, *Empire*, 181–82.
23. Hardt and Negri, *Empire*, 189.
24. Hardt and Negri, *Empire*, 198.
25. Mills, *Power Elite,* 219.
26. Mills, *Power Elite,* 223.
27. Fred J. Cook, *The Warfare State* (New York: Collier, 1962), 100.
28. Cook, *Warfare State*, 189.
29. Cook, *Warfare State*, 354.
30. Chomsky, *Turning the Tide,* 213.
31. Helen Caldicott, *The New Nuclear Danger* (New York: New Press, 2002), 20.
32. Ken Silverstein, *Private Warriors* (London: Verso, 2000), ix.
33. See Chalmers Johnson, "The War Business," *Harpers*, November 2003, 53–58.
34. Cook, *Warfare State,* 189.
35. On the decline of the U.S. economy as a function of the militarized society, see Melman, *Demilitarized Society,* ch. 1; and James Petras and Morris Morley, *Empire or Republic?* (New York: Routledge, 1995), ch. 2.

CHAPTER 2

1. See Gilbert Achcar, "After September 11: The Clash of Barbarisms," *Monthly Review*, September 2002.
2. The main neoconservative geopolitical strategy is contained in Project for the New American Century, "Rebuilding America's Defenses: Strategy, Forces, and Resources for a New American Century," September 2000, at http://new americancentury.org.
3. Donald Rumsfeld, *Pentagon Quadrennial Review* (Washington, DC: U.S. Department of Defense (2001), 30.
4. Karl Grossman, *Weapons in Space* (New York: Seven Stories, 2001).
5. Kagan, *Of Paradise*, 3.
6. Kagan, *Of Paradise*, 73–75.
7. Kagan, *Of Paradise*, 88.
8. Kagan, *Of Paradise*, 41.
9. On the development of neoliberal fundamentalism, see Tariq Ali, *The Clash of Fundamentalisms* (London: Verso, 2002), 285–89.
10. Klare, *Resource Wars*, 213.
11. See Achcar, "After September 11."
12. Johnson, *Blowback*, 7–8.
13. Michael Fischback, op-ed in *Los Angeles Times*, June 2, 2003.
14. Johnson, *Blowback*, 7, 10.

15. Walter Laqueur, *The New Terrorism* (New York: Oxford University Press, 1999), 254.

16. See Michael Scott Doran, "Somebody Else's Civil War," in *How Did This Happen? Terrorism and the New War*, ed. James M. Hoge Jr. and Gideon Rose (New York: Public Affairs, 2001), 38.

17. Doran, "Somebody Else's," 44.

18. *Los Angeles Times*, May 14, 2003.

19. Walter Laqueur, *No End to War* (New York: Continuum, 2003), ch. 3.

20. Laqueur, *No End to War,* 19.

21. Ralph W. McGeehee, *Deadly Deceits* (New York: Sheridan Square, 1983).

22. See Diana Johnstone, *Fool's Crusade* (New York: Monthly Review, 2002).

23. Khalid Khawaja (an observer being interviewed), *Los Angeles Times*, March 2, 2003.

24. Laqueur, *New Terrorism,* 4.

25. Laqueur, *New Terrorism*, 213, 216.

26. Johnstone, *Fool's Crusade*, 1.

27. Michael Parenti, *To Kill a Nation* (London: Verso, 2000), 91.

28. Johnstone, *Fool's Crusade*, 74.

29. Johnstone, *Fool's Crusade*, 122.

30. George W. Bush, quoted in *Los Angeles Times*, January 29, 2003.

31. John Berger, *Nation*, May 12, 2003.

32. Robin Anderson, *Extra!* May–June 2003, 7, 8.

33. Robert Byrd, quoted in *Los Angeles Times*, January 23, 2003.

34. *Los Angeles Times*, June 18, 2003.

35. See Tim Shorrock, *Nation*, June 23, 2003.

36. Mark Baxter, quoted in *Los Angeles Times*, June 23, 2003.

37. Joy Gordon, "Cool War," *Harper's*, November 2002, 43.

38. William Blum, *Rogue State* (Monroe, ME: Common Courage, 2000), 105–6.

39. See Peter Pringle, "Chemical Weapons," in *Crimes of War*, ed. Roy Gutman and David Rieff (New York: Norton, 1999), 74–75.

40. Blum, *Rogue State*, 121–22.

41. *Los Angeles Times*, October 9, 2002.

42. See Stephen Endicott and Edward Hagerman, *The United States and Biological Warfare* (Bloomington: University of Indiana Press, 1998).

43. Endicott and Hagerman, *United States*, 100.

44. Endicott and Hagerman, *United States*, 103.

45. Robert Aldrich, *First Strike!* (Boston: South End, 1983), ch. 1.

46. See Sven Lindqvist, *A History of Bombing* (New York: New Press, 2001), 126.

47. Grossman, *Weapons in Space*.

48. Caldicott, *New Nuclear Danger*, 5.

49. Donald Rumsfeld, *Quadrennial Defense Review* (Washington, DC: U.S. Department of Defense, 2001).

50. Grossman, *Weapons in Space*, 17.

51. Grossman, *Weapons in Space*, 61.

52. Michio Kaku, "Depleted Uranium: Huge Quantities of Dangerous Waste," in *Metal of Dishonor* (New York: International Action Center, 1999), 111–15.

53. See Peter L. Pellett, "Sanctions, Food, Nutrition, and Health in Iraq," in *Iraq Under Siege*, ed. Anthony Arnove (Boston: South End Press, 2000), 151–68.

CHAPTER 3

1. E. J. Dionne Jr., *Why Americans Hate Politics* (New York: Touchstone, 1991), 332.

2. William Greider, *Who Will Tell the People?* (New York: Simon and Schuster, 1992), 44.

3. Martin Wattenberg, *The Decline of American Political Parties* (Cambridge: Harvard University Press, 1994), ix.

4. Zinn, *Peoples' History*, 631.

5. Bill Clinton, quoted in William Greider, *Nation*, February 17, 2003.

6. Tom Lantos, quoted in *Los Angeles Times*, October 9, 2002.

7. Robert Byrd, quoted in *Los Angeles Times*, October 11, 2002.

8. Robert Scheer, *Los Angeles Times*, March 5, 2003.

9. Robert Byrd, quoted in *Los Angeles Times*, March 3, 2003.

10. Barbara Ehrenreich, *Blood Rites* (New York: Henry Holt, 1997), 217.

11. See Douglas Kellner, *The Persian Gulf TV War* (Boulder, CO: Westview, 1992).

12. Cokie Roberts, quoted in Kathleen Hall Jamieson and Paul Waldman, *The Press Effect* (New York: Oxford University Press, 2003), 138.

13. *Los Angeles Times*, September 15, 2002.

14. Norman Mailer, *Why Are We at War?* (New York: Random House, 2003), 15.

15. Mailer, *Why*, 12.

16. Mailer, *Why*, 63.

17. Robert McChesney, *Corporate Media and the Threat to Democracy* (New York: Seven Stories, 1997), 7.

18. See David Croteau and William Hoynes, *By Invitation Only* (Monroe, ME: Common Courage, 1994), ch.3.

19. Norman Solomon and Reese Erlich, *Target Iraq* (New York: Context Books, 2003), 31.

20. Scott Ritter, quoted in *Extra!* August 2002.

21. Kellner, *Persian Gulf TV War*, 420–26.

22. Kellner, *Persian Gulf TV War*, 420.

23. Jamieson and Waldman, *Press Effect*, 152.

24. Michael Massing, *Nation*, November 11, 2002.

25. Ziauddin Sardar and Merryl Wyn Davies, *Why Do People Hate America?* (New York: Disinformation, 2002).

26. Sheldon Rampton and John Stauber, *Weapons of Mass Deception* (New York: Penguin, 2003), ch. 3.

27. Noam Chomsky, "The Cold War and the University," in *The Cold War and the University* (New York: New Press, 1997), 184.

28. Domhoff, *Who Rules America?* 85.

29. Lawrence C. Solely, *Leasing the Ivory Tower* (Boston: South End, 1995), 116–18.

30. Laurence Shoup, in *Z Magazine*, March 2003, 36.

31. Alan Wolfe, "The Home Front," in *How Did This Happen?* ed. James F. Hoge Jr. and Gideon Rose (New York: Public Affairs, 2001), 287.

32. Wolfe, "Home Front," 291.

33. Wolfe, "Home Front," 293.

34. Martin Peretz, in *New Republic*, December 31, 2001.

35. Christopher Hitchens, *A Long Short War* (New York: Plume, 2003), 10.

36. Hitchens, *Long Short War*, 31.

37. Hitchens, *Long Short War*, 99.

38. Hitchens, *Long Short War*, 102.

39. Hitchens, *Long Short War*, 103.

40. Hitchens, *Long Short War*, 11.

41. *Los Angeles Times*, December 12, 2001.

42. Nancy Chang, *Silencing Political Dissent* (New York: Seven Stories, 2002), 43–44.

43. Chang, *Silencing Political Dissent*, 119.

44. Robert Dreyfuss, in *Nation*, March 25, 2002.

45. James Bamford, *Body of Secrets* (New York: Anchor Books, 2002), 617.

46. Bamford, *Body of Secrets*, 647.

47. *Los Angeles Times*, October 11, 2002.

48. Steven Shapiro, quoted in *Los Angeles Times*, January 12, 2004.

CHAPTER 4

1. Mary Edwards Wertsch, *Military Brats* (New York: Random House, 1991), 381.

2. Ehrenreich, *Blood Rites,* ch. 10.

3. Ward Churchill, *Fantasies of the Master Race* (San Francisco: City Lights, 1998), 25.

4. Chris Hedges, *War Is a Force That Gives Us Meaning* (New York: Public Affairs, 2002), 3.

5. Hedges, *War*, 103.

6. Hedges, *War*, 150.

7. Frank Dorrel, *Addicted to War* (Oakland, CA: AK, 2002).

8. Richard Rhodes, *Why They Kill* (New York: Vintage, 1999), 290–93.

9. Rhodes, *Why*, 296.

10. Rhodes, *Why*, 304.

11. James William Gibson, *Warrior Dreams* (New York: Hill and Wang, 1994).

12. Gibson, *Warrior Dreams*, introduction.

13. Gibson, *Warrior Dreams*, 11.

14. William W. Zellner, *Countercultures* (New York: St. Martin's, 1995), 52.

15. On the growth of paranoid images and visions within American culture, see Ray Pratt, *Projecting Paranoia* (Lawrence: University of Kansas Press, 2001), ch. 1.

16. William Colby, quoted in Gore Vidal, *Perpetual War for Perpetual Peace* (New York: Nation Books, 2001), 117.

17. Joel Dyer, *Harvest of Rage* (Boulder, CO: Westview, 1997), 216.

18. Dyer, *Harvest of Rage*, 215–23.

19. Vidal, *Perpetual War,* 109–10.

20. Vidal, *Perpetual War,* 107.

21. See Zellner, *Countercultures,* ch. 1.

22. Darrell Y. Hamamoto, "Empire of Death and the Plague of Civic Violence," in *Masters of War*, ed. Carl Boggs (New York: Routledge, 2003), 277–92.

23. See Philip Carlo, *The Night Stalker* (New York: Pinnacle Books, 1997), 160.

24. James B. Stewart, *Blind Eye* (New York: Touchstone, 1999), 290.

25. Stewart, *Blind Eye*, 291.

26. See Hamamoto, "Empire," 286.

27. See Rampton and Stauber, *Weapons*, 139.

28. Zygmunt Bauman, "The Uniqueness and Normality of the Holocaust," in *Violence: A Reader*, ed. Catherine Besteman (New York: New York University Press, 2002), 173.

29. Bauman, "Uniqueness," 83.

30. Wertsch, *Military Brats*, 375–76.

31. Wertsch, *Military Brats*, 94.

32. Wertsch, *Military Brats*, 119.

33. Wertsch, *Military Brats*, 196.

34. See R. Claire Snyder, "Patriarchal Militarism," in Boggs, *Masters of War*, 264–68.

35. See Joshua Goldstein, *War and Gender* (New York: Cambridge University Press, 2001).

36. Catherine Lutz and John Elliston, "Domestic Terror," *Nation*, October 14, 2002.

37. *Los Angeles Times*, March 15, 2003.

38. See Tom Pollard, "The Hollywood War Machine," in Boggs, *Masters of War,* 132–38.

39. Churchill, *Fantasies*, 175.

40. Churchill, *Fantasies*, 177.

41. Pollard, "Hollywood," 124–25.

42. Douglas Kellner, *Media Culture* (New York: Routledge, 1995), 75–82.

43. Ronnie Lipschutz, *Cold War Fantasies* (Lanham, MD: Rowman & Littlefield, 2001), 164.

44. Susan Jeffords, quoted in Robert Sklar, *Movie-Made America* (New York: Random House, 1994), 346.

45. Ronald Reagan, quoted in Michael Rogin, *Ronald Reagan: The Movie* (Berkeley and Los Angeles: University of California Press, 1987), 7.

46. Rogin, *Ronald Reagan*, 29.

47. Jonathan Mostrow, quoted in *Los Angeles Times*, April 25, 2000.

48. On the events leading up to Pearl Harbor, see Robert B. Stinnett, *Day of Deceit* (New York: Free Press, 2000).

49. M. Mehdi Semati, "Sex, Violence, and Terrorism in Hollywood's International Political Imagery," in *Media, Sex, Violence, and Drugs*, ed. Yahya R. Kamalipour and Kuldip R. Rampal (Lanham, MD: Rowman & Littlefield, 2001), 241–42.

50. Semati, "Sex," 244.

51. Semati, "Sex," 256.

52. *Terminator* magazine, 2003, 52–53.

CHAPTER 5

1. Chalmers Johnson, *Blowback* (New York: Henry Holt, 2000), 7.

2. Roy Gutman and David Rieff, *Crimes of War* (New York: Norton, 1999), 8.

3. Gutman and Rieff, *Crimes of War*, 9.

4. Lawrence Wechsler, "International Humanitarian Law: An Overview," in Gutman and Rieff, *Crimes of War*, 19.

5. Sven Lindqvist, *A History of Bombing* (New York: New Press, 2000), 2.

6. See William Blum, *Rogue State* (Monroe, ME: Common Courage, 2000).

7. *Los Angeles Times*, July 13, 2002.

8. *New York Times*, February 11, 2002.

9. Madeleine Albright, quoted in Gary Jonathan Bass, *Stay the Hand of Vengeance* (Princeton, NJ: Princeton University Press, 2000), 282.

10. Norman Cigar and Paul Williams, *Indictment at The Hague: The Milosevic Regime and Crimes of the Balkans Wars* (New York: New York University Press, 2002), 17, 21.

11. Sara Flounders, "Bosnia Tragedy: The Unknown Role of the Pentagon," in *NATO in the Balkans: Voices of Opposition*, by Ramsey Clark et al. (New York: International Action Center, 1998), 63.

12. See Sean Gervasi, "Why Is NATO in Yugoslavia?" in Clark et al., *NATO in the Balkans*, 29–46.

13. Wesley Clark, quoted in Michael Parenti, *To Kill a Nation* (London: Verso, 2000), 124.

14. Parenti, *To Kill a Nation*, 164.

15. See Gervasi, "Why."

16. *New York Times*, March 8, 1992.

17. Flounders, "Bosnia Tragedy," 71.

18. David Chandler, "International Justice," *New Left Review*, November–December, 2000, 65.

19. Telford Taylor, *Nuremberg and Vietnam* (Chicago: Quadrangle Books, 1970), 39.

20. Steven R. Ratner, "Aggression," in Gutman and Rieff, *Crimes of War*, 25.

21. Blum, *Rogue State*, 125–67.

22. On President Kennedy's involvement in the Vietnam war planning and escalation, see Bruce Miroff, *Pragmatic Illusions* (New York: David McKay, 1976), 142–66; and Marilyn B. Young, *The Vietnam Wars* (New York: HarperCollins, 1991), 60–105.

23. Christopher Hitchens, *The Trial of Henry Kissinger* (London: Verso, 2001).

24. See Philip E. Wheaton, *Panama Invaded* (Trenton, NJ: Red Sea, 1992), 143–58.

25. Anthony Arnove, ed., *Iraq under Siege* (Boston: South End, 2000), especially chs. 1–3, 11, 12, 13.

26. On the attack in Yemen, see the *Los Angeles Times*, November 5, 2002.

27. Lindqvist, *History of Bombing*, 26.

28. Lindqvist, *History of Bombing*, 121.

29. Bonner Fuller, quoted in John Dower, *War without Mercy* (New York: Pantheon, 1986), 41.

30. William O. Douglas, cited in Lindqvist, *History of Bombing*, 128.

31. Lindqvist, *History of Bombing*, 121.

32. James William Gibson, *The Perfect War* (New York: Atlantic Monthly, 1986), 327.

33. Gibson, *Perfect War*, 327.

34. Young, *Vietnam Wars*, 301–2.

35. Lindqvist, *History of Bombing*, 162.

36. See Arnove, *Iraq under Siege*, chs. 1, 4.

37. Ramsey Clark et al., *War Crimes* (Washington, DC: Masionneuve, 1992), parts 1–3.

38. Wesley Clark, "Indictment of the U.S./NATO," in *Hidden Agenda: U.S./NATO Takeover of Yugoslavia*, ed. John Catalinotto and Sara Flounders (New York: IAC, 2002), 33–45.

39. Parenti, *To Kill a Nation*, 124.

40. Tariq Ali, *The Clash of Fundamentalisms* (London: Verso, 2002), 267.

41. Edward Herman, "'Tragic Errors' in U.S. Military Policy," *Z Magazine*, September 2002, 27.

42. Ward Churchill, *A Little Matter of Genocide* (San Francisco: City Lights, 1997), 188.

43. Caleb Carr, *The Lessons of Terror* (New York: Random House, 2002), 172–73.

44. Carr, *Lessons of Terror*, 255.

45. Dower, *War without Mercy*, 69.

46. Stephen Endicott and Edward Hagerman, *The United States and Biological Warfare* (Bloomington: University of Indiana Press, 1998), 89.

47. Cited in Gibson, *Perfect War*, 141–42.

48. Gibson, *Perfect War*, 199.

49. Wheaton, *Panama Invaded*, 115–16.

50. Wheaton, *Panama Invaded*, 31.

51. Chu Chu Martinez, quoted in Wheaton, *Panama Invaded*, 53.

52. See the anthology *Metal of Dishonor* (New York: International Action Center, 1999), especially chs. 1, 3, and 8.

53. Joy Gordon, "Cool War," *Harpers*, November 2002, 43.

54. *Los Angeles Times*, January 4, 2002.

55. See *Newsweek*, August 6, 2002.

56. Phyllis Bennis, *Before and After: U.S. Foreign Policy and the September 11 Crisis* (New York: Olive Branch, 2003), 104.

57. Barbara Ehrenreich, *Blood Rites* (New York: Henry Holt, 1997), 222–23.

58. Richard Rhodes, *Why They Kill* (New York: Vintage Books, 1999), 287.

59. Cigar and Williams, *Indictment at The Hague*, 96–97.

60. On the Contra wars against Nicaragua and the U.S. role, see Noam Chomsky, *Turning the Tide* (Boston: South End, 1986), 127–46.

61. See Gregory Elich, "The Invasion of Serbian Krajina," in Clark et al., *NATO in the Balkans*, 130–40.

62. Richard Stutsman, "CIA Death Squads in Guatemala" (accessed April 7, 1995).

63. Edward Said, "America's Last Taboo," *New Left Review*, November–December, 2000, 47.

64. Gilbert Achcar, "After September 11," *Monthly Review*, September 2002.

65. See Henry T. Nash, "The Bureaucratization of Homicide," in *Protest and Survive*, ed. E. P. Thompson and Dan Smith (New York: Monthly Review, 1981), 149–62.

66. Gibson, *Perfect War*, 464.

67. William Calley, quoted in Herbert Kelman and V. Lee Hamilton, "The My Lai Massacre," in *Sociology: Readings*, ed. David Newman (Newbury Park, CA: Pine Forge, 1995).

68. See Richard Falk's account in the *Nation*, July 9, 2001.

69. Joseph E. Persico, *Nuremberg* (New York: Penguin, 1995), 188.

70. Hannah Arendt, *Eichmann in Jerusalem* (New York: Penguin, 1963), 276.

71. Richard Falk, *Human Rights Horizons* (New York: Routledge, 2000), ch. 10.

72. Chandler, "International Justice," 63.

73. Noam Chomsky, *Rogue States* (Boston: South End, 2000), 17.

74. Lindqvist, *History of Bombing*, 184.

75. Kellner, *Persian Gulf*, 420–29.

CHAPTER 6

1. Perry Anderson, "Force and Consent," *New Left Review*, September–October, 2002, 12.

2. Antonio Gramsci, "State and Civil Society," in *Selections from the Prison Notebooks*, ed. Quintin Hoare and Geoffrey Nowell Smith (New York: International Publishers, 1971), 218.

3. Gramsci, "State and Civil Society," 232.

4. For Gramsci's discussion of "Caesarism" and "Bonapartism," see his "State and Civil Society," 219–23.

5. Gramsci, "Notes on Italian History," in *Selections*, 88.

6. See Eric Wolf, *Peasant Wars in the Twentieth Century* (New York: Harper and Row, 1969), ch. 1.

7. Chalmers Johnson, *Peasant Nationalism and Communist Power* (Stanford: Stanford University Press, 1962), 69.

8. Istvan Meszaros, "Militarism and Coming Wars," *Monthly Review*, June 2003, 23.

9. Johnson, *Blowback*, 10–17.

10. Giovanni Arrighi and Beverly J. Silver, *Chaos and Governance in the Modern World System* (Minneapolis: University of Minnesota Press, 1999), 278.

11. Seymour Melman, *The Demilitarized Society* (Montreal: Harvest House, 1988), ch. 1.

12. Immanuel Wallerstein, "U.S. Weakness and the Struggle for Hegemony," *Monthly Review*, July–August, 2003, 27.

13. Edward Said, Commentary in *Los Angeles Times*, July 20, 2003.

INDEX

ABOUT THE AUTHOR

Carl Boggs is a professor in the School of Arts and Sciences at National University. His previous books include *Masters of War: Militarism and Blowback in the Era of American Empire; The End of Politics: Corporate Power and the Decline of the Public Sphere; and The Socialist Tradition: From Crisis to Decline.*